SWITZERLAND'S PRIVATE INTERNATIONAL LAW STATUTE

Switzerland's Private International Law Statute

of December 18, 1987

The Swiss Code on Conflict of Laws
and Related Legislation

Introduced,
Translated and Annotated

by

Pierre A. Karrer   and   **Karl W. Arnold**

Dr. iur. (Zurich)   *Dr. iur. (Fribourg)*
LL.M (Yale)

Partners, Pestalozzi Gmuer & Heiz, Zurich

Kluwer Law and Taxation Publishers
Deventer ● Boston

Kluwer Law and Taxation Publishers
P.O. Box 23   Tel.: 31 5700 47265
7400 GA Deventer   Telex: 49295
The Netherlands   Fax: 31 5700 22244

Library of Congress Cataloging in Publication Data

Switzerland's Private International Law Statute of
    December 18. 1987.

    Bibliography: p.
    1. Conflict of laws--Switzerland.   I. Karrer,
Pierre A.   II. Arnold, Karl W.
KKW480.S94   1988   340.9   88-8942
ISBN 90-6544-290-1

ISBN 90 6544 290 1

Preface and Acknowledgements

Where to begin? This book seeks to give a practical answer to this very question. The starting point must be the text of the applicable legal provisions, – the Constitution, the Treaties, the Statute. But all of us who are active in the international field experience every day: To understand a text one must go behind and beyond the mere words. In the limited space of this annotated edition, we are trying to give a few pointers. Only a beginning.

We are indebted for numerous suggestions and criticism to Margaret Gilmore, Marcel Kahan and Alisa Jonas. The translation of the chapter on international arbitration is the result of a joint effort with Dr. Robert Briner, Geneva/The Hague, and Dr. Marc Blessing, Zurich.

We would like to thank our partners at Pestalozzi Gmuer & Heiz for their understanding and support.

Zurich, November 1988   *Pierre Karrer and Karl Arnold*

Table of Contents

Page

INTRODUCTION

1. The Beginnings of Switzerland: Independence, Diversity, Neutrality   1
2. Switzerland after the French Revolution: The Federal Structure Takes Shape   2
3. Modern Switzerland: Industrialization and Services   2
4. Civil Law Codified in the Cantons: The Nineteenth Century   3
5. Conflict of Laws and the Swiss Federal System   3
6. Conflict of Laws in the Federal Constitution of 1848   4
7. Conflict of Laws in Treaties of the Early Federal Period: 1848 to 1874   5
8. Conflict of Laws in Federal Case Law   5
9. Codification of Civil Law on the Federal Level: 1874 to 1912   5
10. The NAG of 1891: The First Swiss Statute on Conflict of Laws and Jurisdictions   7
11. Private International Law under the NAG: 1912 to 1988   7
12. The Genesis of the Private International Law Statute   8
13. The Constitution and the Private International Law Statute   12
14. International Treaties and the Private International Law Statute   13
15. A Comprehensive Codification: Rules and Exceptions   14
16. Conflict of Jurisdictions: The Policies of the PIL Statute   16
17. Private International Law: The Policies of the PIL Statute   17
18. Recognition and Enforcement of Foreign Decisions: The Policies of the Private International Law Statute   18
19. International Bankruptcy in the Private International Law Statute   18
20. International Arbitration in the Private International Law Statute   18
21. A Look Ahead   19

A Note on Liechtenstein   21

Abbreviations   23

ANNOTATED TRANSLATION OF SWITZERLAND'S PRIVATE INTERNATIONAL LAW STATUTE

Art.

	Juris-diction	Applicable Law	Recogni-tion and Enforce-ment
FIRST CHAPTER: GENERAL PROVISIONS			
First Section: Field of Application		1	
Second Section: Jurisdiction			
I. In General	2		
II. Subsidiary Jurisdiction	3		
III. Validation of Attachment	4		
IV. Choice of Jurisdiction	5		
V. Unconditional Appearance	6		
VI. Arbitration Agreement	7		
VII. Counterclaim	8		
VIII. Lis Pendens	9		
IX. Provisional Measures	10		
X. Acts of Judicial Assistance	11		
XI. Time Limits	12		
Third Section: Applicable Law			
I. Scope of Conflicts Rule		13	
II. Renvoi		14	
III. Exception Clause		15	
IV. Ascertaining Foreign Law		16	
V. Swiss Public Policy Exception		17	
VI. Mandatory Application of Swiss Law		18	
VII. Taking into Account Mandatory Provisions of a Foreign Law		19	
Fourth Section: Domicile, Seat and Citizenship			
I. Domicile, Habitual Residence, and Business Establishment of an Individual		20	
II. Seat and Business Establishment of Companies		21	

Art.

	Juris-diction	Applicable Law	Recognition and Enforcement
III. Citizenship		22	
IV. Multiple Citizenship		23	
V. Persons without Citizenship and Refugees		24	

Fifth Section: Recognition and Enforcement of Foreign Decisions
I. Recognition			
1. General Rule			25
2. Jurisdiction of Foreign Authorities			26
3. Grounds for Non-recognition			27
II. Enforceability			28
III. Procedure			29
IV. Settlement in Court			30
V. Noncontentious Jurisdiction			31
VI. Entry in Register of Civil Status			32

SECOND CHAPTER: INDIVIDUALS

	Juris-diction	Applicable Law	Recognition and Enforcement
I. General Rule	33	33	
II. Capacity to Have Rights		34	
III. Capacity to Act			
1. General Rule		35	
2. Protection of Legal Transactions		36	
IV. Name			
1. General Rule		37	
2. Change of Name	38	38	
3. Change of Name Abroad			39
4. Entry in Register of Civil Status		40	
V. Declaration of Disappearance			
1. Jurisdiction and Applicable Law	41	41	
2. Declaration of Disappearance or Death Issued Abroad			42

	Art.		
	Juris-diction	Applicable Law	Recognition and Enforcement

THIRD CHAPTER: MARRIAGE

First Section: *Conclusion of Marriage*

I. Jurisdiction	43		
II. Applicable Law		44	
III. Marriage Concluded Abroad			45

Second Section: *Effects of Marriage in General*

I. Jurisdiction			
1. General Rule	46		
2. Jurisdiction at Place of Citizenship	47		
II. Applicable Law			
1. General Rule		48	
2. Support and Alimony		49	
III. Foreign Decisions or Measures			50

Third Section: *Marital Property*

I. Jurisdiction	51		
II. Applicable Law			
1. Choice of Applicable Law			
(a) General Rule		52	
(b) Modalities		53	
2. No Applicable Law Chosen			
(a) General Rule		54	
(b) Mutability and Retroactivity in Case of Change of Domicile		55	
3. Form of Marital Property Contract		56	
4. Legal Relationships with Third Parties		57	
III. Foreign Decisions			58

| | Art. | | |
---	Juris- diction	Applicable Law	Recogni- tion and Enforce- ment
Fourth Section: *Divorce and Separation*			
I. Jurisdiction			
1. General Rule	59		
2. Jurisdiction at Place of Citizenship	60		
II. Applicable Law		61	
III. Provisional Measures		62	
IV. Ancillary Measures		63	
V. Supplement to or Modification of Decrees		64	
VI. Foreign Decrees			65

FOURTH CHAPTER: PARENT-CHILD RELATIONSHIP

	Juris- diction	Applicable Law	Recogni- tion and Enforce- ment
First Section: *Parent-Child Relationship by Descent*			
I. Jurisdiction			
1. General Rule	66		
2. Jurisdiction at Place of Citizenship	67		
II. Applicable Law			
1. General Rule		68	
2. Decisive Time		69	
III. Foreign Decisions			70
Second Section: *Acknowledgement*			
I. Jurisdiction	71		
II. Applicable Law		72	
III. Foreign Acknowledgement and Challenge of Acknowledgement			73
IV. Legitimation			74

	Juris-diction	*Applicable Law*	*Recogni-tion and Enforce-ment*
Third Section: Adoption			
I. Jurisdiction			
1. General Rule	75		
2. Jurisdiction at Place of Citizenship	76		
II. Applicable Law		77	
III. Foreign Adoptions and Similar Measures			78
Fourth Section: Effects of Parent-Child Relationship			
I. Jurisdiction			
1. General Rule	79		
2. Jurisdiction at Place of Citizenship	80		
3. Third Party Claims	81		
II. Applicable Law			
1. General Rule		82	
2. Support Obligation		83	
III. Foreign Decisions			84
FIFTH CHAPTER: GUARDIANSHIP AND OTHER PROTECTIVE MEASURES		85	
SIXTH CHAPTER: INHERITANCE LAW			
I. Jurisdiction			
1. General Rule	86		
2. Jurisdiction at Place of Citizenship	87		
3. Jurisdiction at Place of Assets	88		
4. Conservatory Measures	89		

Art.

	Juris-diction	Applicable Law	Recognition and Enforcement
II. Applicable Law			
1. Last Domicile in Switzerland		90	
2. Last Domicile Abroad		91	
3. Scope of the Law on Succession and Distribution of the Estate		92	
4. Form		93	
5. Capacity to Dispose for Cause of Death		94	
6. Successorial Pacts and Mutual Dispositions for Cause of Death		95	
III. Foreign Decisions, Measures, Certificates, and Rights			96

SEVENTH CHAPTER: REAL RIGHTS

	Juris-diction	Applicable Law	Recognition and Enforcement
I. Jurisdiction			
1. Immovable Property	97		
2. Movable Goods	98		
II. Applicable Law			
1. Immovable Property		99	
2. Movable Goods			
(a) General Rule		100	
(b) Goods in Transit		101	
(c) Goods Entering Switzerland		102	
(d) Retention of Title on Exports		103	
(e) Choice of Applicable Law		104	
3. Special Rules			
(a) Pledge of Claims, Securites and Other Rights		105	
(b) Document of Title		106	
(c) Means of Transportation		107	
III. Foreign Decisions			108

	Art.		
	Juris-diction	*Applicable Law*	*Recogni-tion and Enforce-ment*

EIGHTH CHAPTER:
INTELLECTUAL PROPERTY

I. Jurisdiction	109		
II. Applicable Law		110	
III. Foreign Decisions			111

NINTH CHAPTER: OBLIGATIONS

First Section: *Contracts*

I. Jurisdiction			
1. General Rule	112		
2. Place of Performance	113		
3. Contracts with Consumers	114		
4. Employment Contracts	115		
II. Applicable Law			
1. In General			
(a) Choice of Applicable Law		116	
(b) No Applicable Law Chosen		117	
2. In Particular			
(a) Contracts to Sell Movable Goods		118	
(b) Immovable Property		119	
(c) Contracts with Consumers		120	
(d) Employment Contracts		121	
(e) Contracts on Intellectual Property		122	
3. Common Provisions			
(a) Silence in Response to an Offer		123	
(b) Form		124	
(c) Performance and Inspections Modalities		125	
(d) Agency		126	

Art.

	Juris-diction	Applicable Law	Recognition and Enforcement

Second Section: *Unjust Enrichment*
I. Jurisdiction 127
II. Applicable Law 128

Third Section: *Unlawful Acts*
I. Jurisdiction
  1. General Rule 129
  2. In Particular 130
  3. Direct Claim 131
II. Applicable Law
  1. In General
    (a) Choice of Applicable Law 132
    (b) No Applicable Law Chosen 133
  2. In Particular
    (a) Traffic Accidents 134
    (b) Products Liability 135
    (c) Unfair Competition 136
    (d) Restraint of Competition 137
    (e) Nuisance 138
    (f) Violation of the Right of
        Personality 139
  3. Special Provisions
    (a) More than One Person Liable 140
    (b) Direct Claim 141
  4. Scope of Application 142

Fourth Section: *Common Provisions*
I. Plurality of Debtors
  1. Claims against More than One
      Debtor 143
  2. Recovery among Debtors 144
II. Transfer of Claims
  1. By Contractual Assignment 145
  2. By Operation of Law 146
III. Currency 147
IV. Statute of Limitations and
    Extinction of Claim 148

Fifth Section: *Foreign Decisions* 149

	Art.		
	Juris-diction	Applicable Law	Recognition and Enforcement
TENTH CHAPTER: COMPANIES			
I. Definitions		150	
II. Jurisdiction			
1. General Rule	151		
2. Liability for Foreign Companies	152		
3. Protective Measures	153		
III. Applicable Law			
1. General Rule		154	
2. Scope		155	
IV. Special Rules			
1. Claims from Public Issue of Shares or Bonds		156	
2. Protection of Name and Business Designation		157	
3. Limitations of Power of Representation		158	
4. Liability for Foreign Companies		159	
V. Swiss Branch Offices of Foreign Companies		160	
VI. Transfer of Company from Abroad			
1. General Rule		161	
2. Decisive Time		162	
VII. Transfer of Company from Switzerland to Foreign Country			
1. General Rule		163	
2. Company Debts		164	
VIII. Foreign Decisions			165

ELEVENTH CHAPTER:
BANKRUPTCY AND COMPOSITION

I. Recognition   166
II. Procedure
   1. Jurisdiction   167
   2. Conservatory Measures   168
   3. Publication   169
III. Legal Consequences
   1. In General   170
   2. Undue Preference   171
   3. Schedule of Claims   172
   4. Distribution
     (a) Recognition of Foreign
        Schedules of Claims   173
     (b) Non-recognition of Foreign
        Schedules of Claims   174
IV. Recognition of Foreign Composition
   and Similar Proceedings   175

TWELFTH CHAPTER:
INTERNATIONAL ARBITRATION

I. Scope: Seat of the Arbitral Tribunal   176
II. Arbitrability   177
III. Arbitration Agreement   178
IV. Arbitrators
   1. Constitution of the Arbitral
     Tribunal   179
   2. Challenge of an Arbitrator   180
V. Lis Pendens   181
VI. Procedure
   1. General Rule   182
   2. Provisional and Conservatory
     Measures   183

3. Taking of Evidence 184
4. Other Judicial Assistance 185
VII. Jurisdiction 186
VIII. Decision on the Merits
1. Applicable Law 187
2. Partial Award 188
3. Arbitral Award 189
IX. Finality, Action for Annulment
1. General Rule 190
2. Competent Authority 191
X. Waiver of Annulment 192
XI. Deposit and Certificate of
Enforceability 193
XII. Foreign Arbitral Awards 194

THIRTEENTH CHAPTER: FINAL
PROVISIONS

First Section: *Abrogation and Amendment
of Federal Law Presently in Force* 195

Second Section: *Transitory
Provisions*
I. Non-retroactivity 196
II. Transitory Law
1. Jurisdiction 197
2. Applicable Law 198
3. Recognition and Enforcement
of Foreign Decisions 199

Third Section: *Referendum and Enactment* 200

Appendix

APPENDICES: Page

Swiss Federal Constitution
(Excerpts)   175
Swiss Federal Statute on the
Organization of the Federal Judiciary
(Excerpts)   180
Swiss Intercantonal Concordat
on Arbitration   196

Bibliography   219

Index and Glossary   239

Introduction

> *The life of the law has not been logic, it has been experience . . . in order to know what it is, we must know what it has been, and what it tends to become.*

Oliver Wendell Holmes
The Common Law, p. 5.

Switzerland's Private International Law Statute is the fruit of considerable experience in international matters and of lengthy drafting. Centuries of constitutional and legal history shaped modern Swiss conflict of laws.

1. The Beginnings of Switzerland: Independence, Diversity, Neutrality

The *Swiss Confederation* traces its history to the late *thirteenth* century. During that period the Holy Roman Empire which extended from Germany to Italy across much of what is now Switzerland was without an emperor, and regional lords were seeking to solidify their power. In central Switzerland, a more direct route across the Alps had just opened, the Gotthard pass. The original cantons in the area united their forces against outsiders who might try to dominate their newly opened alpine crossing. With the blessing of a distant emperor, they wished to run their own affairs and did not want foreign judges to interfere.

Over the years, a number of neighboring towns and valleys joined or associated themselves with their alliance. Now a regional power, the cantons acquired buffer territories in the surrounding areas and won victories against the rising Habsburgs (1315, 1386, 1388), the Dukes of Burgundy (1476, 1477), and even against the emperor (1499). By the *end of the 15th century*, the Cantons had gained independence in fact from the Holy Roman Empire. They controlled various German, French and Italian speaking regions.

After 1515, following an unsuccessful foray into northern Italy, Switzerland no longer fought wars to expand its territory. The policy of neutrality so initiated is followed by the Swiss Confederation to this day.

1

Switzerland's independence was legally recognized by the European powers in the *Treaty of Westfalia of 1648*. By that time, the Reformation had been successful in Zurich, Geneva and other parts of Switzerland, but other cantons remained Roman Catholic. Consequently, the cantons became deeply divided by religious strife. Despite this and other tensions among the cantons, the Swiss Confederation survived for another 150 years as a loose alliance. Its neighbors were too weak and involved in their own conflicts to conquer it.

2. Switzerland after the French Revolution: The Federal Structure Takes Shape

In 1798, in the aftermath of the French Revolution, Switzerland's 'ancien régime' was finally overrun by the armies of France. Under French influence, a constitution providing for central government was enacted, but in 1803, Napoleon granted Switzerland a *Federal Constitution* which appeared better suited to the character of the country. The constitution was influenced by the recently-enacted Constitution of the United States of America.

The Napoleonic period ended with the Congress of Vienna in 1815, and with it the French domination of Switzerland. Thereafter Switzerland once more became a loose confederation of cantons ('*Restauration period*', 1815–1830).

The nineteenth century liberals gained power in a majority of the cantons ('*Regeneration period*', 1830–1848). After a brief secession of the Roman Catholic cantons was put down with little bloodshed (1847), Switzerland once more adopted a Federal Constitution.

The *Federal Constitution of 1848* embodied liberal ideas. It was reenacted in 1874. Substantially amended since, it survives to this day.[1]

3. Modern Switzerland: Industrialization and Services

Until the mid-nineteenth century, Switzerland was one of the poorer agrarian countries of Europe. Many Swiss found employment abroad.

Today, having experienced the industrial revolution and survived various European and world wars, Switzerland has become an important exporter of sophisticated equipment and services. Of its six million inhabitants, one million are immigrants who have found employment in Switzerland. International relations are thus particularly important for Switzerland.

---

1. Swiss Federal Constitution, SR 101. Translation used here: Unofficial translation by Swiss Federal Department of Foreign Affairs (1960); other translations in Constitutions of the World, (1979); Christopher Hugh, Silverwood Press, Westport CT (1982).

4. Civil Law Codified in the Cantons: The Nineteenth Century

Switzerland has always been a *civil law* country. From the fifteenth century onwards, Swiss scholars studied Roman law in the universities of northern Italy and in Basel. Although some aspects of Roman law found their way into local laws, Roman law was never considered the law of the land.

In the nineteenth century, the example and university teaching of neighboring countries influenced private law and conflict of laws in Switzerland. The cantons enacted civil codes of their own. Some cantons in the west and south modelled their *civil codes* after the French Civil Code. Some cantons in the east followed the Austrian Civil Code. Other codes were the original work of local scholars seeking to reflect local traditions.

5. Conflict of Laws and the Swiss Federal System

5.1. Issues

After its re-establishment as a union in 1848, Switzerland had to address the following questions:[2] (1) Should citizens of any canton be entitled to equal protection in all other cantons as a matter of federal law? (2) Should (a) intercantonal conflict of jurisdictions, and (b) intercantonal conflict of laws be resolved by federal conflicts rules (and, if so, by a federal statute rather than case law?)[3] and (c) should decisions rendered in other cantons be entitled to full faith and credit in all other cantons as a matter of federal law? (3) Should (a) international conflict of jurisdictions, (b) international conflict of laws (Private International Law), and (c) international recognition and enforcement be a federal matter (and, if so, should there be a federal statute rather than case law)?

5.2. Answers

There was no doubt that the theoretical answer to be given to all these questions should be yes, but for a long time little was done in practice to spell out more precise answers. The federal judiciary and the federal parliament were slow to act even in intercantonal and international conflict of laws, and until the coming into force of the PIL Statute, in practice, most of international conflict of jurisdictions and recognitions and enforcement of foreign decisions remained an area where the federal contribution was limited to constitutional (below, point 6) and treaty law (below, point 7), to be supplemented by cantonal law.

---

2. These same questions must be addressed in all federal states where the members of the union have private laws of their own, such as today, for example, the United States of America, Canada, Australia, Mexico.
3. In the 'Restauration' period, the cantons had made intercantonal treaties ('concordats') on some questions of intercantonal conflict of laws. These stayed in force until 1892.

6. Conflict of Laws in the Federal Constitution of 1848

6.1.

A number of provisions of the *Swiss Federal Constitution* granted *equal treatment and protection* to all Swiss citizens regardless of their canton of origin (Art. 4, 43, 46, 47, 60).

Art. 60 reads as follows:

> All Cantons are bound to afford all Swiss citizens the same treatment as their own citizens in the fields of legislation and of judicial proceedings.

Art. 46 paragraph 1 reads as follows:

> In matters of civil law, permanent residents shall, as a rule, be subject to the jurisdiction and legislation of their domicile.

Art. 47 reads as follows:

> A federal law shall specify the difference between establishment and residence and at the same time lay down provisions regulating the political and civil rights of resident Swiss citizens.

6.2.

The Swiss Federal Constitution also provided certain minimum guarantees limiting the scope of *jurisdiction over Swiss persons*. Art. 59 of the Swiss Federal Constitution[4] reads as follows:

> *1.* A solvent debtor having a domicile in Switzerland must be sued for personal debts before the judge of his domicile; therefore, his property outside the canton in which he is domiciled may not be seized or attached for personal claims.
> *2.* In the case of aliens the pertinent provisions of international treaties remain applicable.[5]
> *3.* Imprisonment for debts is abolished.

---

4. 1874 Version. The constitutional provision already existed in essence in the 1848 Federal Constitution, and may be said to have its origins in the late thirteenth century, see above, point 1.
5. This refers especially to the treaties with the United States of America and France, below Notes 6 and 7.

4

6.3.

Art. 61 of the Swiss Federal Constitution also provided that *full faith and credit* should be given to judgments rendered in other cantons:

> Final judgments rendered in civil law cases in all cantons shall be enforceable in the whole of Switzerland.

7. Conflict of Laws in Treaties of the Early Federal Period: 1848 to 1874

In the first years of the federal period, Switzerland entered into bilateral international *treaties* concerning the conflict of laws and mutual recognition and enforcement of judgments, in particular with the United States of America (1850)[6] and France (1869).[7]

8. Conflict of Laws in Federal Case Law

Apart from express provisions of the Constitution (above, point 6) and treaties (above, point 7), the resolution of international and intercantonal conflicts was initially left to a slowly-growing body of federal case law.[8]

9. Codification of Civil Law on the Federal Level: 1874 to 1912

9.1.

In the latter half of the 19th century, under the influence of the Swiss (centralistic and populistic) 'democratic' movement[9] Switzerland became more centralized.

---

6. Convention of Friendship, Commerce and Extradition signed in Berne on November 25, 1850, SR 0.142.113.361; entered into force on November 8, 1855. 11 Stat. 587; TS 353; 11 Bevans 894; Nussbaum, American-Swiss Private International Law, page 75.

Art. 8 to 12 were terminated on March 23, 1900, as a result of notice given by the United States on March 23, 1899; Art. 13 to 17 relating to extradition were superseded and expressly repealed by the extradition treaty signed on May 14, 1900 (31 Stat. 1928; TS 354; 11 Bevans 904). Provisions on inheritance law are still in force.

7. Convention du 15 juin 1869 entre la Suisse et la France sur la compétence judiciaire et l'exécution des jugements en matière civile (avec prot. explicatif), SR 0.276.193.491. Still in force.

8. The first unsuccessful attempts at federal codification of conflict of laws were made between 1862 and 1887. See also above, note 3.

9. The Swiss democratic movement held ideals similar to those of the movement for Jacksonian democracy in the United States of America.

This trend was evident in the re-enacted Swiss Federal Constitution of 1874, which granted the federal state the power to make laws regarding individuals, marriage, the law of obligations (contracts and torts), bills of exchange, intellectual property, and bankruptcy. Soon after the re-enactment of the Constitution the federal state exercised these powers: Federal statutes were enacted in the areas of marriage law (1874, replaced in 1912 by the Swiss Civil Code) and personal capacity law (1881, mostly replaced by the 1912 Swiss Civil Code). The *Swiss Federal Code of Obligations* of 1881 (re-enacted in 1912), covering mostly contracts and unlawful acts, was modelled after the Dresdner draft of the German Bürgerliches Gesetzbuch prepared after the unification of Germany in 1866. Federal statutes were also enacted in the field of intellectual property law (1890, still in force), and bankruptcy law (1889, still in force, currently undergoing revision), thus intercantonal conflicts in all these areas were eliminated.

9.2.
In 1904, the federal powers were extended to *all* areas of private law. Art. 64 of the Swiss Federal Constitution still reflects the gradual extension of the federal powers:

> *1.* The Confederation is entitled to legislate on civil capacity, on all legal matters relating to commerce and movable property transactions (law of contracts and tort including commercial law and law of bills of exchange), on copyrights in literature and arts, on protection of inventions suitable for industrial use, including designs and models, on suits for debts and bankruptcy.
> *2.* The Confederation is also entitled to legislate in the other fields of civil law.
> *3.* The organization of the courts, procedure and jurisdiction shall remain a matter for the Cantons as before.

By 1912, the Swiss Confederation availed itself of its power in all areas of private law. The *Swiss Federal Civil Code*, encompassing persons, family, inheritance and property, was enacted. Simultaneously, the *Swiss Federal Code of Obligations* was adapted.[10]

---

10. The chapters on contracts and unlawful acts, the first half of the Swiss Federal Code of Obligations as it exists today, were rewritten. The law of corporations and negotiable instruments was substantially modernized only in 1937.

10. The NAG of 1891: The First Swiss Statue on Conflict of Laws and Jurisdictions

Codification of private international law took much longer and is fully achieved only today.

After two unsuccessful attempts at codification in 1876 and 1887, a statute curiously named *'Statute on the private law conditions of domiciliaries and sojourners' (NAG)*[11] was enacted in 1891. The statute was primarily designed to resolve the *then* remaining *intercantonal conflicts* of jurisdiction and of laws. Family and inheritance law were still cantonal, but the other areas of private law were already federal, see above, point 7.1. NAG was based on Art. 46, subs. 1 of the Swiss Federal Constitution cited above, which provided that the law of the canton of domicile of a Swiss permanent resident should apply.

11. Private International Law under the NAG: 1912 to 1988

When the Swiss Federal Civil Code of 1912 was drafted, an unsuccessful attempt was made to include new provisions on *international conflicts* (as in the civil codes of Italy (1865) and Germany (1900)). Instead, the NAG, which upon the enactment of the Swiss Federal Civil Code was no longer required to resolve intercantonal conflicts since those had now disappeared, received a new purpose: It was applied by analogy to international conflicts, and this remained throughout much of the twentieth century.[12]

The analogous application of the NAG had a double effect: Since the NAG referred to the *law of the domicile* Switzerland did not follow the nationality principle then favored by many countries in Europe and the early Hague Conventions. Since the NAG did not cover contracts and torts, the resolution of international conflicts in these areas was left to *case law*.

From 1912 until 1988 legislation enacted in Switzerland on Private International Law remained virtually unchanged, except for the addition of a few *scattered*, independent *statutory provisions*.[13] Swiss Private International Law nevertheless changed considerably within this time period. For example, Switzerland became a party to a number of important *international treaties*, the most important of which are the Geneva Conventions on Bills and Notes[14]

---

11. Bundesgesetz vom 25. Juni 1891 betreffend die zivilrechtlichen Verhältnisse der Niedergelassenen und Aufenthalter. The Statute is now replaced by the PIL Statute; see Art. 195 PIL Statute, and Appendix, subs. Ia.
12. Art. 28, 32 NAG; Art. 59 final title of CC.
13. Art. 7a to 7i NAG were added in 1912. They principally covered the areas of marriage and divorce. Art. 8a to 8e f. NAG were added in 1973. Other statutory provisions are listed in the Appendix of the PIL Statute.
14. Art. 1086 to 1095 CO (1937); Art. 1138 to 1142 CO (1937). These remain the principal statutory sources of Swiss Private International Law outside the PIL Statute.

and several of the later Hague Conventions on Private International Law.[15]

Above all, Swiss case law on the conflict of laws developed further after 1912, especially in the areas of contracts and family law.

As enthusiasm for the nationality principle abated in the surrounding countries, Swiss law on the conflict of laws once again approached the mainstream. Switzerland contributed increasingly to the general international development of the conflict of laws.[16]

> *In the present edition*, very limited *references to the law* replaced by the PIL Statute are provided. The references to former law are meant to be a starting point for those readers who are interested in the development of the policies of Swiss private international law. Does the new PIL Statute merely continue a policy that existed before? If so, the previous case law and doctrinal writing remain a valuable source of law. However, no more than a starting point can be given. While the previous law is much more completely and adequately discussed in the Experts Report, that Report may not be as readily available to the foreign reader as the Statutes, the Swiss Federal Supreme Court decisions and the books in English cited herein may be.

12. The Genesis of the Private International Law Statute

12.1.

The desire for a *comprehensive codification of Private International Law* remained. In 1925, the Swiss Lawyers Association (whose membership includes judges, law professors, lawyers in private practice and corporate lawyers from throughout Switzerland) resolved that a new attempt should be made to achieve that goal. However, as a result of the overriding concerns caused by the

---

15. This annotated edition lists the treaties country by country and refers to the relevant provisions within the treaty. Practitioners will find a convenient guide to the treaties in Anton K. Schnyder, Staatsverträge im Internationalen Privat- und Zivilverfahrensrecht der Schweiz, ein systematischer Führer, Zürich, 1983. Some bilateral treaties on conflicts of jurisdiction and recognition and enforcement of foreign decisions are discussed in Leonard Dutoit/François Knoepfler/ Pierre Lalive/Pierre Mercier, Répertoire de Droit International Privé Suisse, vol. 2, Berne (Stämpfli) 1983.
16. An outstanding example is the *contract type formula* developed by the Swiss Federal Supreme Court, BGE 78 II 74, 91 II 44, 102 II 146. The formula's basic premise is that in the absence of a choice of law there should be neither a general rule for all contracts (for instance, that one must apply the lex loci contractus to all contracts) nor a different rule applied to each case. Rather, for each *type* of contract (sale, sole distributorship, licensing, construction, etc.), the applicable law should be determined by the domicile of the party (i.e., the seller, distributor, licensor, contractor etc.) providing the performance distinctive for that type of contract.

The more recent Hague Conventions and legislation on Private International Law by certain other European countries reflect the contract type formula.

See Art. 117 PIL Statute.

economic crisis of the 1920's and World War II, this goal once again remained unfulfilled.

The subject was discussed once more by the same association in 1971.[17]

This time, conditions were favorable:[18] An intricate lawmaking procedure[19] was set into motion which led to the present PIL Statute.

12.2.

In 1973[20] the Swiss Federal Ministry of Justice, acting on a 1972 motion by Parliament,[21] set up a Committee of Experts chaired by Professor Frank Vischer.[22]

The committee was requested to study whether the conflict of laws could be codified. It prepared a draft statute in three phases:

In the first phase (1973 to 1975), each of six subcommittees produced a draft for its respective area of law.

The second phase (March 1975 through March 1976) began with a meeting of subcommittee chairmen, at which the six portions of the draft statute were analyzed and assembled into a first preliminary draft statute. In 1975, the draft was presented to the full membership of the Experts Committee for their comments and was again reviewed by the subcommittee chairmen. These critiques indicated the need for fundamental revision of numerous parts of the statute, revisions which were substantially completed by early 1976.

In the third and last phase (early 1976 through early 1977), the subcommittee chairmen again reviewed the various drafts and developed a second preliminary draft statute from which the Chairman and Secretary of the Committee of Experts produced the *Experts Draft* on February 24, 1978. This draft was submitted to the Federal Department of Justice and Police on June 30, 1978 together with the *Experts Report*.[23]

12.3.

The entire Experts Draft was also presented to a wider circle of lawyers both from Switzerland and abroad at the *Fribourg Colloque* on April 27–28, 1979.[24]

17. 90 ZSR page 1a et seq.
18. Over the last two decades, new codifications of the conflict of laws were enacted in the Federal Republic of Germany, the German Democratic Republic, Yugoslavia, Greece, Austria, Poland, Portugal, Spain, Czechoslovakia, Hungary and Turkey. Italy and the Netherlands may follow.
19. See Geschäftsverkehrsgesetz, SR 171.11. Translation in 14 Constitutional and Parliamentary Information, 100 (1983).
20. Schweizerisches Bundesblatt 1973 I 1676.
21. House Debate, Amtliches Bulletin 1972, page 1556.
22. For a list of the members, of the Committee of Experts, see Experts Report, page 16.
23. Bundesgesetz über das Internationale Privatrecht (IPR-Gesetz), Schlussbericht der Experten-kommission zum Gesetzesentwurf, 13 Schweizer Studien zum Internationalen Recht (1979) (an abbreviated version appeared in 1978 as 12 Schweizer Studien zum Internationalen Recht).
24. Freiburger Kolloquium, 14 Studien zum Internationalen Recht (1979).

12.4.

Thereupon the Swiss Federal Department of Justice and Police, with Dr. Paul Volken as its chief expert, prepared a departmental draft. Comments were invited from interested parties and the public at large, and then compiled in a voluminous publication.[25]

12.5.

On the basis of these comments, the Swiss Federal Department of Justice and Police prepared a second draft statute which was accepted by the executive branch of the Swiss Federal Government. In 1983, the *Government Draft* was sent to Parliament with the *Government Report*.[26]

12.6.

Discussion of the Government Draft continued among interested groups. In particular, the Swiss Federal Institute of Comparative Law in Lausanne organized a symposium on October 14–15, 1983 to compare the first half of Swiss Federal Government draft statute with the German Federal Government draft of its new statute. This symposium was again attended by numerous Swiss and foreign specialists, particularly from Germany.[27] Its proceedings were published as *Lausanne Colloque*.

12.7.

The Government Draft was then submitted to parliament. The Senate and the House both set up special committees to evaluate the draft and report to the full session.

The Senate's committee suggested a number of changes to the draft. It collected the provisions on intellectual property into a separate chapter. In *1985*, the *Senate* followed most of its Committee's recommendations. Against the Committee's recommendation, the chapter on international arbitration was defeated by a narrow margin.[28]

---

25. Bundesamt für Justiz, Bundesgesetz über das Internationale Privatrecht, Darstellung der Stellungnahmen auf Grund des Gesetzesentwurfs der Expertenkommission und des entsprechenden Begleitberichts (1980).
26. Bundesblatt 1983, the Government Report is cited to its points, and to the pages of the separate German edition.
27. Lausanner Kolloquium über den deutschen und den schweizerischen Gesetzesentwurf zur Neuregelung des Internationalen Privatrechts, Veröffentlichung des Schweizerischen Instituts für Rechtsvergleichung (1984). The German PIL Statute of July 25, 1986, Bundesblatt 1986 I 1142, is in force since November 1986.
28. Senate Debate, Amtliches Bulletin, page 183.

12.8.

The draft was then considered by the *House*. The House Committee recommended passing the Senate's version in most respects, but prepared a substantially amended draft for the chapter on international arbitration.

In the House, the draft thus amended passed swiftly and was accepted unanimously in *1986*.[29]

12.9.

On November 4–5, 1986 a third important meeting took place in St. Gallen to consider the second half of the House draft as it then was. This was published as *Festschrift Rudolf Moser*.[30]

12.10.

In *June 1987*, the *Senate* aligned itself with the House on many points, including the chapter on international arbitration, but some hundred smaller differences remained.[31]

12.11.

In *September 1987*, the *House* accepted the Senate's version[32] with a few exceptions.

12.12.

On *October 10, 1987*, the *Senate* accepted the House version[33] as it was.

29. House Debate, Amtliches Bulietin, 1986, page 1370.
30. Beiträge zum neuen IPR des Sachen-, Schuld- und Gesellschaftsrechts, Festschrift für Prof. Rudolf Moser.
31. Senate Debate, Amtliches Bulletin 1987, page 200.
32. House Debate, Amtliches Bulletin 1987, page 1073. 1987 Herbstsession House 8. Tagung der 42. Amtsdauer, Session de printemps – 8ᵉ session de la 42ᵉ législature Amtliches Bulletin 1985; Amtliches Bulletin der Bundesversammlung – Bulletin officiel de l'Assemblée fédérale, Ständerat – Conseil des Etats
33. Senate Debate, Amtliches Bulletin 1987, page 510. 1985 Frühjahrssession, 8. Tagung der 42. Amtsdaurer, Session de printemps – 8ᵉ session de la 42ᵉ législature Amtliches Bulletin 1985; Amtliches Bulletin der Bundesversammlung – Bulletin officiel de l'Assemblée fédérale, Ständerat – Conseil des Etats

12.13.
Finally, on *December 18, 1987* both House and Senate accepted a slightly edited text.[34] It was published in Schweizerisches Bundesblatt on January 12, 1988. Fifty thousand Swiss voters or eight cantons could have forced a referendum but this did not happen within the statutory deadline.

12.14.
The PIL Statute is scheduled to come into force on January 1, 1989.

> *In the present edition*, full citations to the '*travaux préparatoires*' in the widest sense are provided. The 'travaux préparatoires' for a statute of such a highly technical nature as the Private International Law Statute will provide, for some time at least, guidance to practitioners.

13. The Constitution and the Private International Law Statute

13.1.
Throughout the law-making process, there was no doubt that the federal lawgiver had power to legislate on (a) international conflict of jurisdictions, (b) international conflict of laws (Private International Law), (c) international recognition and enforcement, even though, apart from federal constitutional and treaty law, international conflict of jurisdictions and recognition and enforcement of foreign decisions had, in practice, remained cantonal.

There was no doubt either that international bankruptcy and composition was within the federal powers.

There was some doubt whether the Confederation could legislate on international arbitration. Some argued that arbitration was a procedural matter and thus in the domain of the cantons. However, the view eventually prevailed that international arbitration, as distinguished from domestic arbitration, had sufficient international and contractual elements to make it a federal matter.

As is customary, the constitutional basis is spelled out in the Preamble to the PIL Statute.

---

34. Senate final vote, Amtliches Bulletin 1987, page 685; House final vote, Amtliches Bulletin 1987, page 1894. Unfortunately, some mistakes were introduced in the editing process, see German text of margin to Art. 158, German and French text of margin to 179.

13.2.
The Swiss Federal Constitution remains of course the paramount source of law
in Switzerland. Many provisions of the PIL Statute take into account provisions
of the Swiss Federal Constitution, particularly its Art. 59.

> *In the present edition*, references to the relevant provisions of the *Swiss
> Federal Constitution* are provided. Excerpts appear as Appendix I. The
> references serve essentially as background for understanding the provisions
> of the Private International Law Statute.

14. International Treaties and the Private International Law Statute

14.1.
Under Swiss concepts, the Law of Nations (*'International Law'*), is the law of
the land in Switzerland, and there is no need for implementing statutes once a
treaty has been ratified by Switzerland, except where the treaty is not capable of
direct application ('non-self-executing'). As a source of law the Law of Nations
is second only to federal constitutional law. It takes precedence over federal
statutes such as the PIL Statute.

14.2.
The PIL Statute adopts the convenient practice of referring to the *multilateral*
treaties that have introduced private international law rules of general application ('lois uniformes') into the national system.
    The Statute is not making new law in any sense but is simply referring to a
higher source of law already in existence.

14.3.
The PIL Statute does make law in other cases by extending the application of
certain existing multilateral treaties to Switzerland's relationship with non-treaty
countries (in case of treaties that do not provide for a 'loi uniforme'), or, by
analogy, to areas of law not covered by the treaty.

14.4.
Some mutlilateral treaties remain of non-universal application. These are not
mentioned in the PIL Statute, but they retain precedence over the PIL Statute,
Art. 1 PIL Statute.

14.5.

Where *bilateral treaties* exist, for example, the *Treaties with the United States (1850) and with France (1869)*, it is essential that these not be overlooked, because bilateral treaties retain precedence over the PIL Statute.

14.6.

Some international treaties exercised a considerable influence on the PIL Statute, particulary the Brussels/European Convention 1968, as amended 1978 and 1982.

In the present edition, full references to all treaties are provided.

15. *A Comprehensive Codification*: *Rules and Exceptions*

15.1.

The PIL Statute has three official texts, one in German, one in French and one in Italian. None takes precedence.

In the present edition, the *original official German, French and Italian terms* are provided in footnotes whenever there is no precise, obvious and current English equivalent. Where the texts appear to diverge, the texts or text primarily translated are identified. Short notes explaining legal terms peculiar to Swiss law are added. *Shorthand expressions*, mostly in Latin, commonly used by specialists of the conflict of laws are also given.

15.2.

The PIL Statute is a civil law-type *code*. It stands alone as a separate piece of legislation (containing 200 articles). It is not integrated into the Swiss Federal Civil Code and the Swiss Federal Code of Obligations, but the system upon which the Statute is built follows the Swiss Federal Civil Code and Federal Code of Obligations loosely.

Art. 1 of the Swiss Civil Code applies in conjunction with the Private International Law Statute. Art. 1 reads as follows:

[1]The Law must be applied in all cases which come within the letter or the spirit of any of its provisions.
[2]Where no provision is applicable, the judge shall decide according to the existing Customary Law and, in default thereof, according to the rules which he would lay down if he had himself to act as legislator.
[3]Herein he must be guided by approved legal doctrine and case-law.

15.3.
Less than half of the PIL Statute deals with international conflict of laws *in a narrow sense*. Related areas, including intellectual property, bankruptcy and international arbitration are also covered. The PIL Statute also addresses international conflict of jurisdictions[35] (depending on how one counts, some 60 articles) and the recognition and enforcement of foreign decisions (some 30 articles). Especially in the more remote areas just mentioned, the PIL Statute does more than codify previous case law. It makes new law.

15.4.
The PIL Statute begins in typical civil law code fashion with a first chapter of *general provisions*. On renvoi, the PIL Statute avoids dogma (Art. 13 and 14 PIL Statute). The PIL Statute has a customary Ordre Public exception clause, (Art. 17 PIL Statute), but there are also innovative provisions in favor of Swiss (Art. 18 PIL Statute) and even foreign (Art. 19 PIL Statute) Lois d'Ordre Public or Lois d'Application Immédiate. There are no provisions on characterization,[35] preliminary question,[36] fraus legis,[37] or conflit mobile.[38]

15.5.
In its *later chapters*, the PIL Statute is not limited to general rules. Rather, it spells out the specific rules and exceptions in considerable detail.

The PIL Statute's conflicts rules are in the traditional form: For a particular *legal issue* they designate the applicable law by means of a *point de rattachement*.

Most conflict of laws rules are worded as rules that conceivably could appear, worded the same way, in the legislation of other countries (e.g., Art. 68 PIL). By contrast, most conflict of jurisdictions rules, and all recognition and enforcement rules state only what Switzerland will or will not do (e.g., Art. 66, 70 PIL Statute).

As in the more recent Hague Conventions, the conflict rules use non-technical autonomous concepts such as 'habitual residence' rather than technical terms appearing in other Swiss statutes.

15.6.
Some statutory definitions are provided, for example the terms 'domicile', 'habitual residence', 'business establishment', 'seat' (Art. 20, 21 PIL Statute), or 'company' (Art. 150 PIL Statute).

35. See Lausanne Colloque, page 35. Generally, Swiss courts may be expected to characterize according to the lex fori, but take the purpose of the conflict of laws into consideration.
36. Generally, Swiss Courts may be expected to answer preliminary questions according to the lex causae, Art. 13 PIL Statute.
37. See Art. 2 of the Swiss Civil Code, and Art. 45 PIL Statute.
38. See Art. 101 to 104, 107 PIL Statute.

In the present edition, cross-references to the statutory definitions are given throughout.

In the present edition some references to the *Swiss federal substantive and cantonal (Zurich) procedural law* in the areas covered by particular provisions of the PIL Statute are provided.

For a better understanding of the PIL Statute in the context of the Swiss legal system some considerations of Swiss substantive law may occasionally be helpful even though expressions used in the PIL Statute should not necessarily be characterized according to the lex fori.

Secondary sources available in English are emphasized. These should provide readers with further citations to Swiss substantive law.

The references to Swiss substantive law are also meant to provide some convenient assistance to those practioners who come to the conclusion that Swiss substantive law is likely to be applied to a particular case.[39]

16. Conflict of Jurisdictions: The Policies of the PIL Statute

16.1.
Partly as mandated by Art. 59 of the Federal Constitution, provisions on conflict of jurisdictions in the PIL Statute secure jurisdiction at the (last) domicile (or seat) of the defendant (Art. 2, 33, 38, 46, 57, 75, 84, 98, 109, 112, 127, 129, 151).

16.2.
For persons without a domicile but with habitual residence in Switzerland, particularly children, many provisions secure jurisidiction at the place of habitual residence.

16.3.
Swiss jurisdiction is also provided subsidiarily to avoid denial of justice, (Art. 3 PIL Statute) or if the case has some factual connection with Switzerland.

16.4.
Normally, parties are free to make a choice of jurisdiction, in which case the choice is exclusive (Art. 5, see also Art. 6, 7). Occasionally, their choice is limited (Art. 59, 60, 66, 67, PIL Statute) or even excluded (Art. 114, 151 PIL Statute).

---

39. This is not to say that the 'homeward trend' should be encouraged.

16.5.
Swiss nationalist policies are particularly protected in the field of *forum arresti* (Art. 4 PIL Statute), and by granting special protection to Swiss citizens residing abroad.

17. *Private International Law: The policies of the PIL Statute*

17.1.
Following a recent individualistic trend, relatively wide application is given to the law chosen by the parties (*lex voluntatis* and *professio iuris*) (e.g., Art. 48, 52, 90, 104, 116, 132, 154 PIL Statute). In the absence of a choice of law by the parties, the Statute generally follows the domicile principle traditional in Switzerland (e.g., Art. 35, 37 PIL Statute), and, for companies, the principle of *lex loci incorporationis* (Art. 154 PIL Statute).

17.2.
Previous law tried to avoid "limping" marriages and to preserve unity of citizenship within families, but not always successfully. The PIL statute has abandoned this policy in many cases.

17.3.
Perhaps more than the previous law, the PIL Statute furthers substantive policies. Thus, traditional policies of *favor matrimonii* (Art. 45 PIL Statute), *legitimitatis* (Art. 74 PIL Statute), *negotii* (Art. 36 PIL Statute), *validitatis* (Art. 69, 83, 86 PIL Statute), are pervasive, but also individualistic *favor divortii* (Art. 65 PIL Statute), and social *favor laesi* (Art. 135, 138, 139 PIL Statute), and *favor infantis* (Art. 69, 83, 86 PIL Statute).

17.4.
In the area of contracts, the PIL Statute essentially codifies case law. In the area of unlawful acts, the statute continues the policy in favor of *lex loci delicti* (Art. 133 PIL Statute), but carves out some exceptions for *lex stabuli* (Art. 134 PIL Statute) or *lex domicilii communis* (Art. 133 PIL Statute).

17.5.
Some provisions protect Swiss defendants against foreign (particularly American) laws that provide for punitive damages, treble damages, and excessive damages (Art. 135, 137 PIL Statute).

*18. Recognition and Enforcement of Foreign Decisions: The Policies of the
Private International Law Statute*

The general policy of the PIL Statute is to grant recognition to foreign decisions,
(*favor recognitionis*) provided certain safeguards are observed.

19. *International Bankruptcy in the Private International Law Statute*

The provisions of the PIL Statute on International Bankruptcy and Composition
are the result of a development similar to the development in the area of the law
of obligations. Enforcement of debts and bankruptcy became a federal matter in
1874. A federal statute was enacted in 1891.

The law of international bankruptcy and composition was case law, and was
dominated by the principle of territoriality of bankruptcy.

The PIL Statute makes new law by trying not to duplicate unnecessarily in
Switzerland at the expense of the creditor what has been done abroad.

20. International Arbitration in the Private International Law Statute

20.1.
International arbitration has a long history in *Switzerland*, going back to the
'Alabama' arbitration of 1812. For a long time, arbitration law was considered
part of civil procedure, and thus in the domain of the cantons. Accordingly, it
was covered in the codes of civil procedure of the various cantons.

20.2.
Since 1969, the Swiss Intercantonal Concordat on Arbitration has replaced the
regulations in the cantonal codes of civil procedure in most cantons.[40]

20.3.
With the PIL Statute, international arbitration – newly distinguished from
domestic arbitration (Art. 176 PIL Statute) – in Switzerland becomes a federal
matter subject to very liberal rules. The following articles are particularly
interesting: Art. 176–180, 182, 187, 189–192 PIL Statute.

40. Zurich joined the Concordat on July 1, 1985.

21. A Look Ahead

Swiss case law will *develop* further within the framework of the new statute. Courts will occasionally interpret the statutory text without reference to its drafters. Furthermore, Swiss legal practice, which faces practical problems of private international law daily, will probably depart over time from an excessively literal reading of the text of Switzerland's Private International Law Statute.

A Note on Liechtenstein

The Principality of Liechtenstein is a sovereign country associated with Switzerland since 1923 in customs, monetary, postal, diplomatic, and some tax and other matters. The Swiss Private International Law Statute does not apply in Liechtenstein.

Liechtenstein has fewer international treaties than Switzerland.

International conflict of jurisdictions is governed in Liechtenstein by the Zivilprozessordnung of 1912.

International conflict of laws is governed by the ABGB, and case law.

International recognition and enforcement is governed by case law.

Liechtenstein's substantive law is codified in the ABGB, in the Personen- und Gesellschaftsrecht of 1928, in the Liechtensteinisches Sachenrecht of 1923, and in the AHGB.

Abbreviations

Amtliches Bulletin

Amtliches Bulletin der Bundesversammlung, Eidgenössische Drucksachen- und Material-verwaltung, Bern.

Art.

Article

CC

Swiss Civil Code, Schweizerisches Zivilgesetz-buch (ZGB), Code civil suisse du 10 dé-cembre 1907, SR 210.

Translated: by Williams, 1925; by Wil-liams, Wyler and Wyler, 1987.

Excerpts translated: by American Cham-ber of Commerce in Switzerland, 1974, in 'Swiss Corporation Law', (Art. 52 to 49); Becchio, Phillips and Wehinger, 1984, in 'Swiss Company Law' (Art. 52 to 89 bis): by Russotto and Samuel, 1965, 'Swiss Family Law' (Art. 22 to 38, 90 to 177, 252 to 456).

CO

Swiss Federal Code of Obligations, Schweizeris-ches Obligationenrecht (OR), Loi fédérale du 30 mars 1911 complétant le code civil suisse (Livre cinquième: Droit des obliga-tion), SR 220.

Translated: by Wettstein, 1928/1939, Foreign Tax Law Association, under the title of 'Commercial law of Switzerland, 1958, Simon L. Goren, 1987.

Excerpts translated: by Lidgard, Rohwa and Campbell, A Survey of Commercial Agencies, 1984, (Art. 394 to 422); by Bec-chio, Phillips and Wehinger, 1984, (Art. 458 to 465, and 530 to 964); Swiss-American Chamber of Commerce, 1984, (Art. 1 to 238; 253 to 343; 356 to 362; 394 to 439); by American Chamber of Com-merce in Switzerland, 1974, (Art. 620 to 763; 927 to 944, 950 to 952; 956 to 964).

23

Concordat	Concordat intercantonal sur l'arbitrage, Concordat sur l'arbitrage du 27 mars 1969, SR 279. See Appendix III.
E	English
Experts Draft	Bundesgesetz über das internationale Privatrecht (IPRGesetz), Gesetzesentwurf der Expertenkommission und Begleitbericht – Loi fédérale sur le droit international privé (loi de d.i.p), projet de loi de la commission d'experts et rapport explicatif, Etudes suisses de droit international, volume 12, Zurich 1978.
	Revue critique de droit international privé 1979, No 1, p. 185; Rabels Zeitschrift für ausländisches und internationales Privatrecht 1978, No 4, p. 716.
Experts Report	Bundesgesetz über das internationale Privatrecht (IPRGsetz), Schlussbericht der Expertenkommission zum Gesetzesentwurf, Etudes suisses de droit international, volume 13, Zürich 1979.
F	French
Festschrift Moser	Beiträge zum neuen IPR des Sachen-, Schuld- und Gesellschaftsrechts, Festschrift für Prof. Rudolf Moser, Schweizer Studien zum internationalen Recht 51.
Fribourg Colloque	Freiburger Kolloquium über den schweizerischen Entwurf zu einem Bundesgesetz über das internationale Privatrecht, Freiburg (Schweiz), 27.–28. April 1979 = Colloque de Fribourg relatif au projet suisse de loi fédérale sur le droit international privé, Zürich, 1979. Schweizer Studien zum internationalen Recht 14.
G	German
Government Draft	Appendix to Government Report.
Government Report	Botschaft zum Bundesgesetz über das internationale Privatrecht (IPR-Gesetz) vom 10. November 1982.
House Debate	Amtliches Bulletin – Nationalrat.
House Draft	Amtliches Bulletin – Nationalrat.

I	Italian
L	Latin
Lausanne Colloque	Lausanner Kolloquium über den deutschen und den schweizerischen Gesetzenwurf zur Neuregelung des Internationalen Privatrechts, Lausanne. 14–15. Oktober 1983, veranstaltet vom Schweizerischen Institut für Rechtsvergleichung, Lausanne. Zürich, 1984. – Veröffentlichungen des Schweizerischen Instituts für Rechtsvergleichung 1.
Lit	Letter.
NAG	Bundesgesetz vom 25. Juni 1891 betreffend die zivilrechtlichen Verhältnisse der Niedergelassenen und Aufenthalter, Loi fédérale du 25 juin 1891 sur les rapports de droit civil des citoyens établis ou en séjour, SR 211.435.1 repealed by Appendix to the PIL Statute.
	Excerpts translated: by Nussbaum, 1958, in 'American-Swiss Private International Law', (Art. 7 b to 7 h; 22; 24; 28 and 32); by Russotto and Samuel, 1965, in 'Swiss Family Law' (Art. 1 to 21; 28 to 34).
Para.	Paragraph
PIL Statute	Private International Law Statute, Bundesgesetz über das internationale Privatrecht (IPR-Gesetz), Loi fédérale sur le droit international privé (loi de DIP) du 18 décembre 1987.
SchKG	Bundesgesetz über Schuldbetreibung und Konkurs, Loi fédérale du 11 avril 1889 sur la poursuite pour dettes et la faillite, SR 281.1.
Senate Debate	Amtliches Bulletin – Ständerat.
Senate Draft	Amtliches Bulletin – Ständerat.
SJ1R	Schweizerisches Jahrbuch für Internationales Recht.
SJZ	Schweizerische Juristenzeitung.

25

SR	Systematische Sammlung des Bundesrechts, Recueil systématique du droit fédéral (RS) [Looseleaf in German, French and Italian] 1970 ff.
Subs.	Subsection.
Swiss Federal Constitution	Bundesverfassung der Schweizerischen Eidgenossenschaft Constitution fédérale de la Conféderation suisse du 29 mai 1874, SR 101.
	Translated: by Swiss Federal Department of Foreign Affairs, 1980; by Blaustein, Flanz und Siegenthaler, 1979 in 'Constitutions of the Countries of the World'; by Hughes, 1954. See Appendix I.
ZPO	Zivilprozessordnung, Code of Civil Procedure.
ZSR	Zeitschrift für schweizerisches Recht.

Federal Statute on Private International Law (PIL Statute)

of December 18, 1987

The Federal Parliament of the Swiss Confederation,[1]

- based on the federal power in foreign affairs;[2]
- based on Art. 64[3] of the Federal Constitution;
- based on the Report of the Federal Council,[4] of November 10, 1982;

resolves:

Legislative history of the preamble: Lausanne Colloque, page 255, 257, 261; Senate Debate, Amtliches Bulletin 1985; pages 113, 116, 135, 176, 177, 178, 179; House Debate, Amtliches Bulletin 1986, page 1293.

1. The official text was published in Schweizerisches Bundesblatt 1988 I 5 and in the loose-leaf edition, Systematische Sammlung des Bundesrechts, SR 291.435.1 in German, French and Italian. As with all Swiss statutes, the versions in French, German and Italian are equally original, see Art. 116 Swiss Federal Constitution. The titles and margin titles are part of the text. Any amendments would again be published in Schweizerisches Bundesblatt and would appear in the loose-leaf edition, Systematische Sammlung des Bundesrechts, in SR 291.4235.1.

2. Federal power in foreign affairs (E), compétence de la Confédération en matière de relations extérieures (F), Zuständigkeit des Bundes in auswärtigen Angelegenheiten (G), competenza della Confederazione in materia di affari esteri (I). The 'foreign power' is not granted in any particular Article of the Swiss Federal Constitution, but is apparent from Swiss Federal Constitution, Art. 8 to 11, 85, subs. 5 and 6 and Art. 102, subs. 8 and 9. See Appendix I.

3. Art. 64 of the Swiss Federal Constitution, see Appendix I, grants the power to make law in civil and bankruptcy matters. See Introduction, points 9.2 and 13.

4. Government Report of November 10, 1982, Schweizerisches Bundesblatt 1983 I 263, available in German, French and Italian, also in separate editions.

First Chapter: General Provisions[1]

First Section: Field of Application[2]

Art. 1

1. This Statute regulates[3] in international matters:[4]
(a) the jurisdiction of the Swiss judicial or administrative authorities;[5]
(b) the applicable law;[6]
(c) the conditions for recognition and enforcement of foreign decisions;[7]
(d) bankruptcy and composition;[8]
(e) arbitration.[9]

2. The international treaties[10] are reserved.

> *Previous law:* See Introduction, points 10 and 11, Art. 34 NAG, repealed in Appendix to PIL Statute.
> *Legislative history:* Experts Draft, *Art. 1;* Experts Report, page 5 ff.; Fribourg Colloque, page 9, 11, 29, 65, 66; Government Draft, *Art. 1;* Government Report, point 111.3, page 7; point 112, pages 34 to 36; Lausanne Colloque, page 276; Senate Debate, Amtliches Bulletin 1985, page 128; House Debate, Amtliches Bulletin 1986, page 1295, 1296; Senate Debate, Amtliches Bulletin 1987, page 181.

1. General Provisions (E), dispositions communes (F), Gemeinsame Bestimmungen (G), disposizioni comuni (I).

2. Field of Application (E), champ d'application (F), Geltungsbereich (G), campo di applicazione (I).

3. Regulates (E), régit (F), regelt (G), disciplina (I).

4. In international matters (E), en matière internationale (F), im internationalen Verhältnis (G), nell'ambito internazionale (I).
    What makes a matter international is not defined. The field of application of the chapter on international arbitration is defined in Art. 176 of the PIL Statute.
    In this subsection, the general structure of the Statute is not announced with any precision. As may be seen from the Table of Contents, most chapters first deal with international jurisdiction, then with choice of law, and finally with recognition and enforcement of foreign decisions. The chapter on international bankruptcy may be said to deal with the recognition and enforcement of foreign bankruptcy decrees. Letters (d) and (e) refer to areas of the law not generally expected to be covered by a PIL statute.

5. Swiss judicial or administrative authorities (E), autorités judiciaires ou administratives suissees (F), schweizerische Gerichte oder Behörden (G), tribunali e autorità svizzeri (I). These include cantonal and local authorities.

6. The applicable law (E), le droit applicable (F), das anzuwendende Recht (G), il diritto applicabile (I). The law applicable to the merits in international arbitration is governed by Art. 187 of the PIL Statute exclusively.

7. Conditions for recognition and enforcement of foreign decisions (E), condition de la reconnaissance et de l'exécution des décisions étrangères (F), Voraussetzungen der Anerkennung und Vollstreckung ausländischer Entscheidungen (G), presupposti del riconoscimento e dell'esecuzione di decisioni straniere (I).

8. Bankruptcy and composition (E), la faillite et le concordat (F), den Konkurs und den Nachlassvertrag (G), il fallimento e il concordato (I). See Art. 166 to 175. 'Concordat' is in French also used for an intercantonal treaty providing for uniform law.

9. Arbitration (E), l'arbitrage (F), die Schiedsgerichtbarkeit (G), l'arbitrato (I). See Art. 176 to 194.

10. International treaties (E), traités internationaux (F), völkerrechtliche Verträge (G), trattati internazionali (I). The German text avoids the term 'Staatsverträge'. That makes clear that such treaties need not be closed by States exclusively. See Introduction, point 14.
   The term 'treaty' is too narrow. What is meant is Public International Law or the Law of Nations, which includes areas of customary law, for instance, on state and diplomatic immunity.
   Treaties that provide for uniform substantive law in particular areas are also reserved by subsection 2, such as the Geneva convention on bills and notes, an area not covered by the PIL Statute at all, the treaties on international rail transportation, and the Vienna convention on the law of international sales that Switzerland has not yet joined, but probably will. These treaties are mentioned in the annotations of the present edition under 'substantive law'.

Second Section: Jurisdiction[1]

Art. 2

I. In General Unless otherwise provided by this Statute[2], jurisdiction[1] lies with the Swiss judicial or administrative authorities[3] at the defendant's domicile.[4]

Swiss Federal Constitution: Art. 59, see Appendix I. Introduction, points 1, 6.2.2, 13, and 16. This applies also in favor of Swiss companies, even owned by non-Swiss persons. Compare Para. 2. Zurich ZPO.
Multilateral treaties: With most countries: Convention de Vienne du 18 avril 1961 sur les relations diplomatiques, Art. 30 to 41, SR 0.191.01; Convention de Vienne du 24 avril 1963 sur les relations consulaires, Art. 43, 53, SR 0.191.02.

With Austria, Belgium, the U.K. and Cyprus: also Convention européenne du 16 mai 1972 sur l'immunité des Etats (avec annexe), Art. 1 to 15, SR 0.273.1. International organizations: in general, SR 0.192.11 et seq.

Bilateral treaties: With *France:* Convention du 15 juin 1869 entre la Suisse et la France sur la compétence judiciare et l'exécution des jugements en matière civile (avec protocole explicatif), Art. 1 to 12, SR 0.276.193.491. With *Italy:* Accord avec l'Italie sur la compétence judiciaire; Convention d'établissement et consulaire du 22 juillet 1868, entre la Suisse et l'Italie (avec décl.), Art. 1, 2, 8, SR 0.142.114.541; Protocole du 1 mai 1869 concernant l'exécution des conventions conclues et signées à Berne et à Florence entre la Suisse et l'Italie le 22 juillet 1868, Art. IV, SR 0.142.114.541.1; Convention du 3 janvier 1933 entre la Suisse et l'Italie sur la reconnaissance et l'exécution de décisions judiciaires, Art. 8, SR 0.276.194.541.

Previous law: Art. 2 NAG, repealed in Appendix to PIL Statute; Cantonal law.

Legislative history: Experts Draft, *Art. 2;* Experts Report, page 43; Government Draft, *Art. 2;* Government Report, point 213, 213.1, page 36; Lausanne Colloque, page 227; Senate Debate, Amtliches Bulletin 1986, page 129; House Debate, Amtliches Bulletin 1986, page 1295, 1296; Festschrift Moser, page 249; Senate Debate, Amtliches Bulletin, 1987, page 181.

1. See Art. 1.

2. The PIL Statute states for each type of cases, in the first section of each chapter, whether the Swiss courts have international jurisdiction, and which courts within Switzerland have venue. See Table of Contents. Examples: Art. 3, 4, 5, 6 etc. This article applies only if other articles of the PIL Statute do not provide otherwise.

3. See Preamble of the PIL Statute.

4. See Art. 20 and Art. 21. Introduction, points 1, 6.2.2, 13, and 16.

Art. 3

II.
Subsidiary
Jurisdiction[1]

If this Statute does not provide for jurisdiction in Switzerland, and proceedings abroad are impossible or highly impracticable,[2] jurisdiction lies with the Swiss judicial or administrative authorities[3] at the place which has a sufficient connection[4] with the case.[5]

Treaties: See Art. 2.
Previous law: Cantonal.
Legislative history: Experts Draft, *Art. 4;* Experts Report, page 45; Fribourg Colloque, page 8, 17, 66, 67; Government Draft, *Art. 3;* Government Report, point 213.3, page 37; Lausanne Colloque, page 269; Senate Debate, Amtliches Bulletin 1985, page 129; House Debate, Amtliches Bulletin 1986, page 1295, 1296; Senate Debate, Amtliches Bulletin, 1987, page 181; House Debate,

Amtliches Bulletin, 1987, page 1066; Senate Debate, Amtliches Bulletin 1987, page 506.

1. Subsidiary jurisdiction (E), for de nécessité (F), Notzuständigkeit (G), foro di necessità (I), forum necessitatis (L).
This section applies subsidiarily to the special provisions on international jurisdiction in each chapter, and to Art. 2. See Table of Contents.

2. Impossible or highly impracticable (E), impossible ou qu'on ne peut raisonnablement exiger qu'elle le soit (F), nicht möglich oder unzumutbar (G), non è possibile o non può essere ragionevolmente preteso (I).

3. See Art. 1.

4. Sufficient connection (E), lien suffisant (F), genügender Zusammenhang (G), sufficiente connessione (I). Art. 15 is a similar provision on applicable law.

5. With the case (E), avec la cause présente (F), mit dem Sachverhalt (G), colla fattispecie (I).

Art. 4

III.
Validation of
Attachment[1]

Unless this Statute provides for another jurisdiction in Switzerland, a lawsuit in validation of attachment[1] may be brought at the Swiss place of attachment.[2]

Treaties: See Art. 2.
Previous law: Cantonal, e.g. Para. 9 Zurich ZPO.
Legislative history: Experts Draft, *Art. 12;* Experts Report, page 55; Fribourg Colloque, page 44; Government Draft, *Art. 4;* Government Report, point 213.4, page 37; Senate Debate, Amtliches Bulletin 1985, page 129; House Debate, Amtliches Bulletin 1986, page 1295, 1302; Festschrift Moser, page 253; Senate Debate, Amtliches Bulletin 1987, page 181.
Bankruptcy and Composition: See Art. 166 to 175.
Swiss substantive law: Art. 278 SchKG.

1. Lawsuit in validation of attachment (E), action en validition de séquestre (F), Klage auf Arrestprosequierung (G), azione di convalida del sequestro (I).
A lawsuit in validation of attachment is an ordinary civil suit for a money judgment. However, a judgment becomes immediately enforceable into the assets that were attached.
Attachment in Switzerland (similar to Mareva injunction) is possible if (1) the main debtor does not have his domicile in Switzerland, (2) a prima facie case can be made that the main debt exists and is due, and (3) the main debtor has assets in Switzerland (e.g. a receivable from a debtor domiciled in Switzerland).

31

To attach a Swiss bank account, the branch office must be identified, though not the account number. There is no need to trace assets to Switzerland in connection with the main debt. Initial proceedings are ex parte. Once attachment has been made, an ordinary lawsuit must be filed against the debtor. Article 4 makes this possible at the place of attachment (quasi in rem jurisdiction at the forum arresti). The ultimate decision on the merits has only quasi in rem effect: It can be enforced only against the assets under attachment.

2. Swiss place of attachment (E), for suisse du séquestre (F), schweizerischer Arrestort (G), luogo svizzero del sequestro (I), forum arresti (L).

Art. 5

IV. Choice of Jurisdiction[1]

1. For an existing or future dispute of financial interest[2] arising from a specific legal relationship[3] the parties may agree on a place of jurisdiction. The agreement may be made[4] in writing, by telegram, by telex, telecopier or any other means of communication which permits it to be evidenced by a text. Unless otherwise provided by the agreement, the choice of jurisdiction is exclusive.

2. A choice of jurisdiction is ineffective if a party is abusively[5] deprived of protection at a place of jurisdiction provided by Swiss law.

3. The court chosen may not decline jurisdiction:[6]
(a) if one of the parties has its domicile,[7] habitual residence,[7] or business establishment[7] in the canton of the chosen court, or
(b) if this Statute[8] declares Swiss law applicable to the case.[9]

Treaties: See Art. 2.
Previous law: Cantonal, e.g. Para. 9 Zurich ZPO. BGE 111 II 175.
Legislative history: Experts Draft, *Art. 5 and 6;* Experts Report, page 46; Fribourg Colloque, page 67, 68, 69; Government Draft, *Art. 5;* Government Report, point 213.5, page 38; Lausanne Colloque, page 117, 227; Senate Debate, Amtliches Bulletin 1985, page 121, 129; House Debate, Amtliches Bulletin 1986, page 1288, 1295, 1302; Festschrift Moser, page 250; Senate Debate, Amtliches Bulletin 1987 page 181; House Debate, Amtliches Bulletin 1987, page 1067; Senate Debate, Amtliches Bulletin 1987, page 506.

1. Choice of jurisdiction (E), élection de for (F), Gerichtsstandvereinbarung (G), proroga di foro (I), forum prorogatum (L).

2. Dispute of financial interest (E), différences en matière patrimoniale (F), Rechtsstreit um vermögensrechtliche Ansprüche (G), controversia in materia di pretese patrimoniali (I).

3. Specific legal relationship (E), rapport de droit déterminé (F), bestimmten Rechtsverhältnis (G), determinato rapporto giuridico (I).

4. One may suggest that to *make* the agreement *both* parties must use writing, telex etc. (though not both the same means), not just one of them. Whether this is correct is unclear, especially if one compares Art. 178.

5. Abusively (E), d'une manière abusive (F), missbräuchlich (G), abusivamente (I).

6. Decline jurisdiction (E), décliner sa compétence (F), Zuständigkeit ablehnen (G), declina la propria competenza (I).

7. See Art. 20 and Art. 21.

8. Probably too narrow. May the court chosen decline jurisdiction if Swiss law becomes applicable by treaty or by other legislation? Probably not.

9. More fully: Swiss substantive law applicable to the merits of the case.

Art. 6

V.
Unconditional
Appearance[1]

In disputes of financial interest,[2] an unconditional appearance[1] gives jurisdiction to the Swiss court if it may not decline jurisdiction according to Article 5 subsection 3.

Treaties: See Art. 2.
Previous law: Cantonal, e.g. Para. 12 Zurich ZPO.
Leglislative history: Experts Draft, *Art. 7*; Experts Report, page 50; Government Draft, *Art. 6*; Government Report, point 213.7, page 40; Senate Debate, Amtliches Bulletin 1985, page 129; House Debate, Amtliches Bulletin 1986, page 1295, 1302; Festschrift Moser, page 250, 251.
Cantonal procedural law: e.g. Para. 111 Zurich ZPO.

1. Unconditional appearance (E), le défendeur procède au fond sans faire de réserve (F), vorbehaltlose Einlassung (G), incondizionata costituzione in giudizio del convenuto (I). By what time an appearance becomes unconditional depends on the applicable civil procedure. See, e.g. Para. 111 Zurich ZPO.

2. See Art. 5.

Art. 7

If, in an arbitrable dispute,[1] the parties have concluded an arbitration agreement,[2] the Swiss courts must decline jurisdiction[3] unless
  (a) the defendant has entered an unconditional appearance;[4]
  (b) the court finds that the arbitration agreement fails, is inoperative, or cannot be implemented;[5] or
  (c) the arbitral tribunal cannot be formed for reasons for which evidently the respondent in the arbitration[6] is answerable.

Multilateral treaty: (New York) Convention du 10 juin 1958 pour la reconnaissance et l'exécution des sentences arbitrales étrangères, Art. II, SR 0.277.12.
Treaties: see Art. 2.
Previous law: Cantonal, e.g. Para. 111 Zurich ZPO.
Legislative history: Experts Draft, *Art. 8;* Experts Report, page 51; Fribourg Colloque, page 69; Government Draft, *Art. 7;* Government Report, point 213.8, page 41; Senate Debate, Amtliches Bulletin 1985, page 129, 130; House Debate, Amtliches Bulletin 1986, page 1295, 1302; Festschrift Moser, page 205, 251.

1. Arbitrable dispute (E), différend arbitrable (F), schiedsfähige Streitsache (G), controversia compromettibile (I). See Art. 181.

2. This includes an arbitration clause. On the validity of an arbitration clause where the seat of the arbitral tribunal is Switzerland and where at least one of the parties had neither its domicile nor its habitual residence (Art. 20) in Switzerland (Art. 176), see Art. 178. If both or all parties have their domicile or habitual residence in Switzerland and the seat of the arbitral tribunal is in a Concordat Canton, Art. 6 Concordat and through it Art. 13 CC applies. If the seat is outside Switzerland, the Swiss courts should decline jurisdiction if an award would be enforceable in Switzerland, see Art. 194 which refers in many cases to Art. 3 of the New York Convention of 1958.

3. See Art. 5.

4. See Art. 6.

5. Agreement fails, is inoperative or cannot be implemented (E), convention d'arbitrage est caduque, inopérante ou non susceptible d'être appliquée (F), Schiedsvereinbarung hinfällig, unwirksam oder nicht erfüllbar (G), caducità, inefficacia o inadempibilità del patto d'arbitrato (I).

6. Respondent in the arbitration (E), défendeur à l'arbitrage (F), der Beklagte im Schiedsverfahren (G), convenuto nel procedimento arbitrale (I).

Art. 8

VII.
Counter-
claim[1]

The court before which the principal claim is pending has jurisdiction over the counterclaim[1] if both claims are factually connected.[2]

> *Swiss Federal Constitution:* Art. 59, see Appendix I.
> *Treaties:* See Art. 2.
> *Previous law:* Cantonal, e.g. Para. 15 Zurich ZPO.
> *Legislative history:* Experts Draft, *Art. 9;* Experts Report, page 52; Fribourg Colloque, page 69; Government Draft, *Art. 8;* Government Report, point 213.9, page 41; Senate Debate, Amtliches Bulletin 1985, page 120; House Debate, Amtliches Bulletin 1986, page 1295, 1302.
>
> 1. Counterclaim (E), demande reconventionnelle (F), Widerklage (G), domanda riconvenzionale (I).
> A set-off defense should be distinguished from a counterclaim. Set-off is governed by Art. 148. Jurisdiction exists if there is jurisdiction on the principal claim.
>
> 2. Factually connected (E), connexité (F), sachlicher Zusammenhang (G), materialmente connesse (I). Here this translation follows the German and Italian text. Any connection is sufficient that is more than the mere identity of the parties. See Art. 3.

Art. 9

VIII. Lis
Pendens[1]

1. If a lawsuit on the same matter between the same parties is already pending[1] abroad, the Swiss court must stay the proceedings if it is to be expected that the foreign court will, within a reasonable time,[2] render a judgment recognizable in Switzerland.

2. A lawsuit becomes pending in Switzerland when the first act necessary to commence the lawsuit is performed.[3] To commence the lawsuit it is sufficient to initiate conciliation proceedings.[4]

3. The Swiss court must dismiss a lawsuit without prejudice[5] as soon as a foreign judgment recognizable in Switzerland[6] is submitted to it.

> *Treaties:* See Art. 2.
> *Previous law:* Cantonal, e.g. Para. 102 Zurich ZPO. In intercantonal cases, the time when a matter becomes pending for purposes of determining jurisdication continues to be determined by the cantonal law of the forum. The present article is likely to influence cantonal lawmakers in the future.

35

Legislative history: Experts Draft, *Art. 10;* Experts Report, page 53; Fribourg Colloque, page 69; Government Draft, *Art. 9;* Government Report, point 213.10, page 42; Senate Debate, Amtliches Bulletin 1985, page 121, 120; House Debate, Amtliches Bulletin 1986, page 1295, 1302.

1. Lis pendens (L), litispendence (F), Rechtshängigkeit (G), litispendenza (I). Subsection 3 actually deals with res iudicata.

2. Reasonable time (E), délai convenable (F), angemessene Frist (G), congruo termine (I).

3. Lis pendens in international arbitration proceedings is regulated in a similar way in Art. 172.

4. Conciliation proceeding (E), citation en conciliation (F), Sühneverfahren (G), procedura di conciliazione (I).
   In most cantons, conciliation proceedings are compulsory in most cases. They are conducted before the Justice of the Peace, e.g., Para. 93 et seq. Zurich ZPO.

5. Dismiss without prejudice (E), se dessaisit (F), weist zurück (G), stralcia la causa del ruolo (I). Here, the translation follows the French and Italian texts.

6. For recognition of foreign arbitral awards, see Art. 194.

Art. 10

IX.
Provisional
Measures[1]

The Swiss judicial or administrative authorities may order provisional measures[1] even if they have no jurisdiction to render a decision on the merits.[2]

Treaties: See Art. 2.
Previous law: Cantonal.
Legislative history: Experts Draft, *Art. 11;* Experts Report, page 55; Government Draft, *Art. 10;* Government Report, point 213.11, page 43; Senate Debate, Amtliches Bulletin 1985, page 130; House Debate, Amtliches Bulletin 1986, page 1295, 1302.
Cantonal procedural law: e.g. Para. 110, 231 Zurich ZPO.

1. Provisional measures (G), mesures provisoires (F), vorsorgliche Massnahmen (G), provvedimenti cautelari (I). This is similar to a temporary restraining order.

2. See Art. 1.
   The procedure remains cantonal. For Zurich, see ZPO.

36

Art. 11

1. Acts of judicial assistance[1] are accomplished[2] in Switzerland according to the law of the Canton where they are performed.

2. On motion of the requesting authority, foreign forms of procedure may also be applied or taken into account if this is necessary to enforce a legal claim abroad and if the party concerned has no important countervailing reasons.[3]

3. The Swiss[4] judicial or administrative authorities[5] may issue documents pursuant to a form of foreign law or take a sworn statement from a petitioner if a form pursuant to Swiss[6] law is not recognized abroad and if, therefore, a legitimate claim could not be enforced abroad.

Treaties: See Art. 2.
Multilateral Treaties: Hague Convention of 1905 and 1954; see ad Art. 25. New York Convention of 1956 on Support and Maintenance; see Art. 83. European Information Agreement of 1968, see Art. 16. Switzerland will probably join the Hague Conventions of November 15, 1965, March 18, 1970 and October 25, 1980.
Bilateral treaties: With *Austria:* Accord du 26 août 1968 entre la Confédération suisse et la République d'Autriche visant à compléter la convention de La Haye du 1er mars 1954 sur la procédure civile, SR 0.274.181.631; With *Bahamas:* Echange de lettres des 3 mars/3 mai 1977 concernant l'application entre la Suisse et les Bahamas de la convention conclue le 3 décembre 1937 par la Suisse et la Grande-Bretagne en matière de procédure civile, SR 0.274.181.641; With *Belgium:* Déclaration du 29 novembre 1900 entre la Suisse et la Belgique concernant la transmission directe des actes judiciaires, etc., SR 0.274.181.721; Déclaration du 29 novembre 1900 entre la Suisse et la Belgique concernant la transmission directe des actes judiciaires, SR 0.274.181.721, Convention du 9 décembre 1886 entre la Suisse et la Belgique sur l'assistance judiciaire devant les tribunaux (bénéfice du pauvre), SR 0.274.181.722; With *Czechoslovakia:* Accord du 21 décembre 1926 entre la Suisse et la République tchécoslovaque concernant l'assistance judiciaire réciproque en matière civile et commerciale (avec protocole additionnel), SR 0.274.187.411; With *Estonia:* Déclaration du 29 octobre 1926 entre la Suisse et l'Estonie concernant l'application réciproque de la Convention de La Haye relative à la procédure civile, SR 0.274.181.341; With *France:* Déclaration du 1er février 1913 entre la Suisse et la France relative à la transmission des actes judiciaires et extrajudiciaires et des commissions rogatoires en matière civile et commerciale (avec annexe), SR 0.274.181.491; With (Federal Republic of) *Germany:* Déclaration du 1er/13 décembre 1878 entre la Suisse et l'Empire allemand au sujet de la correspondance directe entre les autorités judiciaires des deux pays, SR 0.274.181.361; With *Greece:* Convention du 30 mars 1934 réglant l'entraide judiciaire en matière civile et commerciale entre la Suisse et la Grèce, SR 0.274.183.721; With *Hungary:* Echange de notes du 20 octobre 1972 entre la Suisse et la Hongrie concernant la transmission d'actes judiciaires et extrajudiciaires et de commisssions rogatoires, SR 0.274.184.181; With *Kenya:* Echange de notes des 19 mai/21 septembre 1965 entre la Suisse et le Kenya concernant le maintien en vigueur dans leurs

rapports de la convention du 3 décembre 1937 entre la Suisse et la Grand-Bretagne en matière de procédure civile, SR 0.274.184.721; With *Luxemburg:* Echange de lettres des 12/15 février 1979 entre la Suisse et le Grand-Duché de Luxembourg sur l'acheminement des actes judiciaires et extrajudiciaires en matière civile et commerciale (avec annexe), SR 0.274.185.181; With *Nauru:* Echange de notes des 23 août 1978/10 janvier 1979 concernant l'application entre la Suisse et la République de Nauru de la convention du 3 décembre 1937 conclue entre la Suisse et la Grande-Bretagne en matière de procédure civile, SR 0.274.185.761; With *Pakistan:* Echange de lettres des 12 mai/7 juillet 1960 entre la Suisse et le Pakistan concernant l'entraide judiciaire en matière civile, SR 0.274.186.231; With *Poland:* Echange de notes des 15 mars/18 août 1928 entre la Suisse et la Pologne concernant l'application de la Convention de La Haye relative à la procédure civile, SR 0.274.186.491; With *Spain:* Accord avec l'Espagne sur la transmission des actes judiciaires, SR 0.274.183.321; With *Swaziland:* Echange de notes des 20 juillet/24 septembre 1971 concernant l'application entre la Suisse et le Royaume du Swaziland de la convention du 3 décembre 1937 conclue entre la Suisse et la Grande-Bretagne en matière de procédure civile, SR 0.274.187.231; With *Tansania:* Echange de notes des 2 décembre 1963/30 janvier 1964 entre la Suisse et le Tanganyika concernant le maintien en vigueur, dans leurs rapports, de la convention du 3 décembre 1937 entre la Suisse et la Grande-Bretagne en matière de procédure civil, SR 0.274.187.321; With *Tonga:* Echange de lettres des 6 juin/20 août 1973 concernant l'application entre la Suisse et Tonga de la convention conclue le 3 décembre 1937 par la Suisse et la Grande-Bretagne en matière de procédure civile, SR 0.274.187.521; With *Turkey:* Convention du 1 juin 1933 réglant les rapports judiciaires en matière civile et commerciale entre la Suisse et la Turquie, SR 0.274.187.631; With *Uganda:* Echange de notes des 24 mars/26 mai 1965 entre la Suisse et l'Ouganda concernant le maintien en vigueur dans leurs rapports de la convention du 3 décembre 1937 entre la Suisse et la Grande-Bretagne en matière de procédure civile, SR 0.274.186.181; With *United Kingdom:* Convention du 3 décembre 1937 entre la Suisse et la Grande-Bretagne en matière de procédure civile, SR 0.274.183.671.

Previous law: Federal: international comity; some specific provisions, e.g. Art. 177 ZStV; Cantonal: e.g. Para. 114, 116 Zurich GVG.

Legislative history: Experts Draft, *Art. 11;* Experts Report, page 55; Government Draft, *Art, 11;* Government Report, point 213.12, page 44; Lausanne Colloque, page 231; Senate Debate, Amtliches Bulletin 1985, page 130; House Debate, Amtliches Bulletin 1986, page 1295, 1302.

Federal criminal law: Foreign acts of sovereignty on Swiss territory are forbidden and punishable by imprisonment, Swiss Federal Penal Code, SR Art. 273 (translated in 30 Journal of Criminal Law and Criminology, 1938; and in Taxes International, 1984, page 15). This includes private actions that are the functional equivalent of actions normally performed by officials in Switzerland. Delivery (whether in person or by mail) of a summons to appear in a foreign court is forbidden and punishable by imprisonment. Unless a party illegally served in Switzerland enters an unconditional appearance in the foreign court that court's judgment is not recognized and not declared enforceable in Switzerland. It is also forbidden and punishable by imprisonment to serve interrogatories or conduct discovery in Switzerland.

Cantonal procedural law: e.g. Para. 114, 116 Zurich GVG, which do not provide for oath-taking.

1. Acts of judicial assistance (E), actes d'entraide judiciaire (F), Rechtshilfehandlungen (G), atti d'assistenza giudiziaria (I). In private law matters.

2. Accomplished (E), accomplis (F), durchgeführt (G), compiuto (I).
The prerequisities for judicial assistance in civil matters are those in (federal) treaties or cantonal (procedural) law.

3. Party has no important countervailing reasons (E), importants motifs à l'intéressé (F), wichtige Gründe auf Seiten des Betroffenen (G), gravi motivi inerenti all'interessato (I).

4. This includes cantonal.

5. See Art. 1.

6. This means cantonal.

Art. 12

XI. Time
Limits[1]

If a person must observe abroad a time limit[1] before Swiss judicial or administrative authorities,[2] it is sufficient for the submission to arrive on the last day of the time limit at a Swiss diplomatic or consular mission.[3]

Treaties: See Art. 2.
Previous law: Cantonal, e.g. Para. 189 et seq. Zurich GVG.
Legislative history: Experts Draft, *Art. 187;* Experts Report, page 304; Fribourg Colloquium, page 6; Government Draft, *Art. 12;* Government Report, page 44; Lausanne Colloque, page 231; Senate Debate, Amtliches Bulletin 1985, page 130; House Debate, Amtliches Bulletin 1986, page 1295, 1302; Senate Debate, Amtliches Bulletin 1987, page 182.
Swiss substantive law: Multilateral treaty: Convention européenne du 16 mai 1972 sur la computation des délais, SR 0.221.122.3, *Federal substantive law:* Art. 31, 60, 67, 127 ff., 201 CO; Art. 74 SchKG. *Federal procedural law:* Art. 21, OG, Loi fédérale du 20 décembre 1968 sur la procédure administrative, SR 172.021, see Appendix III. *Cantonal procedural law:* e.g., Para. 189 et seq. Zurich GVG; Para. 287 Zurich ZPO.

1. Time limit (E), délai (F), Frist (G), termine (I). The time limit as such may be a time limit set by foreign law, Swiss federal law or cantonal law.

2. See Art. 1.

3. A full list is published every year by Eidgenössische Drucksachen- und Materialzentrale, Bundeshaus West, 3000 Bern.

Selected addresses:

Swiss Embassy in Sidney
'Edgecliff Center', 203-233 New South Head Road
Edgecliff NSW 2027, P.O. Box 82
Tel.: (612) 328 7511 / 328 7925.

Swiss Embassy in Washington
2900 Cathedral Ave, N.W., Washington,
D.C. 20008-3489
Tel.: (1 202) 745 7900.

Swiss Embassy in Ottawa
5, av. Marlborough, Ottawa, ON K1N 8E6
Tel.: (1 613) 235 1837 / 235 0958.

Swiss Embassy in Hong Kong
3703 Glouchester Tower, 11 Pedder Street
Hong Kong
Tel.: (852 5) 227 147/8.

Swiss Embassy in New Delhi
P.O. Box 392, New Delhi 110021
Tel.: (9111) 60 42 25/6/7.

Swiss Embassy in Tokyo
Azabu P.O. Box 38, Tokyo 106-91
Tel.: (81 3) 473 0121.

Swiss Embassy in Lagos
P.O. Box 536, Lagos
Tel.: (2341) 61 38 48/61 3918.

Swiss Embassy in Brasilia
Caixa postal 04 0171, 70000 Brasilia D.F.
Tel.: (55 61) 244 5500 / 244 5611.

Swiss Embassy in Buenos Aires
Casilla de Correo, Central No. 4895
RA-1000 Buenos Aires
Tel.: (541) 311 6491/5.

Third Section: Applicable Law

Art. 13

I. Scope of
Conflicts
Rule[1]

Where this Statute refers to a foreign law, the reference encompasses all provisions that are applicable to the case according to that law.[2] A foreign provision is not inapplicable for the sole reason that it is characterized as public law.[3]

Previous law: BGE 80 II 53; 83 II 313; 95 II 109.
Legislative history: Experts Draft, *Art. 13;* Experts Report, page 57, Fribourg Colloque, page 5, 12; Government Draft, *Art. 13;* subs. 1 and 3; Government Report, point 214.2, page 46; Lausanne Colloque, page 3, 56, 269, 274; Senate Debate, Amtliches Bulletin 1985, page 130; House Debate, Amtliches Bulletin 1986, page 1295, 1303; Festschrift Moser, page 14, 75; Senate Debate, Amtliches Bulletin 1987, page 182.

1. Scope of conflicts rule (E), portée de la règle de conflit (F), Umfang der Verweisung (G), estensione del rinvio (I).

2. While this includes foreign conflict of laws rules, Art. 14 excludes renvoi in many cases. Foreign public law is also included, see second sentence.

3. Characterized as public law (E), caractère de droit public (F), öffentlichrechtlicher Charakter (G), carattere di diritto pubblico (I). The distinction between public and private law is important in other areas of Swiss law, as in any civil law country. Borderline cases: *Public law:* criminal law, civil procedure, antitrust, bankruptcy, (according to some) arbitration, *Private law:* individual employment contract, unfair competition, family law, guardian and ward.

Art. 14

II. Renvoi[1]

1. If the applicable law refers back to Swiss law or onwards to a different foreign law, the reference is followed only if this Statute so provides.[2]

2. In matters concerning personal or family status,[3] a reference back to Swiss law is followed.[4]

Legislative history: Experts Draft, *Art. 13;* Experts Report, page 57; Fribourg Colloque, page 9, 71, 75, 85; Government Draft, *Art. 13;* Government Report, point 214.2, page 46; Lausanne Colloque, page 37, 57, 170, 267; Senate Draft, *Art. 13a;* Senate Debate, Amtliches Bulletin 1985, page 130; House Debate, Amtliches Bulletin 1986, page 1295, 1303; Festschrift Moser, page 11 to 14.

1. Renvoi (E) (F), Verweisung (G), rinvio (I).

2. Such provisions appear in the PIL Statute as follows: Art. 14, subs. 2; Art. 37 subs. 1; Art. 91 subs. 1.

3. See Art. 33 to 85.

4. A reference onwards to a different foreign law is not followed.

Art. 15

III.
Exception
Clause

1. The law designated[1] by this Statute is, by way of exception, not applicable if, under all the circumstances, the case clearly has only a slight connection with the designated law, and has a much closer connection with another law.[2]

2. This provision is not applicable where the parties have made a choice of law.[3]

Previous law: Art. 8e subs. 3 NAG, repealed by Appendix to PIL Statute; BGE 94 II 355, 78 II 190, 76 II 45.
Legislative history: Experts Draft, *Art. 14;* Experts Report, page 59; Fribourg Colloque, page 2, 3, 5, 9, 11, 13, 17, 44, 47, 59, 70, 76, 82, 83, 85, 87; Government Draft, *Art. 14;* Government Report, point 214.3, page 48; Lausanne Colloque, page 10, 49, 57, 265, 276; Senate Debate, Amtliches Bulletin 1985, page 114, 131; House Debate, Amtliches Bulletin 1986, page 1295, 1303; Festschrift Moser, page 7, 65, 94.

1. Designated (E), désigné (F), verweist (G), richiamata (I).

2. Slight – much closer connection (E), lien très lâche-relation beaucoup plus étroite (F), geringer – viel engerer Zusammenhang (G), esiguamente – più strettamente connesso (I). More stringent requirements than in Art. 3.

3. Where the parties have made a choice of law (E), en cas d'élection de droit (F), wenn eine Rechtswahl vorliegt (G), diritto applicabile scelto dalle parti (I). The choice of law must be permissible as provided in the PIL Statute, see e.g. Art. 52, 104, 116, 120, 121.

Art. 16

1. The content of the applicable foreign law[1] must be established ex officio.[2] For this purpose the collaboration of the parties may be requested. For claims of financial interest,[3] proof may be imposed on the parties.

2. If the content of the foreign law is not ascertainable, Swiss law applies.

> *Multilateral treaty:* With Austria, Belgium, Costa Rica, Cyprus, Denmark, France, (Federal Republic of) Germany, Greece, Iceland, Italy, Liechtenstein, Luxemburg, Malta, Netherlands, Norway, Portugal, Spain, Sweden, Turkey and United Kingdom: Convention européenne dans le domaine de l'information sur le droit étranger, du 7 juin 1968, SR 0.274.161. Members of the public can use the assistance of Schweizerisches Institut für Rechtsvergleichung, 1015 Dorigny, Lausanne, Tel. international (4122) 46 43 11.
> *Previous law:* Cantonal Law, e.g. Para. 133 Zurich ZPO; BGE 92 II 111.
> *Legislative history:* Experts Draft, *Art. 15;* Experts Report, page 60; Fribourg Colloque, page 4, 5, 9, 10, 11, 12, 13, 69, 75, 77; Government Draft, *Art. 15;* Government Report, point 214.4, page 49; Lausanne Colloque, page 240, 251; Senate Debate, Amtliches Bulletin 1985, page 132; House Debate, Amtliches Bulletin 1986, page 1288, 1295, 1303; Festschrift Moser, page 4, 6, 8, 78; Senate Debate, Amtliches Bulletin 1987, page 182, House Debate, Amtliches Bulletin 1987, page 1086; Senate Debate, Amtliches Bulletin 1987, page 506.

1. Art. 16 of the Experts Draft provided: 'If this Statute refers to the law of a country with more than one internal state laws, without also indicating the applicable internal law, the law is defined according to the interlocal or interpersonal law of the state whose internal law is to be applied'. This was not included in the text of the Statute probably because it was considered too technical. It must be considered to be implied.

2. Ex officio (L), d'office (F), von Amtes wegen (G), d'ufficio (I).

3. For claims of financial interest (E), en matière patrimoniale (F), bei vermögensrechtlichen Ansprüchen (G), in caso di pretese partimoniali (I).
   Procedure on these matters follows the adversarial system (Verhandlungsmaxime, contradictoire)

Art. 17

The application of provisions of a foreign law is excluded if the outcome[2] is incompatible with Swiss public policy.

Treaties: Some have public policy exception clauses of their own.
Previous law: BGE 103 Ib 69; 102 Ia 308, 574.
Legislative history: Experts Draft, *Art. 17;* Experts Report, page 63; Fribourg Colloque, page 9, 44, 82; Government Draft, *Art. 16;* Government Report, point 214.5, 214.51, page 50; Lausanne Colloque, page 25; Senate Debate, Amtliches Bulletin 1985, page 133; House Debate, Amtliches Bulletin 1986, page 1295, 1306; Festschrift Moser, page 22.

1. Swiss public policy exception (E), réserve de l'ordre public suisse (F), Vorbehaltsklausel, schweizerischer Ordre public (G), clausola di riserva, ordine pubblico svizzero (I).

2. Outcome (E), résultat (F), Ergebnis (G), esito (I).

Art. 18

VI. Mandatory Application of Swiss Law

Provisions of Swiss law which, in view of their special policy,[1] must be applied without regard to the law designated by this Statute remain reserved.

Legislative history: Experts Draft, *Art. 17;* Experts Report, page 65; Fribourg Colloque, page 3, 32, 44, 82, 83; Government Draft, *Art. 17;* Government Report, point 214.53, page 52; Lausanne Colloque, page 42, 55, 274; Senate Debate, Amtliches Bulletin 1985, page 133; House Debate, Amtliches Bulletin 1986, page 1295, 1306; Festschrift Moser, page 22, 73, 94.

1. Policy (E), but (F), Zweck (G), scopo (I). Lois d'ordre public in the French sense. Lois d'application immédiate
Examples: 'Lex Friedrich', Loi fédérale du 16 décembre 1983 sur l'acquisition d'immeubles par des personnes à l'étranger (LFAEI), SR 211.412.41 (non-literal translation by Swiss-American Chamber of Commerce, 1985); Public labor protection laws; Human rights legislation.

Art. 19

VII. Taking in Account Mandatory Provisions of a Foreign Law

1. A provision of a law other than the one designated by this Statute that is meant to be applied mandatorily may be taken into account[1] if interests of a party that are according to Swiss views[2] legitimate and clearly overriding[3] so require and the case is closely connected[4] to that law.

2. Whether such a provision should be taken into account depends on its policy and its consequences for a judgment that is fair according to Swiss views.[5]

Legislative history: Experts Draft, *Art. 18;* Experts Report, page 65; Fribourg Colloque, page 3, 9, 44; Government Draft, *Art. 18;* Government Report, point 214.54, page 52; Lausanne Colloque, page 42, 49, 55, 119, 274, 276; Senate Debate, Amtliches Bulletin 1985, page 133; House Debate, Amtliches Bulletin 1986, page 1295, 1306; Festschrift Moser, page 13, 16 to 22, 94, 95, 96, Senate Debate, Amtliches Bulletin 1987 page 182.

1. May be taken in account (E), peut être prise en considération (F), kann berücksichtig werden (G), può essere tenuto conto (I).

2. Swiss views (E), conception suisse du droit (F), nach schweizerischer Rechtsauffassung (G), concezione giuridica svizzera (I).

3. Legitimate and clearly overriding interests of a party (E), intérêts légitimes et manifestement prépondérants (F), schützenswerte und offensichtlich überwiegende Interessen einer Partei (G), interessi degni di protezione e manifestamente preponderanti di una parte (I).

4. Closely connected (E), lien étroit (F), enger Zusammenhang (G), strettamente connesso (I). More stringent requirements than in Art. 3 and Art. 15.

5. Whether such a provision should be taken into account depends on its policy and its consequences for a judgment that is fair according to Swiss views (E). Pour juger si une telle disposition doit être prise en considération, on tiendra compte du but qu'elle vise et des conséquences qu'aurait son application pour arriver à une décision adéquate au regard de la conception suisse du droit (F). Ob eine solche Bestimmung zu berücksichtigen ist, beurteilt sich nach ihrem Zweck und den daraus sich ergebenden Folgen für eine nach schweizerischer Rechtsauffassung sachgerechte Entscheidung (G). Per stabilire se si debba tener conto di tale norma, se ne esaminerà lo scopo e le conseguenze per una decisione equanime secondo la concezione giuridica svizzera (I).

Fourth Section: Domicile, Seat, and Citizenship

Art. 20

I. Domicile, Habitual Residence, and Business Establishment of an Individual[1]

1. For the purpose of this Statute, an individual[1] has
(a) his domicile in the country in which he is living with the intention of staying permanently;[2]
(b) his habitual residence[3] in the country in which he is living for a certain time, even if this time is limited from the outset;
(c) his business establishment[4] in the country in which his business activities[5] are centered.

45

2. No individual can be domiciled in more than one place at the same time. If an individual has no domicile, his habitual residence serves to replace domicile. The provisions of the Civil Code on domicile and residence are not applicable.

Treaties: Where an international treaty uses concepts such as residence, domicile, or permanent establishment they must be interpreted independently from the PIL Statute.
Previous law: Art. 7a NAG, repealed in Appendix to PIL Statute; BGE 97 II 3.
Legislative history: Experts Draft, *Art. 19;* Experts Report, page 67, 71; Fribourg Colloque, page 8, 13, 18; Government Draft, *Art. 19, subs. 1;* Government Report, point 215, 215.1, page 53; Lausanne Colloque, page 133; Senate Draft, *Art. 19;* Senate Debate, Amtliches Bulletin 1985, page 121, 125, 134; House Debate, Amtliches Bulletin 1986, page 1295, 1296, 1307; Senate Debate, Amtliches Bulletin 1987, page 183.
Swiss substantive law: Art. 23 CC; Art. 25, 26 CO.

1. Individual (E), personne physique (F), natürliche Person (G), persona fisica (I).

2. The definition of domicile follows word by word the definition in Art. 23, Swiss Civil Code *but* (1) a line of cases interprets Art. 23 CC to mean that the domicile is at the 'Mittelpunkt der Lebensbeziehungen', i.e. the place where, in a person's life, a person's relationships are centered. See BGE 97 II 3. These cases are meant to apply to Art. 20 of the PIL Statute. (2) Under the Swiss Civil Code, persons under guardianship, and children (Art. 25, CC) are deemed to be domiciled where their guardian or parents are domiciled, and under Art. 26 CC a student has no domicile at the residence taken up to attend school. This is not reproduced in the PIL Statute and does not apply for its purposes.

3. Habitual residence (E), résidence habituelle (F), gewöhnlicher Aufenthalt (G), dimora abituale (I). The concept of habitual residence is an autonomous concept of private international law created by various Hague conventions, for instance Convention du 5 octobre 1961 concernant la cempétence des autorités et la loi applicable en matière de protection des mineurs, SR 0.211.231.01. It is not identical with the concept of residence in Art. 24 CC. A similar concept was created in Art. 115 of the PIL Statute.

4. Business establishment (E), établissement (F), Niederlassung (G), stabile organizzazione (I). The concept of business establishment is an autonomous concept created by the Statute in analogy to the concept of domicile, the tax concept of permanent establishment and concept of permanent business establishment in 'Lex Friedrich', Acquisition d'immeubles par des personnes domiciliées à l'étranger, SR 211.412.4 (non-literal translation by Swiss-American Chamber of Commerce, 1985).

5. Business activities (E), activités professionnelles ou commerciales (F), geschäftliche Tätigkeit (G), attività economica (I).

Art. 21

1. Companies[3] are domiciled at their seat.[1]

2. The seat of a company is at the place designated in the articles or the contract of association. If there is no such designation, the seat is at the place where the company is in fact administered.

3. The business establishment[2] of a company[3] is in the country in which it has its seat or a branch office.[4]

> *Previous law:* Cantonal, e.g. Para. 3 Zurich ZPO; BGE 97 II 3.
>
> *Legislative history:* Experts Draft, *Art. 19;* Experts Report, page 67, 72; Government Draft, *Art. 19; subs. 3;* Government Report, point 215.4, page 59; Senate Draft, *Art. 19a;* Senate Debate, Amtliches Bulletin 1985, page 134; House Debate, Amtliches Bulletin 1986, page 1295, 1296, 1307; Festschrift Moser, page 179; Senate Debate, Amtliches Bulletin 1987, page 183; House Debate, Amtliches Bulletin, 1987, page 1068.
>
> *Swiss substantive law:* See Art. 69 et seq. Handelsregisterverordnung, Ordonnance du 7 juin 1937 sur le registre du commerce, SR 221.411 (translated by American Chamber of Commerce in Switzerland, 1974).
>
> In most cantons, the Register of Commerce is kept in the cantonal capital. In the following cantons, the Register is kept in the districts: Bern, Fribourg, Solothurn, Ticino, Vaud, Wallis, Neuchâtel, Jura. A private publication of all firms registered in Switzerland is Schweizerisches Ragionenbuch, published yearly by Orell Füssli, Zurich.
>
> 1. Seat (E), siège (F), Sitz (G), sede (I).
>
> 2. See Art. 20, 150.
>
> 3. Companies (E), sociétés (F), Gesellschaften (G), società (I).
>
> 4. Branch office (E), succursale (F), Zweigniederlassung (G), succursale (I). In Swiss law, this is used for an office that is legally part of the company as a whole but may make contracts on its own. Offices just for payment or deliveries are not considered branch offices.

Art. 22

The citizenship[1] of a person[2] is determined by the law of the country[3] whose citizenship is in question.

Previous law: BGE 85 I 165.

Legislative history: Experts Draft, *Art. 20;* Experts Report, page 76; Fribourg Colloque, page 7; Government Draft, *Art. 20;* Government Report, point 215.5, page 59; Senate Debate, Amtliches Bulletin 1985, page 134; House Debate, Amtliches Bulletin 1986, page 1307.

Multiple citizenship: See Art. 23.

Persons without citizenship and refugees: See Art. 24.

Swiss substantive law: Swiss citizenship may be acquired by descent in accordance with the Swiss federal Statute on citizenship, Loi fédérale du 29 septembre 1952 sur l'acquisition et la perte de la nationalité suisse (Loi sur la nationalité [LN]), SR 141.0, presently under revision. Swiss citizenship is necessarily coupled with citizenship of a town or village and of the canton of that place. The place of citizenship has nothing to do with the place of birth. Rather, it might be described as the place of family origin. Acquisition of citizenship (naturalization) is possible only through acquisition of the citizenship of a town or a village. The requirements that must be met vary from place to place, but are very stringent everywhere. Honorary citizenship of a town or village does not confer cantonal or Swiss citizenship and is thus without civil effect. It is possible for a Swiss to be a citizen of several places and cantons.

1. Citizenship (E), nationalité (F), Staatsangehörigkeit (G), cittadinanza (I).

2. Person (E), personne (F), Person (G), persona (I). This applies only to individuals, since the PIL Statute does not use the concept of a company's 'citizenship', see Art. 20 and 21.

3. Country (E), l'Etat (F), Staat (G), Stato (I). A more literal, but probably misleading, translation would be 'state'.

Art. 23

IV. Multiple Citizenship[1]

1. If a person with Swiss citizenship also has the citizenship of another country, then for the determination of the jurisdiction at the place of citizenship[2] the Swiss citizenship alone is relevant.[3]

2. Unless this Statute provides otherwise,[4] if a person has multiple citizenship, for the purpose of determining the applicable law, the citizenship of that country is relevant with which the person has the closest connection.[5]

3. If a particular citizenship of a person is a prerequisite for the recognition of a foreign decision in Switzerland, it is sufficient if the person has that citizenship.

Treaties: Switzerland is not a party to any treaty on multiple citizenship.
Previous law: Art. 5 NAG repealed; BGE 89 I 303.
Legislative history: Experts Draft *Art. 21;* Experts Report, page 78; Fribourg Colloque, page 3/4, 25, 29; Government Draft, *Art. 21;* Government Report, point 215.6, page 60, 64, 89; Senate Debate, Amtliches Bulletin 1985, page 134; House Debate, Amtliches Bulletin 1986, page 1295, 1291, 1296, 1307.

1. Multiple citizenship (E), pluralité de nationalité (F), mehrfache Staatsangehörigkeit (G), pluricittadinanza (I).

2. Jurisdiction at the place of citizenship (E), Heimatgerichtsstand (G), for d'origine (F), foro di origine (I), forum originis (L). The effect of subs. 1 is to guarantee jurisdiction at the places of citizenship to Swiss citizens regardless of closeness of connections whenever the PIL Statute provides for that jurisdiction. The preferential treatment of Swiss citizens applies only to jurisdiction at the place of citizenship.

3. Regardless whether the person has the citizenship of a country with which the person has a close connection.

4. See Art. 52 subs. 2, Art. 90 subs. 2, Art. 94.

5. Regardless whether the person has Swiss citizenship.
   In keeping with the general policy of the PIL Statute the closest connection exists normally with the country that is also the country of habitual residence. Failing that a close connection may exist with the country of which the citizenship has been acquired most recently. Closeness of connection is relevant only for the applicable law; not for conflict of jursdiciton and recognition and enforcement. Where the statute declares the law of common citizenship applicable as in Art. 54 subs. 2, Art. 68 subs. 2, Art. 82 subs. 2, it means common *relevant* citizenship under Art. 23 subs. 2, not *any* citizenship that the parties may have in common iure soli or iure matrimonii.

Art. 24

V. Persons without Citizenship[1] and Refugees

1. A person is deemed[2] to be without citizenship[1] if he is so considered by the New York Convention on the Legal Status of Persons Without Citizenship of September 28, 1954,[3] or if his connection with his country of citizenship is so loose that this is equivalent to a lack of citizenship.

2. A person is deemed[2] to be a refugee if he is so considered pursuant to the Statute on Asylum of October 5, 1979.[4]

3. If this Statute is applied to persons without citizenship or refugees, domicile[5] serves to replace citizenship.[6]

Multilateral treaties: Geneva Convention of 1951 on Refugees, Protocole du 31 janvier 1967, Art. 12, SR 0.142.301, (New York) Convention du 28 septembre 1954 relative au statut des apatrides (avec annexe et modèle), Art. 12, SR 0.142.40.
Previous law: Art. 7a NAG, repealed.
Legislative history: Experts Draft, *Art. 22;* Experts Report, page 81; Government Draft, *Art. 22;* Government Report, point 215.7, page 62; Senate Debate, Amtliches Bulletin 1985, page 134, House Debate, Amtliches Bulletin 1986, page 1295, 1296, 1308; Senate Debate, Amtliches Bulletin 1987, page 183; House Debate, Amtliches Bulletin 1987, page 1086.
Swiss substantive law: Asylgesetz, Loi du 5 octobre 1979 sur l'asile, SR 142.31, Art. 25.

1. Without citizenship (E), apatride (F), staatenlos (G), apolide (I).

2. Deemed (E), réputée (F), gilt (G), considerata (I). Pursuant to Art. 22 the person may still have the original citizenship. Art. 24 makes it possible to apply the law of the domicile regardless of the person's official break with the country of original citizenship and that country's possible insistence on the person's allegiance.

3. Convention du 28 septembre 1954 relatives au statut des apatrides (avec annexe et modèle) SR 0.142.40, Art. 12.

4. Asylgesetz, Loi du 5 octobre 1979 sur l'asile, SR 142.31, Art. 25. Spouses and minor children are also recognized as refugees.

5. See Art. 20.

6. If the individual has no domicile either, Art. 20 subs. 2 applies.

Fifth Section: Recognition and Enforcement of Foreign Decisions

Art. 25

I.
Recognition
1. General
Rule

A foreign decision is recognized in Switzerland:
(a) if jurisdiction lay[1] with the judicial or administrative authorities of the country in which the decision was rendered;
(b) if no ordinary judicial remedy[2] can any longer be brought against the decision or if the decision is final, and
(c) if no ground for non-recognition under Article 27 exists.

Multilateral treaties: With Austria, Belgium, Denmark, Federal Republic of Germany, Finland, France, Hungary, Israel, Italy, Luxemburg, Netherlands, Norway, Poland, Portugal, Spain, Sweden and Turkey: (Hague) Convention du 1 mars 1954 relative à la procédure civile, Art. 18f., SR 0.274.12. With German

Democratic Republic and Iceland: (Hague) Convention du 17 juillet 1905 relative à la procédure civile, Art. 18f., SR 0.274.11. Switzerland is not a member of the Brussels/European Convention of September 27, 1968.
Bilateral treaties: With *Austria:* Convention du 16 décembre 1960 entre la Confédération suisse et la République d'Autriche relative á la reconnaissance et á l'exécution de décisions judiciaires, SR 0.276.191.632. With *Belgium:* Convention du 29 avril 1959 entre la Suisse et la Belgique sur la reconnaissance et l'exécution de décisions judiciaires et de sentences arbitrales, SR 0.276.191.721. With *Czechoslovakia:* Convention du 21 décembre 1926 entre la Suisse et la République tchécoslovaque relative à la reconnaissance et à l'exécution de décisions judiciaires (avec protocole additionnel), SR 0.276.197.411. With *(Federal Republic of)* Germany: Convention du 2 novembre 1929 entre la Confédération suisse et le Reich allemand relative à la reconnaissance et l'exécution de décisions judiciaires et de sentences arbitrales, SR 0.276.191.361. With *France:* Convention du 15 juin 1869 entre la Suisse et la France sur la compétence judiciaire et l'exécution des jugements en matière civile (avec protocole explicatif), SR 0.276.193.491. With *Italy:* Convention du 3 janvier 1933 entre la Suisse et l'Italie sur la reconnaissance et l'exécution de décisions judiciaires, SR 0.276.194.541. With *Liechtenstein:* Convention du 25 avril 1968 entre la Confédération suisse et la Principauté de Liechtenstein sur la reconnaissance et l'exécution de décisions judiciaires et de sentences arbitrales en matière civile, SR 0.276.195.141. With *Spain:* Traité du 19 novembre 1896 entre la Suisse et l'Espagne sur l'exécution réciproque des jugements ou arrêts in matière civile et commerciale (avec protocole additionnel), SR 0.276.193.321. With *Sweden:* Convention du 15 janvier 1936 entre la Suisse et la Suède relative à la reconnaisance et l'exécution de décisions judiciaires et de sentences arbitrales, SR 0.276.197.141.
Previous law: Cantonal, e.g. Para. 302 Zurich ZPO.
Legislative history: Experts Draft, *Art. 23;* Experts Report, page 82; Fribourg Colloque, page 28; Government Draft, *Art. 23;* Government Report, point 217, 217.1, page 65; Senate Debate, Amtliches Bulletin 1985, page 123, 134; House Debate, Amtliches Bulletin 1986, page 1308; Senate Debate, Amtliches Bulletin 1987, page 183; House Debate, Amtliches Bulletin 1987, page 1068.

1. Jurisdiction lay (E), compétence était donnée (F), Zuständigkeit war begründet (G), vi era competenza (I).

2. Ordinary judicial remedy (E), recours ordinaire (F), ordentliches Rechtsmittel (G), rimedio giuridico ordinario (I).

Art. 26

2.
Jurisdiction[1]
of Foreign
Authorities

Jurisdiction[1] lies with a foreign authority,[2]

(a) if a provision of this Statute[3] so provides or, if there is no such provision, if the defendant had his domicile,[4] in the country where the decision was rendered;

51

(b) if, in disputes of financial interest the parties by an agreement valid under this Statute[5] subjected themselves to the jurisdiction of the authority,[2] that rendered the decision;

(c) if in a dispute of financial interest the defendant entered an unconditional appearance,[5] or

(d) if, in the case of a counterclaim, the authority that rendered the decision had jurisdiction over the principal claim, and the two claims are factually connected.[6]

Legislative history: Experts Draft, *Art. 24;* Experts Report, page 83; Fribourg Colloque, page 11, 67; Government Draft, *Art. 24;* Government Report, point 217.2, page 65; Lausanne Colloque, page 245; Senate Debate, Amtliches Bulletin 1985, page 136; House Debate, Amtliches Bulletin 1986, page 1295, 1296, 1309; Festschrift Moser, page 246; Senate Debate, Amtliches Bulletin 1987, page 183.

1. Direct international jurisdiction of the Swiss courts is covered by Art. 2. This Article deals with 'indirect' international jurisdiction of foreign authorities for purposes of recognition and declaration of enforceability in Switzerland. Both articles have only a subsidiary function.

2. See Art. 1.

3. Or an international treaty, e.g. Treaty with France (1869), Convention du 15 juin 1869 entre la Suisse et la France sur la compétence judiciaire et l'exécution des jugements en matière civile (avec protocole explicatif), SR 0.276.193.491.

4. See Art. 20.

5. Compare Art. 6.

6. Compare Art. 8.

Art. 27

3. Grounds for Non-recognition

1. A foreign decision is not recognized in Switzerland if its recognition would be clearly[1] incompatible with Swiss public policy.

2. A foreign decision is also not recognized if a party proves:
(a) that neither according to the law of its domicile nor according to the law of its habitual residence,[2] was the party properly served with process, unless the party entered an unconditional appearance in the proceedings;

(b) that the judgment was rendered in violation of essential principles of Swiss procedural law,[3] especially, the party was denied the
right to be heard;[4]

(c) that a lawsuit between the same parties concerning the same case
was first commenced or decided in Switzerland, or was first
decided in a third country, provided that the prerequisities for
the recognition of that decision are met.

3. In no other respects may the foreign decision be reviewed on the
merits.

Treaties: See Art. 25
Previous law: BGE 102 Ia 308, 574; 105 Ib 47.
Legislative history: Experts Draft, *Art. 25;* Experts Report, page 84; Govern-
ment Draft, *Art. 25;* Government Report, point 217.3, page 66; Lausanne
Colloque, page 150; Senate Debate, Amtliches Bulletin 1985, page 137; House
Debate, Amtliches Bulletin 1986, page 1309; Festschrift Moser, page 118.

1. Clearly (E), manifestement (F), offensichtlich (G), manifestamente (I). This
word does not appear in Art. 17 which deals with the applicable law. It is
designed to indicate a particularly stringent requirement to overcome the basic
policy of favor recognitionis.

2. See Art. 20.

3. Essential principles of Swiss procedural law (E), principes fondamentaux
ressortissant à la conception suisse du droit de procédure (F), wesentliche
Grundsätze des schweizerischen Verfahrensrechts (G), principi procedurali
svizzeri essenziali (I). Such essential principles may be gathered from the
Supreme Court decisions on Art. 4 and 59 of the Swiss Federal Constitution, see
Appendix I. See also Art. 18.

4. Right to be heard (E), possibilité de faire valoir ses moyens (F), rechtliches
Gehör (G), diritto d'essere sentita (I).

Art. 28

II. Enforce-
ability

A decision recognized pursuant to Articles 25 to 27 is declared
enforceable on petition[1] by the interested party.

Treaties: See Art. 25.
Legislative history: Experts Draft, *Art. 27;* Experts Report, page 85; Govern-
ment Draft, *Art. 26;* Government Report, point 217.4, page 68; Senate Debate,
Amtliches Bulletin 1985, page 138; House Debate, Amtliches Bulletin 1986,

page 1295, 1296, 1309; Senate Debate, Amtliches Bulletin 1987, page 183; House Debate, Amtliches Bulletin 1987, page 1068.

Swiss substantive law: The exequatur procedure is cantonal. It may be 'wrapped in' with the enforcement of debt procedure inasmuch as the exequatur question is raised incidentally or preliminarily to mainlevée d'opposition, Rechtsöffnung. See e.g. Para. 302 Zurich ZPO.

1. Petition (E), requête (F), Begehren (G), istanza (I).

Art. 29

III.
Procedure

1. A petition[1] for recognition or declaration of enforceability must be directed to the competent authority of the canton in which the foreign decision is invoked. The following must be attached[2] to the petition:

(a) a complete and certified original of the decision;
(b) a certificate that no ordinary judicial remedy can any longer be brought against the decision or that the decision is final; and
(c) in case of a decision by default, a document[3] establishing that the losing party was properly and timely served with process, and had a reasonable opportunity to defend itself.

2. The party opposing the petition must be heard; the party may present evidence.

3. If a foreign decision is invoked on a preliminary point, the authority seized may itself decide on recognition.

Treaties: See Art. 25.
Legislative history: Experts Draft, *Art. 28;* Experts Report, page 85; Government Draft, *Art. 27;* Government Report, point 217.4, page 68; Lausanne Colloque, page 247; Senate Debate, Amtliches Bulletin 1985, page 135, 138, 139; House Debate, Amtliches Bulletin 1986, page 1295, 1296, 1309.
Swiss substantive law: See Para. 302 Zurich ZPO.

1. Petition (E), requête (F), Begehren (G), istanza (I).

2. Attached (E), accompagnée (F), beizulegen (G) allegati (I), which implies that the petition must be in writing.

3. Document (E), document officiel (F), Urkunde (G), documento (I). This translation follows the German and Italian texts. The French text specifies 'official' document, but in many countries service of process is accomplished privately, not officially by the court.

Art. 30

IV.
Settlement
in Court[1]

Articles 25 to 29 also apply to a settlement in court[1] if in the country in which it was made the settlement is considered equivalent to a judgment.

Treaties: See Art. 25.
Legislative history: Experts Draft, *Art. 26;* Experts Report, page 86; Government Draft, *Art. 28;* Government Report, point 217.4, page 68; Senate Debate, Amtliches Bulletin, page 139; House Debate, Amtliches Bulletin, page 1295, 1296, 1309.
Out-of-court settlement: See Art. 112.
Swiss substantive law: Para. 188 Zurich ZPO.

1. Settlement in court (E), transaction judiciaire (F), gerichtlicher Vergleich (G), transazione giudiziale (I).

Art. 31

V. Noncon-
tentious
Jurisdiction[1]

Articles 25 to 29 apply by analogy to the recognition and enforcement of a judgment[1] or document of noncontentious jurisdiction.

Legislative history: Experts Draft, *Art. 29;* Experts Report, page 86; Government Draft, *Art. 29;* Government Report, point 22, 221, page 69; Senate Debate, Amtliches Bulletin 1985, page 139; House Debate, Amtliches Bulletin 1986, page 1309; Senate Debate, Amtliches Bulletin 1987, page 183.
Swiss substantive law: Para. 211 Zurich ZPO.

1. Noncontentious jurisdiction (E), jurisdiction gracieuse (F), freiwillige Gerichtsbarkeit (G), giurisdizione volontaria (I). This does not include preliminary injunctions, conservatory measures and other provisional decisions, but see Art. 96.

Art. 32

VI. Entry in
Register of
Civil Status[1]

1. A foreign decision or document concerning civil status is recorded in the Register of Civil Status[1] if it is so ordered by the cantonal supervisory authority.[2]

2. Registration is permitted if the conditions of Articles 25 to 27 are met.

3. If it is unclear whether the procedural rights of the parties were sufficiently safeguarded in the foreign rendering country, the interested parties must be heard[3] before registration.

Multilateral treaties: With Belgium, Federal Republic of Germany, France, Italy, Yugoslavia, Luxemburg, Netherlands, Austria, Portugal, Turkey: (Paris) Convention du 27 septembre 1956 relative à la délivrance de certains extraits d'actes de l'état civil destinés à l'étranger (avec annexe), SR 0.211.112.11. With Federal Republic of Germany, Spain, France, Luxemburg, Netherlands and Turkey: (CIEC) Convention (Nr. 9) du 10 septembre 1964 relative aux décisions de rectification d'actes de l'état civil (avec annexes), SR 0.211.112.14; Convention du 26 septembre 1957 relative à la délivrance gratuite et à la dispense de légalisation des expéditions d'actes de l'état civil (avec annexes), SR 0.211.112.12; Convention du 10 septembre 1964 relative aux décisions de rectification d'actes de l'état civil (avec annexes), SR 0.211.112.14. Germany and Austria: Arrangement du 29 novembre 1878 entre la Suisse et les Etats riverains du lac de Constance au sujet de l'inscription des actes de l'état civil concernant les cas de naissance et de décès sur le lac de Constance ou lorsqu'un cadavre vient à être retiré de l'eau, SR 0.211.112.491.1.
Bilateral treaties: With *Austria:* Accord du 26 avril 1962 entre la Confédération suisse et la République d'Autriche sur la suppression de la légalisation et sur l'échange des actes de l'état civil, ainsi que sur la délivrance de certificats de capacité matrimoniale (avec annexes), SR 0.211.112.416.3. With *France:* Déclaration du 3 décembre 1937 entre la Suisse et la France concernant la délivrance d'actes de l'état civil, SR 0.211.112.434.9. With (*Federal Republic of*) *Germany:* Accord du 6 juin 1956 entre la Confédération suisse et la Règublique fédérale d'Allemagne sur la suppression de la légalisation et l'échange des actes de l'état civil, ainsi que sur la délivrance de certificats de capacité matrimoniale (avec annexes), SR 0.211.112.413.6. With *Italy:* Accord du 16 novembre 1966 entre la Confédération suisse et la République italienne sur la dispense de légalisation, l'échange des actes de l'état civil et la présentation des certificats requis pour contracter mariage, SR 0.211.112.445.4.
Legislative history: Experts Draft, *Art. 30;* Experts Report, page 86; Government Draft, *Art. 30;* Government Report, point 222, page 70; Senate Debate, Amtliches Bulletin 1985, page 139; House Debate, Amtliches Bulletin 1986, page 1295, 1296, 1309.
Swiss substantive law: Zivilstandsverordnung, Ordonnance du 1 juin 1953 sur l'état civil, SR 211.112.1; BG über das Verwaltungsverfahren, Loi fédérale du 20 décembre 1968 sur la procédure administrative, Art. 6., SR 172.021.

1. Register of Civil Status (E), registre de l'état civil (F), Zivilstandsregister (G), registro dello stato civile (I). See Art. 14.

2. Supervisory authority (E), l'autorité de surveillance (F), Aufsichtsbehörde (G) autorità di vigilanza (I). See Zivilstandsverordnung, Ordonnance du 1 juin 1953 sur l'état civil, SR 211.112.1 and cantonal law.

3. Must be heard (E), sont entendues (F), anzuhören (G), devono essere sentiti (I). The procedure follows Bundesgesetz über das Verwaltungsverfahren, Loi fédérale du 20 décembre 1968 sur la procédure administrative, SR 172.021.

Second Chapter: Individuals[1]

Art. 33

I. General
Rule

1. Unless otherwise provided by this Statute, jurisdiction on matters of personal status[2] lies with the Swiss judicial or administrative authorities,[3] at the domicile;[4] these authorities apply the law of the domicile.

2. For claims of violation of the right of personality,[5] the provisions of this Statute on unlawful acts apply (Art. 129 et seq.).

> *Swiss Federal Constitution:* Art. 46, see Appendix I.
> *Bilateral treaty:* With Iran: Convention d'établissement du 25 avril 1934 entre la Confédération suisse et l'Empire de Perse (Iran) (avec annexe), Art. 8, SR 0.142.114.362.
> *Previous laws:* Art. 2, 34 NAG, repealed
> *Legislative history:* Experts Draft, *Art. 31;* Experts Report, page 87; Government Draft, *Art. 31;* Government Report, point 223, page 69; Lausanne Colloque, page 61, 83, 96, 279, 281; Senate Debate, Amtliches Bulletin 1985, page 139; House Debate, Amtliches Bulletin 1986, page 1309, 1310.
> *Companies:* See Art. 150 et seq.
> *Swiss substantive law: Treaty:* (European) Convention de sauvegarde des droits de l'homme et des libertès fondamentales, du 4 novembre 1950, SR 0.101.
> *Statute:* Art. 11 et seq. CC, Art. 28 et seq. SR. 210

1. Individuals (E), personnes physiques (F), natürliche Personen (G), persone fisiche (I).

2. Matters of personal status (E), en matière de droit des personnes (F), personenrechtliche Verhältnisse (G), rapporti di diritto delle persone (I).

3. See Art. 1.

4. See Art. 20.

5. Violation of the right of personality (E), atteintes aux intérêts personnels (F), Persönlichkeitsverletzung (G), lesioni arrecate alla personalità (I).

Art. 34

1. The capacity to have rights[1] is governed by Swiss law.[2]

2. Commencement and termination of personality[3] are determined by the law governing the legal relationship that presupposes the capacity to have rights.

Bilateral treaty: With Iran: see Art. 33.
Legislative history: Experts Draft, *Art. 32;* Experts Report, page 87; Government Draft, *Art. 32;* Government Report, point 222, page 70; Lausanne Colloque, page 63, 84, 273; Senate Debate, Amtliches Bulletin 1985, page 140; House Debate, Amtliches Bulletin 1986, page 1309, 1310.
Swiss substantive law: Art. 11 CC.

1. Capacity to have rights (E), jouissance des droits civils (F), Rechtsfähigkeit (G), capacità giuridica (I).

2. Under Swiss law, Art. 11 subs. 1 of the Civil Code, every person has the capacity to have rights. This is a provision which falls under Art. 17 of the PIL Statute. In effect, Art. 11 subs. 1 of the Swiss Civil Code is a loi d'application immédiate. For this reason, it was originally reproduced verbatim in Experts Draft, Art. 32. The rights meant are the individual rights of personality that every individual has, and all other rights that an individual may acquire.

3. Personality (E), personnalité (F), Persönlichkeit (G), personalità (I). Personality here means legal existence or personhood. This subsection deals with the question whether nasciturus pro iam nato habetur, when a person is legally dead, and presumptions of survivorship (Kommorientenvermutung).

Art. 35

The capacity to act[1] is governed by the law of the domicile.[2] A change of domicile does not affect the capacity to act[1] once the capacity is acquired.

Bilateral treaty: With Iran: see Art. 33.
Previous law: Art. 7, 34 NAG, repealed; BGE 106 1b 196.
Legislative history: Experts Draft, *Art. 33;* Experts Report, page 88; Fribourg Colloque, page 69; Government Draft, *Art. 33;* Government Report, point 223, page 70; Lausanne Colloque, page 85; Senate Debate, Amtliches Bulletin 1985, page 140; House Debate, Amtliches Bulletin 1986, page 1309, 1310, Art. 33a; Senate Debate, Amtliches Bulletin 1987, page 183, Art. 33.

Capacity to get married: See Art. 44.
Capacity to dispose for cause of death: See Art. 94.
Capacity to commit an unlawful act: See Art. 142.
Swiss substantive law: See Art. 12 CC, SR 210.

1. Capacity to act (E), exercice des droits civils (F), Handlungsfähigkeit (G), capacità d'agire (I). To 'act' means to issue transactional declarations of will and other declarations of will or opinion of legal consequence.

2. See Art. 20.

Art. 36

2. Protection of Legal Transactions[1]

1. A person who has made a legal transaction[2] even though he lacked the capacity to act[3] under the law of his domicile,[4] cannot invoke his incapacity to act if he had the capacity to act under the law of the country in which the legal transaction[2] was made,[5] provided that the other party did not know nor should have known of his incapacity.[6]

2. This provision does not apply to legal transactions in family and inheritance law[7] or concerning real rights in immovable property.[8]

Bilateral treaty: With Iran: see Art. 33.
Previous law: Art. 7b NAG, repealed.
Legislative history: Experts Draft, *Art. 34;* Experts Report, page 89; Fribourg Colloque, page 69; Government Draft, *Art. 34;* Government Report, point 224, page 71; Lausanne Colloque, page 85; Senate Debate, Amtliches Bulletin 1985, page 141; House Debate, Amtliches Bulletin 1986, page 1309, 1310.
Swiss substantive law: Art. 3 CC. Under Swiss law, individuals come of age at the age of 20 or through marriage, Art. 14 CC.

1. Protection of legal transactions (E), sécurité des transactions (F), Verkehrsschutz (G), protezione del commercio giuridico (I). This Article protects not only legal transactions made in Switzerland but also abroad. The Article deals not only with contracts made by parties in the same country, but how it applies to contracts made across borders is not clear.

2. Legal transaction (E), acte juridique (F), Rechtsgeschäft (G), negozio giuridico (I). These are transactions where rights or obligations are created pursuant to one or several declarations of will. Examples: contracts, partnership agreements, wills, marriage.

3. See Art. 35.

4. See Art. 20.

59

5. Made (E), accompli (F), vorgenommen (G), compiuto (I). Some legal transactions involve only *one* declaration of will, hence 'made' rather than 'concluded'.

6. Incapacity, did not know nor should have known (E), incapacité, n'ait connu ou dû connaître (F), Handlungsunfähigkeit, gekannt oder hätte sie kennen müssen (G), incapacità, abbia saputo o dovuto sapere (I). In case of a declaration of will made from a different country the foreign origin may be recognizable. Under continental principles, a declaration of will is made when and where it is received (simplified).

7. See Art. 43 to 96.

8. See Art. 119.

Art. 37

IV. Name
1. General Rule

1. The name of a person domiciled in Switzerland is governed by Swiss law; the name of a person domiciled abroad is governed by the law designated by the conflict of laws rules of the country of domicile.[1]

2. A person may, however, claim[2] that his name be governed by the law of his country of citizenship.[3]

Previous law: Art. 8 NAG, repealed; BGE 106 II 103, 106 II 236, 109 II 81.
Legislative history: Experts Draft, *Art. 35;* Experts Report, page 91; Fribourg Colloque, page 5, 7; Government Draft, *Art. 35;* Government Report, point 225, 225.1, page 72, 64; Lausanne Colloque, page 66, 86, 95; Senate Debate, Amtliches Bulletin 1985; House Debate, Amtliches Bulletin 1986, page 1309, 1310; Senate Debate, Amtliches Bulletin 1987, page 184.
Swiss substantive law: Art. 29 CC.
In Switzerland, an individual has no freedom to adopt whatever name he pleases. Titles of nobility are not recognized in Switzerland, Art. 4 subs. 1 Swiss Federal Constitution. In some cantons, prepositions denoting nobility such as 'von', 'de' are not registered in the Register of Civil Status.

1. This is an example of renvoi under Art. 14 subs. 1.

2. Claim (E), demander (F), verlangen (G), esigere (I). The declaration should be made in writing. Swiss citizens not domiciled in Switzerland may make this declaration to the authorities of their canton of citizenship (usually the cantonal Government or the cantonal Supreme Court) or at a Swiss diplomatic or consular mission. (For selected addresses see Art. 12).

3. See Art. 22, Art. 23 subs. 2, Art. 24.

Art. 38

2. Change of Name[1] *1.* For a change of name, jurisdiction lies with the Swiss authorities[2] at the domicile[3] of the petitioner.[4]

2. A Swiss citizen not domiciled in Switzerland may request a change of name from the authority[2] of his Canton of citizenship.

3. Conditions for and effects of a change of name are governed by Swiss law.[5]

> *Legislative history:* Experts Draft, *Art. 36;* Experts Report, page 92; Government Draft, *Art. 36;* Government Report; point 225.3, page 74; Senate Debate, Amtliches Bulletin 1985, page 141; House Debate, Amtliche Bulletin 1986, page 1309, 1310.
> *Change of name abroad:* Art. 39.
> *Swiss substantive law:* Art. 30 CC.

1. In Switzerland. Subs. 1 and 2 deal with jurisdiction, subs. 3 with applicable law.

2. Usually just one administrative authority in each canton.

3. See Art. 20.

4. Petitioner (E), requérant (F), Gesuchssteller (G), instante (I).

5. Lex fori, in most cases lex domicilii.

Art. 39

3. Change of Name Abroad[1] A change of name which occurred[2] abroad[1] is recognized in Switzerland if it is valid[3] in the country of either the petitioner's domicile[4] or his citizenship.[5]

> *Legislative history:* Experts Draft, *Art. 37;* Experts Report, page 93; Government Draft, *Art. 37;* Government Report, point 225.3, page 74; Senate Debate, Amtliches Bulletin 1985, page 140, 141; House Debate, Amtliches Bulletin 1986, page 1309, 1310.

1. Change of name abroad (E), changement de nom intervenu à l'étranger (F), Namensänderung im Ausland (G), cambiamento dell nome all'estero (I).

2. Occurred (E), intervenu (F), erfolgt (G), avvenuto (I). The word 'occur' rather than 'made' is designed to include changes of name abroad that come

through marriage. The Government Report points out that changes of name that occurred in a country where a change of name can be declared unilaterally by the interested party without a decision by an authority can be recognized in Switzerland only if they were made 'with the collaboration' of a foreign authority. This goes beyond the text of the present article.

3. Valid (E), valable (F), gültig (G), valido (I).

4. See Art. 20.

5. See Art. 22, 23 subs. 3, Art. 24.

Art. 40

4. Entry in Register of Civil Status

Names are recorded in the Register of Civil Status in accordance with the Swiss principles of registration (Art. 37).[1]

> *Previous law:* BGE 106 II 103.
> *Legislative history:* Experts Draft, *Art. 36;* Experts Report, page 93; Government Draft, *Art. 38;* Government Report, point 225.3, page 74; Senate Debate, Amtliches Bulletin 1985, page 141; House Debate, Amtliches Bulletin 1986, page 1309, 1310.
> *Swiss substantive law:* Art. 39 ff. CC; Zivilstandsverordnung, Etat civil, SR 211.112; Arrêté du Conseil fédéral du 30 avril 1969 concernant l'exercice des activités de l'état civil par des représentations suisses á l'étranger, Etablissement et suppression d'offices de l'état civil à l'étranger, SR 211.112.20.
> Names are registered in Latin script as they appear in the registers or passport of the country of citizenship. Titles of nobility are not registered. In some cantons, prepositions denoting nobility such as 'von', 'de' are not registered in the Register of Civil Statuts.

1. See Art. 37.

Art. 41

V. Declaration of Disappearance[1]

1. Jurisdiction and Applicable Law

1. For the declaration of a person's disappearance[1] jurisdiction lies with the Swiss courts at the last known domicile[2] of the disappeared person.[3]

2. The Swiss courts also have jurisdiction to issue a declaration of disappearance if a legitimate interest[4] justifies this.

3. The prerequisites and effects of a declaration of disappearance are governed by Swiss law.[5]

62

Previous law: BGE 107 II 97.
Legislative history: Experts Draft, *Art. 39;* Experts Report, page 93; Government Draft, *Art. 39;* Government Report, point 226, page 75; Lausanne Colloque, page 85; Senate Debate, Amtliches Bulletin 1985, page 140, 142; House Debate, Amtliches Bulletin 1986, page 1310.
Declaration of disappearance or death issued abroad: See Art. 42.
Swiss substantive law: Art. 35 et seq. CC, SR 210.

1. Declaration of disappearance (E), déclaration d'absence (F), Verschollenerklärung (G), dichiarazione di scomparsa (I). In Switzerland. subs. 1 and deals with jurisdiction; subs. 3 with applicable law.

2. Art. 20.

3. Disappeared person (E), personne disparue (F), verschwundene Person (G), scomparso (I).

4. Legitimate interest (E), intérêt légitime (F), schützenswertes Interesse (G), interesse degno di protezione (I).

5. Lex fori, in most cases lex domicilii.

Art. 42

2.
Declaration of Disappearance or Death[1] Issued[2] Abroad

A declaration of disappearance or death[1] that was issued[2] abroad is recognized in Switzerland if it was issued[2] in the country of either the person's last known domicile[3] or his citizenship.[4]

Swiss Federal Constitution: Art. 35, see Appendix I.
Legislative history: Experts Draft, *Art. 40;* Experts Report, page 94; Government Draft, *Art. 40;* Government Report, point 226, page 75; Senate Debate, Amtliches Bulletin 1985, page 140, 141, 142; House Debate, Amtliches Bulletin 1986, page 1309, 1310.

1. Declaration of disappearance or death (E), déclaration d'absence et de décès (F), Verschollen- und Todeserklärung (G), dichiarazione di scomparsa e di morte (I).

2. Issued (E), prononcé (F), ausgesprochen (G), pronunciato (I). The declaration will also be recognized in Switzerland if either the country of domicile or citizenship recognizes it.

3. See Art. 20.

4. See Art. 22, 23 subs. 3, Art. 24.

63

Third Chapter: Marriage

First Section: Conclusion of Marriage

Art. 43

1.
Jurisdiction

1. The Swiss authorities have jurisdiction to conduct a marriage ceremony[1] if either the bride or the groom is domiciled[2] in or is a citizen of Switzerland.

2. Foreigners without a domicile in Switzerland may be permitted by the competent authority to marry[3] in Switzerland if the marriage will be recognized in both future spouses' countries of domicile or citizenship.[4]

3. Permission to marry may not be denied for the sole reason that a divorce granted or recognized in Switzerland is not recognized abroad.

Swiss Federal Constitution: Art. 54.
Bilateral treaty: With Iran: see Art. 33.
Previous law: Art. 7c NAG, repealed in Appendix to PIL Statute; BGE 97 I 389; 99 II 4; 102 I 61.
Legislative history: Experts Draft, *Art. 40;* Experts Report, page 102; Fribourg Colloque, page 19; Government Draft, *Art. 41;* Government Report, point 23, 231, page 75, point 232.3, page 79; Lausanne Colloque, page 87; Senate Debate, Amtliches Bulletin 1985, page 142; House Debate, Amtliches Bulletin 1986, page 1310, 1311; Senate Debate, Amtliches Bulletin 1987, page 184; House Debate, Amtliches Bulletin 1987, page 1068.
Applicable law: See Art. 44.
Marriage concluded abroad: See Art. 45.
Swiss substantive law: Art. 90 et seq. CC. In Switzerland, civil marriage is compulsory, and may be conducted only by government officials, not religious authorities. Religious marriage ceremonies may be conducted only *after* the civil marriage ceremony.

1. Conduct a marriage ceremony (E), célébrer le marriage (F), Eheschliessung (G), celebrare il matrimonio (I).

2. See Art. 20.

3. Marry (E), s'y marier (F), Eheschliessung (G), contrarre matrimonio (I).

4. See Art. 22, 23 subs. 3, 24. Here, favor matrimonii leads to a derogation from Art. 23 subs. 2.

Art. 44

1. The substantive prerequisites[1] for a marriage ceremony in Switzerland are determined by Swiss law.[2]

2. If the prerequisites of Swiss law are not met, a marriage ceremony between foreigners may be conducted if the prerequisites of the law of one of their countries of citizenship[3] are met.

3. The form of a marriage ceremony conducted in Switzerland is governed by Swiss law.[2]

Swiss Federal Constitution: Art. 58, Appendix I.
Bilateral treaties: With *Iran:* see Art. 33. With *Austria:* Accord du 26 avril 1962 entre la Confédération suisse et la République d'Autriche sur la suppression de la légalisation et sur l'échange des actes de l'état civil, ainsi que sur la délivrance de certificats de capacité matrimoniale (avec annexes), SR 0.211.112.416.3. With *Federal Republic of Germany:* Accord du 6 juin 1956 entre la Confédération suisse et la République fédérale d'Allemagne sur la suppression de la légalisation et l'échange des actes de l'état civil, ainsi que sur la délivrance de certificats de capacité matrimoniale (avec annexes), SR 0.211.112.413.6. With *Italy:* Accord du 16 novembre 1966 entre la Confédération suisse et la République italienne sur la dispense de légalisation, l'échange des actes de l'état civil et la présentation des certificats requis pour contracter mariage, SR 0.211.112.445.4.
Previous law: Art. 7c, d, e NAG, repealed in Appendix to PIL Statute.
Legislative history: Experts Draft, *Art. 41 and 42;* Experts Report, page 103; Fribourg Colloque, page 7, 19, 24, 26; Government Draft, *Art. 42;* Government Report, point 232.3, page 79; Lausanne Colloque, page 71, 29, 30, 64; Senate Debate, Amtliches Bulletin 1985, page 143; House Debate, Amtliches Bulletin 1986, page 1310, 1312.
Jurisdiction: See Art. 43.
Marriage concluded abroad: See Art. 45.
Swiss substantive law: Treaty: Convention de Vienne du 24 avril 1963 sur les relations consulaires, 1968, Art. 5 subs. f, SR 0.191.02, of limited application in Switzerland.
Statute: Art. 96 et seq. CC. Marriages are concluded only in civil form, and religious marriage is permitted only after civil marriage has been concluded.

1. Substantive prerequisites (E), conditions de fond (F), materiell-rechtliche Voraussetzungen (G), presupposti materiali (I).

2. Lex fori, in most cases lex domicilii.

3. See Art. 23. Here, favor matrimonii leads to a derogation from Art. 23 subs. 2.

Art. 45

III. Marriage Concluded Abroad

1. A marriage validly concluded[1] abroad is recognized in Switzerland.

2. If the bride or the groom is a Swiss citizen or if both are domiciled in Switzerland, a marriage concluded abroad is recognized provided that it was not concluded abroad with the clear intention of evading the grounds for nullity under Swiss law.

> *Swiss Federal Constitution:* Art. 54, see Appendix I.
> *Bilateral treaty:* With Iran, see Art. 33.
> *Previous law:* Art. 7f NAG, repealed in Appendix to PIL Statute.
> *Legislative history:* Experts Draft, *Art. 43;* Experts Report, page 106; Fribourg Colloque, page 22, 27, 65; Government Draft, *Art. 43;* Government Report, point 232.5, page 81; Lausanne Colloque, page 87; Senate Debate, Amtliches Bulletin 1985, page 114, 143; House Debate, Amtliches Bulletin, 1986, page 1310, 1312; Senate Debate, Amtliches Bulletin 1987, page 184.
> *Jurisdiction:* See Art. 43.
> *Applicable law:* See Art. 44.

1. Concluded (E), célébré (F), geschlossen (G) celebrato (I).

Second Section: Effects of Marriage in General

Art. 46

I. Jurisdiction
1. General Rule

For lawsuits or measures[1] concerning marital rights and duties,[2] jurisdiction lies with the Swiss judicial or administrative authorities at the domicile[3] or, if there is none,[4] at the habitual residence[5] of one of the spouses.

> *Multilateral treaties:* See Art. 47.
> *Bilateral treaty:* With Iran: see Art. 33.
> *Previous law:* BGE 100 II 65.
> *Legislative history:* Experts Draft, *Art. 44;* Experts Report, page 108; Fribourg Colloque, page 19; Government Draft, *Art. 44;* Government Report, point 233, 233.1, page 81; Lausanne Colloque, page 88, 120; Senate Debate, Amtliches Bulletin 1985, page 143; House Debate, Amtliches Bulletin 1986, page 1310, 1312.
> *Applicable law:* See Art. 48.
> *Foreign decisions or measures:* See Art. 50.
> *Recognition and declaration of enforceability of decisions concerning support and alimony:* (Hague) Convention du 2 octobre 1973 sur la loi applicable aux

obligations alimentaires, 1977, SR 0.211.213.01; (Hague) Convention du 2 octobre 1973 concernant la reconnaissance et l'exécution de décisions relatives aux obligations alimentaires, 1976, SR 0.211.213.02.
Swiss substantive law: Art. 159 et seq., 169 et seq. CC.

1. Lawsuits or measures (E), actions ou mesures (F), Klagen oder Massnahmen (G), azioni o provvedimenti (I).

2. Marital rights and duties (E), effets du mariage (F), eheliche Rechte und Pflichten (G), diritti e doveri coniugali (I).

3. See Art. 20.

4. If there is none (E), à défaut de domicile (F), wenn ein solcher fehlt (G), in mancanza di domicilio (I).

5. Art. 20 subs. 2 makes the 'or' portion of this article superfluous.

Art. 47

2.
Jurisdiction
at Place of
Citizenship[1]

If neither spouse has his domicile or habitual residence in Switzerland but one of the spouses is a Swiss citizen, jurisdiction for lawsuits or measures concerning marital rights and duties lies with the judicial or administrative authorities at the place of citizenship[1] if it is impossible or highly impracticable to bring a lawsuit or petition at the domicile or habitual residence of one of the spouses.[2]

Bilateral treaty: With Iran, see Art. 33.
Legislative history: Experts Draft, *Art. 45;* Experts Report, page 109; Government Draft, *Art. 45;* Government Report, point 233.2, page 82; Senate Debate, Amtliches Bulletin 1985, page 143; House Debate, Amtliches Bulletin 1986, page 1310, 1312.
Applicable law: See Art. 48.

1. Place of citizenship (E), for d'origine (F), Heimatzuständigkeit (G), foro di origine (I), forum originis (L). See Art. 23.

2. As provided in Art. 46.

Art. 48

II.
Applicable
Law
1. General
Rule

1. Marital rights and duties[1] are governed by the law of the country in which the spouses have their domicile.[2]

2. If the spouses are not domiciled in the same country, the marital rights and duties are governed by the law of the country of domicile that has the closest link with the case.[3]

3. If Article 47 grants jurisdiction to the Swiss judicial or administrative authorities at the place of citizenship, they will apply Swiss law.

> *Bilateral treaty:* With Iran: see Art. 33.
> *Legislative history:* Experts Draft, *Art. 46;* Experts Report, page 111; Fribourg Colloque, page 20, 30, 31, 64; Government Draft, *Art. 46;* Government Report, point 233.3, page 83; Lausanne Colloque, page 88, 276; Senate Debate, Amtliches Bulletin 1985, page 144; House Debate, Amtliches Bulletin 1986, page 1310, 1313.
> *Jurisdiction:* See Art. 46.
> *Foreign decisions or measures:* See Art. 50.
> *Swiss substantive law:* Art. 159 et seq. CC.

1. See Art. 46.

2. See Art. 20, lex domicilii communis, see subs. 2.

3. See Art. 3.

Art. 49

2. Support
and
Alimony

For the support obligations between spouses the Hague Convention of October 2, 1973 concerning the Law Applicable to Maintenance Obligations applies.

> *Bilateral treaty:* With Iran, see Art. 33.
> *Multilateral treaty:* For all countries: (Hague) Convention du 2 octobre 1973 sur la loi applicable aux obligations alimentaires, 1977, SR 0.211.213.01.
> *Legislative history:* Experts Draft, *Art. 47;* Experts Report, page 113; Fribourg Colloque, page 17, 65; Government Draft, *Art. 47;* Government Report, point 233.3, page 84; Senate Debate, Amtliches Bulletin 1985, page 144; House Debate, Amtliches Bulletin 1986, page 1310, 1313; Senate Debate, Amtliches Bulletin 1987, page 184; House Debate, Amtliches Bulletin 1987, page 1068; Senate Debate Amtliches Bulletin 1987, page 506.

Art. 50

Foreign decisions or measures concerning marital rights and duties[1] are recognized[2] in Switzerland if they were rendered or ordered in the country of domicile[3] or habitual residence of one of the spouses.

Swiss Federal Constitution: Art. 59, see Appendix I.

Multilateral treaties: With Austria, Belgium, Czechoslovakia, Denmark, Spain, France, Liechtenstein, United Kingdom, Hungary, Italy, Luxemburg, Norway, Netherlands, Portugal, Spain, Finland, Turkey: (Hague) Convention du 2 octobre 1973 concernant la reconnaissance et l'exécution de décisions relatives aux obligations alimentaires, 1976, SR 0.211.213.02. With 37 countries: (New York) Convention of 1956 on Convention du 20 juin 1956 sur le recouvrement des aliments à l'étranger, 1977, SR 0.274.15.

Bilateral treaties: With Austria, Belgium, Czechoslovakia, (Federal Republic of) Germany, Spain, Liechtenstein, Italy and Sweden: see Art. 25. With Iran: see Art. 33.

Legislative history: Experts Draft, *Art. 48;* Experts Report, page 113; Government Draft, *Art. 48;* Government Report, 233.4, page 84; Lausanne Colloque, page 88; Senate Debate, Amtliches Bulletin 1985, page 144; House Debate, Amtliches Bulletin 1986, page 1310, 1313; Senate Debate, Amtliches Bulletin 1987, page 184; House Debate, Amtliches Bulletin 1987, page 1068; Senate Debate, Amtliches Bulletin 1987, page 507.

Jurisdiction: See Art. 46.

Applicable law: See Art. 48.

1. See Art. 46.

2. Are recognized (E), sont reconnus (F), werden anerkannt (G), sono riconosciuti (I).

3. See Art. 20.

Third Section: Marital Property

Art. 51

For lawsuits or measures concerning marital property, jurisdiction lies as follows:
(a) For the distribution of marital property[1] in case of death of one spouse, with the Swiss judicial or administrative authorities that have jurisdiction over the distribution of the estate[2] (Art. 86 to 89);

69

(b) For the distribution of marital property in case of judicial dissolution or separation of marriage, with the Swiss courts that have jurisdiction over the dissolution or separation of the marriage (Art. 59, 60, 63, 64);

(c) In all other cases, with the Swiss judicial or administrative authorities that have jurisdiction over lawsuits or measures concerning the effects of marriage (Art. 46, 47).

Multilateral treaties: Switzerland is not a member of the Hague Convention of March 14, 1978, on the law applicable to matrimonial property regimes, but the Statute is influenced by it.
Bilateral treaty: With Iran, see Art. 33.
Previous law: Art. 19, 31 NAG, repealed in Appendix to PIL Statute; BGE 34 I 734.
Legislative history: Experts Draft, *Art. 49;* Experts Report, page 118; Fribourg Colloque, page 34; Government Draft, *Art. 49;* Government Report, point 234.2, page 87, point 234, 234.1, 85; Lausanne Colloque, page 116, 120; Senate Debate, Amtliches Bulletin, page 145; House Debate, Amtliches Bulletin, page 1310, 1313; Senate Debate, Amtliches Bulletin 1987, page 184.
Applicable law: See Art. 52, 54.
Foreign decisions: See Art. 58.
Swiss substantive law: Art. 178 CC.

1. Distribution of marital property (E), dissolution du régime matrimonial (F), güterrechtliche Auseinandersetzung (G), liquidazione del regime dei beni (I).

2. Distribution of the estate (E), liquider la succession (F), erbrechtliche Auseinandersetzung (G), liquidare la successione (I).

Art. 52

II.
Applicable Law
1. Choice of Applicable Law
a. General Rule

1. Marital property is governed by the law chosen by the spouses.

2. The spouses may choose between the law of the country in which they both have their domicile, or will have their domicile after the marriage, and the law of one of their countries of citizenship. Article 23 subsection 2 is not applicable.

Bilateral treaty: With Iran: see Art. 33.
Legislative history: Experts Draft, *Art. 50;* Experts Report, page 120; Fribourg Colloque, page 34, 35, 39, 41, 65; Government Draft, *Art. 50;* Government Report, point 234.3, 234.31, page 88; Lausanne Colloque, page 103, 117, 119, 120; Senate Debate, Amtliches Bulletin 1985, page 145; House Debate, Amtliches Bulletin 1986, page 1313.
Jurisdiction: See Art. 51.
Foreign decisions: See Art. 58.

b. Modalities *1.* A choice of law must be made in writing or be clearly evident[1] from the marital property contract.[2] Moreover, it is governed by the law chosen.

2. A choice of law may be made or altered at any time. If it is made after the conclusion of the marriage,[3] it is effective retroactively from the time of conclusion of the marriage,[3] unless otherwise provided by the parties.

3. The chosen law remains applicable until the spouses choose a different law or revoke the choice of law.

> *Bilateral treaty:* With Iran: see Art. 33.
> *Legislative history:* Experts Draft, *Art. 51 and 52;* Experts Report, page 123; Fribourg Colloque, page 35, 40; Government Draft, *Art. 51;* Government Report, 234.31, page 88, 89; Lausanne Colloque, page 104, 122; Senate Debate, Amtliches Bulletin 1985, page 145; House Debate, Amtliches Bulletin 1986, page 1313.
>
> 1. Clearly evident (E), d'une façon certaine (F), eindeutig (G), univocamente (I).
>
> 2. Marital property contract (E), contrat de mariage (F), Ehevertrag (G), convenzione matrimoniale (I).
>
> 3. Conclusion of the marriage (E), célébration du mariage (F), Abschluss der Ehe (G), celebrazione del matrimonio (I).

Art. 54

2. No Applicable Law Chosen a. General Rule *1.* If the spouses have not made a choice of law, their marital property is governed by:
(a) the law of the country in which both spouses are domiciled at the same time,[1] or, if there is none,
(b) the law of the country in which both spouses were last domiciled at the same time.

2. If the spouses were never domiciled at the same time in the same country, the law of the country of their common citizenship applies.[2]

3. If the spouses were never domiciled at the same time in the same country nor have common citizenship, the provisions of Swiss law on separation of property[3] apply.

Bilateral treaty: With Iran: see Art. 33.
Previous law: Art. 19, 31 NAG, repealed in Appendix to PIL Statute.
Legislative history: Experts Draft, *Art. 53;* Experts Report, page 123; Fribourg Colloque, page 35, 39, 40; Government Draft, *Art. 52;* Government Report, point 234.3, 234.31, page 88; point 234.32, 91; Lausanne Colloque, page 106, 123; Senate Debate, Amtliches Bulletin 1985, page 120, 146; House Debate, Amtliches Bulletin 1986, page 1310, 1313.
Jurisdiction: See Art. 51.
Foreign decisions: See Art. 58.
Swiss substantive law: Art. 181 et seq. CC.

1. Domiciled at the same time (E), domiciliés en même temps (F), gleichzeitig Wohnsitz haben (G), simultaneamente domiciliati (I), lex domicilii communis (L).

2. See Art. 22, 23.

3. See Art. 247 et seq. CC. subs. 2, Art. 24.

Art. 55

b.
Mutability
and
Retro-
activity
in Case of
Change
of Domicile

1. If the spouses move their domicile from one country to another, the law of the new domicile applies retroactively from the time of the marriage.[1] The spouses may exclude the retroactivity by an agreement in writing.[2]

2. A change of domicile has no effect on the applicable law if the parties have agreed in writing that the previous law remains applicable, or if they have made a marital property contract.

Bilateral treaty: With Iran: see Art. 33.
Previous law: Art. 19, 20, 21, 31, NAG, repealed in Appendix to PIL Statute.
Legislative history: Experts Draft, *Art. 54;* Experts Report, page 125; Fribourg Colloque, page 41, 65; Government Draft, *Art. 53;* Government Report, point 234.3, 234.31, page 89; point 234.32, page 91; Lausanne Colloque, page 108, 118, 125; Senate Debate, Amtliches Bulletin 1985, page 146; House Debate, Amtliches Bulletin 1986, page 1313.
Swiss substantive law: Art. 181 et seq. CC.

1. Time of the marriage (E), jour du mariage (F), Zeitpunkt der Eheschliessung (G), momento della celebrazione del matrimonio (I).

2. No time limit is specified. Art. 53 para. 2 seems to suggest that retroactivity may be excluded at any time. See Art. 57.

Art. 56

3. Form of
Marital
Property
Contract

A marital property contract is valid as to its form if it conforms to the law governing the marital property contract or to the law at the place where it is concluded.[1]

Bilateral treaty: With Iran, see Art. 33.
Legislative history: Experts Draft, *Art. 55;* Experts Report, page 128; Government Draft, *Art. 54;* Government Report, point 234.4, page 93; Lausanne Colloque, page 128; Senate Debate, Amtliches Bulletin 1985, page 146; House Debate, Amtliches Bulletin 1986, page 1310, 1313.
Swiss substantive law: Art. 182 CC.

1. Law at the place where it is concluded (E), droit du lieu où l'acte a été passé. (F), Recht am Abschlussort (G), diritto del luogo di stipulazione (I), locus regit actum (L).
   The PIL Statute does not exclude that a marital property contract could be closed inter absentes. In that case, in keeping with Swiss substantive law, the place of closing is where the offeror received the acceptance.

Art. 57

4. Legal
Relationships
with Third
Parties

1. The effects of the marital property system on the legal relationship between a spouse and a third party are governed by the law of the spouse's domicile[1] at the time when the legal relationship arose.

2. If, however, when the legal relationship arose, the third party knew or should have known the law governing the marital property, then that law applies.

Bilateral treaty: With Iran: see Art. 33.
Previous law: Art. 19, 21 NAG, repealed in Appendix to PIL Statute.
Legislative history: Experts Draft, *Art. 56;* Experts Report, page 129; Fribourg Colloque, page 36, 39, 65; Government Draft, *Art. 55;* Government Report, point 234.5, page 93; Lausanne Colloque, page 109, 128, 153, 154; Senate Debate, Amtliches Bulletin 1985, page 146; House Debate, Amtliches Bulletin 1986, page 1313.
Swiss substantive law: Art. 181 et seq. CC.

1. See Art. 20.

Art. 58

1. Foreign decisions on marital property rights are recognized in Switzerland if:

(a) they were rendered in the country of the domicile of the defendant spouse, or are recognized there;

(b) they were rendered in the country of the domicile of the plaintiff spouse, or are recognized there, provided that the defendant spouse was not domiciled in Switzerland;

(c) they were rendered in the country whose law is applicable according to this Statute,[1] or are recognized there; or

(d) they concern immovable property and were rendered at the place where the property is situated,[2] or are recognized there.

2. The recognition of decisions on marital property rendered in connection with measures to protect the marital union, or following death, declaration of nullity of marriage, divorce or separation, is governed by the provisions of this Statute on marriage, divorce, or inheritance law (Art. 50, 65 and 96).

Swiss Federal Constitution: Art. 59, see Appendix I.
Bilateral treaties: With Austria, Belgium, Czechoslovakia, (Federal Republic of) Germany, Italy, Liechtenstein, Spain and Sweden; see Art. 25. With Iran: see Art. 33.
Legislative history: Experts Draft, *Art. 57;* Experts Report, page 130; Government Draft, *Art. 56;* Government Report, point 234.6, page 94; Lausanne Colloque, page 129; Senate Debate, Amtliches Bulletin 1985, page 146; House Debate, Amtliches Bulletin 1986, page 1313.
Jurisdiction: See Art. 51.
Applicable law: See Art. 52, 54.

1. See Art. 52, 54.

2. Place where the property is situated (E), l'Etat dans lequel ces immeubles sont situés (F), Ort der gelegenen Sache (G), Stato di situazione dei medesimi (I), forum rei sitae (L).

Fourth Section: Divorce and Separation

Art. 59

I.
Jurisdiction
1. General
Rule

Lawsuits for divorce or separation[1] are subject to the jurisdiction of:
(a) the Swiss courts at the domicile of the defendant spouse;
(b) the Swiss courts at the domicile of the plaintiff spouse, if plaintiff has been residing[2] in Switzerland for one year or is a Swiss citizen.

Bilateral treaty: With Iran: see Art. 33.
Previous law: Art. 7g, 7h NAG, repealed in Appendix to PIL Statute.
Legislative history: Experts Draft, *Art. 58;* Experts Report, page 132; Fribourg Colloque, page 19, 24, 31, 32, 64; Government Draft, *Art. 57;* Government Report, point 235, 235.1 page 94, 95; Lausanne Colloque, page 89, 255, 260; Senate Debate, Amtliches Bulletin 1986, page 147; House Debate, Amtliches Bulletin 1986, page 1310, 1313.
Applicable law: See Art. 61.
Foreign decisions: See Art. 65.
Swiss substantive law: Art. 120 et seq., 137 et seq., 144 CC.

1. This includes actions in nullity, compare Art. 58 subs. 2.

2. Has been residing (E), résider (F), sich aufhalten (G), dimora (I). What is probably meant is habitual residence in the sense of Art. 20 in Switzerland that has lasted at least one year. The same test applies in Art. 61, but for two years.

Art. 60

2.
Jurisdiction
at Place of
Citizenship

If the spouses are not domiciled in Switzerland but one of them is a Swiss citizen, jurisdiction over lawsuits for divorce or separation lies with the courts at the place of citizenship[1] if it is impossible or highly impracticable to bring the lawsuit at the domicile of one of the spouses.

Swiss Federal Constitution: Art. 59, Appendix I.
Bilateral treaty: With Iran: see Art. 33
Previous law: Art. 7g, 7h NAG, repealed in Appendix to PIL Statute.
Legislative history: Experts Draft, *Art. 59;* Experts Report, page 133; Fribourg Colloque, page 31, 64; Government Draft, *Art. 58;* Government Report, point 235.2, page 95; Lausanne Colloque, page 89, 229; Senate Debate, Amtliches Bulletin 1985, page 147; House Debate, Amtliches Bulletin 1986, page 1313, 1314.
Swiss substantive law: Art. 144 CC.

1. Of the Swiss citizen. See Art. 20, 23. See also Art. 61 subs. 4.

75

Art. 61

1. Divorce and separation are governed by Swiss law.[1]

2. If the spouses have a common foreign citizenship and only one of them is domiciled in Switzerland, the law of the country of their common citizenship applies.

3. If under the law of the foreign country of common citizenship a divorce is not permitted at all or only under unusually strict conditions, Swiss law applies[2] if one of the spouses is also a Swiss citizen or has been residing in Switzerland for two years.[3]

4. If Article 60 grants jurisdiction to the Swiss courts at the place of citizenship, they will apply Swiss law.[4]

Bilateral treaty: With Iran: see Art. 33.
Previous law: Art. 7g, 7h, 7i NAG, repealed in Appendix to PIL Statute.
Legislative history: Experts Draft, *Art. 60 and 61;* Experts Report, page 134; Fribourg Colloque, page 32; Government Draft, *Art. 59;* Government Report, point 235.3, page 95, 96; Lausanne Colloque, page 90, 169; Senate Debate, Amtliches Bulletin 1985, page 147; House Debate, Amtliches Bulletin 1986, page 1314; Senate Debate, Amtliches Bulletin 1987, page 184.
Jurisdiction: See Art. 59.
Foreign decisions: See Art. 65.
Swiss substantive law: Art. 137 et seq. CC. A revision of the law is planned.

1. Lex fori, in most cases lex domicilii.

2. Applies (E), est applicable (F), ist anzuwenden (G), si applica (I), favor divortii (L).

3. What is probably meant is habitual residence in Switzerland that has lasted at least two years. The same test applies in Art. 59, but one year is enough.

4. Lex fori.

Art. 62

1. A Swiss court before which a lawsuit for divorce or separation is pending may order provisional measures[1] unless it clearly lacks jurisdiction over the lawsuit or it has been finally determined that it lacks jurisdiction.

2. The provisional measures[1] are governed by Swiss law.

3. The provisions of this Statute on support and alimony obligations between spouses (Art. 49), consequences of parent-child relationship (Art. 82 and 83), and protection of minors (Art. 85) are reserved.

Bilateral treaty: With Iran: see Art. 33.
Previous law: BGE 83 II 495.
Legislative history: Experts Draft, *Art. 62;* Experts Report, page 137; Government Draft, *Art. 60;* Government Report, point 235.4, page 98; Senate Debate, Amtliches Bulletin 1985, page 147; House Debate, Amtliches Bulletin 1986, page 1310, 1314.
Swiss substantive law: Art. 145 CC.

1. Provisional measures (E), mesures provisoires (F), vorsorgliche Massnahmen (G), provvedimenti cautelari (I). Examples: alimony, visiting rights.

Art. 63

IV. Ancillary Measures[1]

1. The Swiss courts that have jurisdiction over actions for divorce or separation also have jurisdiction to issue ancillary measures.[1]

2. The ancillary measures on divorce or separation are determined by the law governing the divorce.[2] The provisions of this Statute on name (Art. 37 to 40),[2] support and alimony obligations between spouses (Art. 49), marital property (Art. 52 to 57), consequences of parent-child relationship (Art. 82 and 83), and protection of minors (Art. 85) are reserved.

Bilateral treaty: With Iran: See Art. 33.
Legislative history: Experts Draft, *Art. 63;* Experts Report, page 138; Government Draft, *Art. 61;* Government Report, point 235.4, page 98; Senate Debate, Amtliches Bulletin 1985, page 148; House Debate, Amtliches Bulletin 1986, page 1310, 1314.
Swiss substantive law: Art. 149 et seq. CC.

1. Ancillary measures (E), effets accessoires (F), Nebenfolgen (G), effetti accessori (I). Examples: Alimony, visiting rights, marital property.

2. Law governing the divorce (E), le droit applicable au divorce (F), auf die Scheidung anzuwendendes Recht (G), diritto applicablile al divorzio (I). See Art. 61.

Art. 64

1. Lawsuits for supplement to or modification of divorce or separation decrees[1] are subject to the jurisdiction of the Swiss courts if the courts have issued the decrees themselves or if they have jurisdiction based on Articles 59 or 60.[2] The provisions of this Statute on protection of minors (Art. 85) are reserved.

2. The supplement to or modification of a divorce or separation decree[1] is governed by the law governing the divorce or separation. The provisions of this statute on name (Art. 37 to 40), support and alimony obligations between spouses (Art. 49), marital property (Art. 52 to 57), consequences of parent-child relationship (Art. 82 and 83), and protection of minors (Art. 85) are reserved.

> *Bilateral treaty:* With Iran: See Art. 33.
> *Legislative history:* Experts Draft, *Art. 64;* Experts Report, page 139; Fribourg Colloque, page 20; Government Draft, *Art. 62;* Government Report, point 235.6, page 99; Lausanne Colloque, page 91; Senate Debate, Amtliches Bulletin 1985, page 148; House Debate, Amtliches Bulletin 1986, page 1310, 1314.

> 1. Decree (E), décision (F), Entscheidung (G), decisione (I).

> 2. This always concerns the ancillary effects in the sense of Art. 63. The conversion of a separation into divorce is governed by Art. 61.

Art. 65

1. Foreign divorce or separation decrees[1] are recognized in Switzerland if they were issued[2] in the country of the domicile, habitual residence, or citizenship[3] of one spouse, or are recognized by one of these countries.

2. If, however, the decree was issued in a country of which neither spouse or only the plaintiff spouse is a citizen, it is recognized in Switzerland only if
(a) at the time when the lawsuit was commenced, at least one spouse had his domicile or his habitual residence in that country and the defendant spouse did not have his domicile in Switzerland;
(b) the defendant spouse entered an unconditional appearance before the foreign court;[4] or

(c) the defendant spouse agrees to the recognition of the decree in Switzerland.

Swiss Federal Constitution: Art. 59, Appendix I.
Multilateral treaty: With Cyprus, Czechoslovakia, Denmark, Egypt, Finland, Netherlands, Norway, Portugal, Sweden and United Kingdom: (Hague) Convention du 1er juin 1970 sur la reconnaissance des divorces et das séparations de corps, SR 0.211.212.3.
Bilateral treaties: With Austria, Belgium, Czechoslovakia, (Federal Republic of) Germany, Italy, Liechtenstein, Spain and Sweden: See Art. 25. With Iran: See Art. 33.
Legislative history: Experts Draft, *Art. 65;* Experts Report, page 139; Fribourg Colloque, page 22, 23, 28, 68; Government Draft, *Art. 63;* Government Report, point 235.7, page 99; point 217.2, page 66; Senate Debate, Amtliches Bulletin 1985, page 148; House Debate, Amtliches Bulletin 1986, page 1315; Senate Debate, Amtliches Bulletin 1987, page 185.
Jurisdiction: See Art. 59.
Applicable law: See Art. 61.

1. Foreign divorce or separation decrees (E), décisions étrangères de divorce ou de séparation de corps (F), ausländische Entscheidungen über die Scheidung oder Trennung (G), decisioni straniere in materia di divorzio o separazione (I).

2. Issued (E), rendu (F), ergangen (D), pronunciato (I). Not necessarily court decrees, but unilateral repudiation of a spouse is insufficient.

3. See Art. 22, 23 subs. 3, 24.

4. See Art. 26 letter c.

Fourth Chapter: Parent-Child Relationship

First Section: Parent-Child Relationship by Descent[1]

Art. 66

I.
Jurisdiction
1. General
Rule

Lawsuits for a declaration or disclaimer of parent-child relationship, are subject to the jurisdiction of the Swiss courts either at the child's habitual residence or at the domicile of either parent.

Bilateral treaty: With Iran: See Art. 33.
Previous law: Art. 8d subs. 1 NAG, repealed in Appendix to PIL Statute.
Legislative history: Experts Draft, *Art. 66;* Experts Report, page 146; Government Draft, *Art. 64;* Government Report, point 24, 241, 241.1, page 100, point

242, page 103; Lausanne Colloque, page 161; Senate Debate, Amtliches Bulletin, page 149; House Debate, Amtliches Bulletin, page 1343, 1344.
Applicable law: See Art. 68.
Foreign decisions: See Art. 70.
Swiss substantive law: Art. 253 CC.

1. Descent (E), naissance (F), Abstammung (G), discendenza (I). This excludes adoption, see Art. 75 et seq.

Art. 67

2.
Jurisdiction
at Place of
Citizenship[1]

If neither parent has domicile and the child has no habitual residence in Switzerland, lawsuits for a declaration or disclaimer of parent-child relationship are subject to the jurisdiction of the courts at the Swiss place of citizenship[1] of either parent, if it is impossible or highly impracticable to bring a lawsuit at either parent's domicile or at the child's habitual residence.

Bilateral treaty: With Iran: See Art. 33.
Previous law: Art. 8d NAG, repealed in Appendix to PIL Statute.
Legislative history: Experts Draft, *Art. 67;* Experts Report, page 147; Government Draft, *Art. 65;* Government Report, point 242.1, page 103; Senate Debate, Amtliches Bulletin 1985, page 149; House Debate, Amtliches Bulletin 1986, page 1288, 1291, 1343, 1344.

1. See Art. 22, 23 subs. 1, Art. 24.

Art. 68

II.
Applicable
Law
1. General
Rule

1. Creation, declaration, and disclaimer of parent-child relationship[1] are governed by the law at the child's habitual residence.

2. If, however, neither parent is domiciled in the country of the child's habitual residence, but the parents and the child are citizens[2] of the same country, the law of the country of their common citizenship[3] applies.

80

Bilateral treaty: With Iran: See Art. 33.
Previous law: Art. 8e NAG, repealed in Appendix to PIL Statute; BGE 107 II 209.
Legislative history: Experts Draft, *Art. 68;* Experts Report, page 147; Fribourg Colloque, page 20, 21, 26; Government Draft, *Art. 66;* Government Report, point 242.2, page 104; Lausanne Colloque, page 166, 176; Senate Debate, Amtliches Bulletin 1985, page 149; House Debate, Amtliches Bulletin 1986, page 1343, 1348.
Jurisdiction: See Art. 66.
Foreign decisions: See Art. 70.
Swiss substantive law: Art. 252, 256, 261 CC.

1. The scope of this Article is limited to the parent-child status created by descent, a presumption of parenthood, or a decision.

2. See Art. 22, 23 subs. 2, Art. 24.

3. Law of the country of their common citizenship (E), si les parents e l'enfant ont la nationalité d'un même État, le droit de cet Etat (F), gemeinsames Heimatrecht (G), diritto nazionale commune (I), lex patriae communis (L).

Art. 69

2. Decisive Time[1]

1. The time of birth is decisive[2] to determine the law governing the creation, declaration, or disclaimer of parent-child relationship.

2. However, the time when the lawsuit is commenced is decisive for a judicial declaration or disclaimer of parent-child relationship if an overriding interest of the child so requires.

Bilateral treaty: With Iran: See Art. 33.
Legislative history: Experts Draft, *Art. 69;* Experts Report, page 151; Government Draft, *Art. 67;* Government Report, point 242.2, page 106; Lausanne Colloque, page 166, 172, 177, 178; Senate Debate, Amtliches Bulletin 1985, page 149; House Debate, Amtliches Bulletin 1986, page 1343, 1348.
Swiss substantive law: Art. 253 CC.

1. Decisive time (E), moment déterminant (F), massgeblicher Zeitpunkt (G), momento determinante (I).

2. Time of birth is decisive (E), on se fondera sur la date de la naissance (F), Zeitpunkt der Geburt ist massgebend (G), momento della nascita determina (I).

Art. 70

Foreign decisions concerning a declaration or disclaimer of parent-child relationship are recognized in Switzerland if they were rendered in the country of the child's habitual residence or citizenship, or in the country of either parent's domicile or citizenship.[1]

> *Bilateral treaty:* With Iran: See Art. 33. With Austria, Belgium, Czechoslovakia, (Federal Republic of) Germany, Italy, Liechtenstein, Spain and Sweden; Art. 25.
> *Legislative history:* Experts Draft, *Art. 70;* Experts Report, page 151; Government Draft, *Art. 68;* Government Report, point 242.3, page 107; Senate Debate, Amtliches Bulletin 1985, page 149, 150; House Debate, Amtliches Bulletin 1986, page 1343, 1348; Senate Debate, Amtliches Bulletin 1987, page 185.
> *Jurisdiction:* See Art. 66.
> *Applicable law:* See Art. 68.

1. Favor validitatis, favor recognitionis (L).

Second Section: Acknowledgement

Art. 71

1. To record an acknowledgement of paternity, jurisdiction lies with the Swiss authorities at the child's place of birth or habitual residence, and at either parent's domicile or place of citizenship.[1]

2. If an acknowledgement is made in a judicial proceeding the judge seized with the lawsuit may also record the acknowledgement.

3. For a challenge of acknowledgement, jurisdiction lies with the same courts as for declaration or disclaimer of parent-child relationship (Art. 66 and 67).

> *Multilateral treaty:* With Belgium, Federal Republic of Germany, France, Greece, Italy, Netherlands, Portugal and Turkey: (CIEC) Convention No. 5 du 14 septembre 1961 portant extension de la compétence des autorités qualifiées pour recevoir lés reconnaissances d'enfants naturels, SR 0.211.112.13.
> *Bilateral treaty:* With Iran: See Art. 33.
> *Legislative history:* Experts Draft, *Art. 71;* Experts Report, page 153; Govern-

ment Draft, *Art. 69;* Government Report, point 243, page 107; Senate Debate, Amtliches Bulletin 1985, page 150; House Debate, Amtliches Bulletin 1986, page 1343, 1348, Senate Debate, Amtliches Bulletin 1987, page 185.
Applicable law: See Art. 72.
Foreign acknowledgement or challenge of acknowledgement: See Art. 73.

1. See Art. 22, 23 subs. 1, Art. 24, favor legitimationis.

Art. 72

II.
Applicable
Law

1. An acknowledgement made in Switzerland[1] is valid if it conforms to the law of the country of the child's habitual residence or citizenship,[2] or of the country of either parent's domicile or citizenship.[2] The time of acknowledgement is decisive.

2. The form of an acknowledgement in Switzerland is governed by Swiss law.

3. The challenge of an acknowledgement is governed by Swiss law.

Bilateral treaty: With Iran: See Art. 33.
Legislative history: Experts Draft, *Art. 71;* Experts Report, page 153, 329; Government Draft, *Art. 70;* Government Report, point 243, page 108; Lausanne Colloque, page 180, 183; Senate Debate, Amtliches Bulletin 1985, page 150; House Debate, Amtliches Bulletin 1986, page 1343, 1349; Senate Debate, Amtliches Bulletin 1987, page 185.
Jurisdiction: See Art. 71.
Foreign acknowledgement or challenge of acknowledgement: See Art. 73.
Swiss substantive law: Art. 260 subs. 3 CC.

1. Acknowledgement made in Switzerland (E), reconnaissance en Suisse (F), Anerdennung in der Schweiz (G), riconoscimento in Svizzera (I).

2. Art. 22, 23 subs. 2, 24.

Art. 73

III.
Foreign
Acknow-
ledgement
and
Challenge of
Acknow-
ledgement

1. A foreign acknowledgement[1] of a child is recognized in Switzerland if it is valid under the law of the country of the child's habitual residence or citizenship,[2] or of the country of either parent's domicile or citizenship.[2]

2. Foreign decisions on a challenge of acknowledgment are recognized in Switzerland if they were rendered in one of the countries mentioned in subsection 1.

Bilateral treaty: With Iran: See Art. 33.
Legislative history: Experts Draft, *Art. 73;* Experts Report, page 154; Government Draft, *Art. 71;* Government Report, point 243, page 108; Lausanne Colloque, page 182; Senate Debate, Amtliches Bulletin 1985, page 150; House Debate, Amtliches Bulletin 1986, page 1343, 1349, Senate Debate, Amtliches Bulletin 1987, page 185.
Jurisdiction: Art. 71
Applicable law: Art. 72
Swiss substantive law: Art. 260 subs. 3 CC.

1. Foreign acknowledgement (E), reconnaissance intervenue à l'étranger (F), im Ausland erfolgte Anerkennung (G), riconoscimento all'estero (I).

2. Art. 22, 23, subs. 3, Art. 24.

Art. 74

IV.
Legitimation

For the recognition of a foreign legitimation, Article 73 applies by analogy.

Bilateral treaty: With Iran: See Art. 33.
Legislative history: Experts Draft, *Art. 72;* Experts Report, page 152; Fribourg Colloque, page 21, 27; Government Draft, *Art. 72;* Government Report, point 243, page 108; Senate Debate, Amtliches Bulletin 1985, page 150; House Debate, Amtliches Bulletin 1985, page 1343, 1349.
Swiss substantive law: The distinction between children born in and out of wedlock is abolished in Switzerland.

84

Third Section: Adoption[1]

Art. 75

I.
Jurisdiction
1. General
Rule

1. Jurisdiction to grant an adoption lies with the Swiss judicial or administrative authorities at the domicile of the adopting person or spouses.

2. For a challenge of an adoption, jurisdiction lies with the same courts as for a declaration or disclaimer of the parent-child relationship (Art. 66 and 67).

Multilateral treaty: With Austria and United Kingdom: (Hague) Convention du 15 novembre 1965 concernant la compétence des autorités, la loi applicable et la reconnaissance des décisions en matière d'adoption, 1978, SR 0.211.221.315.
Bilateral treaty: With Iran: See Art. 33.
Previous law: Art. 8a, 8c NAG, repealed in Appendix to PIL Statute.
Legislative history: Experts Draft, *Art. 74;* Experts Report, page 155; Fribourg Colloque, page 10, 21, 29; Government Draft, *Art. 73;* Government Report, point 244.3, page 110; Senate Debate, Amtliches Bulletin 1985, page 150; House Debate, Amtliches Bulletin 1986, page 1343, 1349.
Applicable law: See Art. 77.
Foreign adoption and similar measures: See Art. 78.
Swiss substantive law: Art. 268, 269 CC.

1. Adoption (E), adoption (F), adoption (G), adozione (I).

Art. 76

2.
Jurisdiction
at Place of
Citizenship[1]

If the adopting person or the adopting spouses are not domiciled in Switzerland but one of is a Swiss citizen, jurisdiction for adoption lies with the judicial or administrative authorities at the place of citizenship if it is impossible or highly impracticable to have an adoption granted at the domicile.

Multilateral treaty: See Art. 75.
Bilateral treaty: With Iran: See Art. 33.
Previous law: Art. 8a subs. 2 NAG, repealed.
Legislative history: Experts Draft, *Art. 75;* Experts Report, page 156; Government Draft, *Art. 74;* Government Report, point 244.2, page 109; Senate Debate, Amtliches Bulletin 1985, page 150, 15; House Debate, Amtliches Bulletin 1986, page 1343, 1349.
Swiss substantive law: Art. 268 CC.

1. See Art. 22.

Art. 77

II.
Applicable
Law

1. The prerequisites for adoption in Switzerland are governed by Swiss law.[1]

2. If it is apparent that an adoption would not be recognized in the country of the adopting person's or adopting spouses' domicile or citizenship,[2] and this would result in serious detriment to the child, then the authority will also take into account the prerequisites of the law of that country. If even then recognition does not appear secured, the adoption may not be granted.

3. The challenge of an adoption granted in Switzerland is governed by Swiss law. A foreign adoption may be challenged in Switzerland only if a reason for challenge is also present under Swiss law.

> *Multilateral treaty:* With Austria and United Kindgom: (Hague) Convention du 15 novembre 1965 concernant la compétence des autorités, la loi applicable et la reconnaissance des décisions en matière d'adoption, 1978, SR 0.211.221.315.
> *Bilateral treaty:* With Iran: See Art. 33.
> *Previous law:* Art. 8b and 8c NAG, repealed in Appendix to PIL Statute.
> *Legislative history:* Experts Draft, *Art. 76;* Experts Report, page 157; Fribourg Colloque, page 21, 27; Government Draft, *Art. 75;* Government Report, point 244.3, page 110; Senate Debate, Amtliches Bulletin 1985, page 151; House Debate, Amtliches Bulletin 1986, page 1343, 1349.
> *Jurisdiction:* See Art. 75.
> *Foreign adoption and similar measures:* See Art. 78.
> *Swiss substantive law: Treaty*: Convention européenne en matière d'adoption des enfants du 24 avril 1967, 1973, SR 0.211.221.310. *Statute:* Art. 269 to 269 b CC.

> 1. Lex fori, in most cases lex domicilii.

> 2. See Art. 22, 23 subs. 2, 24.

Art. 78

III. Foreign
Adoptions
and
Similar
Measures

1. Foreign adoptions are recognized in Switzerland if they were granted in the country of the adopting person's or adopting spouses' domicile or citizenship.[1]

2. Foreign adoptions or similar measures that have effects substantially different from a parent-child relationship under Swiss law are recognized in Switzerland only with the effects given to them in the country in which they were granted.

Multilateral treaty: With Austria and United Kingdom: (Hague) Convention du 15 novembre 1965 concernant la compétence des autorités, la loi applicable et la reconnaissance des décisions en matière d'adoption, 1978, SR 0.211.221.315; *Bilateral treaties:* With Austria, Belgium, Czechoslovakia, Liechtenstein, Italy and Sweden: See Art. 25. With Iran: See Art. 33
Legislative history: Experts Draft, *Art. 77;* Experts Report, page 158; Fribourg Colloque, page 23, 24, 33; Government Draft, *Art. 76;* Government Report, point 244.4, page 110; Lausanne Colloque, page 247; Senate Debate, Amtliches Bulletin 1985, page 151; House Debate, Amtliches Bulletin 1986, page 1343, 1349, Senate Debate, Amtliches Bulletin 1987, page 185.
Jurisdiction: See Art. 75.
Applicable law: See Art. 77.

1. See Art. 22, 23 subs. 3, Art. 24.

Fourth Section: Effects of Parent-Child Relationship

Art. 79

I.
Jurisdiction
1. General
Rule

1. Lawsuits concerning the relationship between parent and child, in particular for child support, are subject to the jurisdiction of the Swiss courts at the child's habitual residence or at the defendant parent's domicile or, if there is none, at his habitual residence.

2. The provisions of this Statute on name (Art. 33, 37 to 40), and protection of minors (Art. 86 to 89) are reserved.

Bilateral treaty: With Iran: See Art. 33.
Legislative history: Experts Draft, *Art. 78;* Experts Report, page 159; Government Draft, *Art. 77;* Government Report, point 245, page 111; Senate Debate, Amtliches Bulletin, page 151; House Debate, Amtliches Bulletin, page 1343, 1350.
Applicable law: See Art. 82.
Foreign decisions: See Art. 84.
Swiss substantive law: Treaty: Art. 270 et seq. CC. (New York, United Nations) Convention du 20 juin 1956 sur le recouvrement des aliments à l'étranger, 1977, SR 0.274.15.

Art. 80

2.
Jurisdiction
at Place of
Citizenship

If neither the child nor the defendant parent has his domicile or habitual residence in Switzerland but one of them is a Swiss citizen, jurisdiction lies with the courts at the place of citizenship.[1]

Bilateral treaty: With Iran: See Art. 33.
Legislative history: Experts Draft, *Art. 79;* Experts Report, page 160; Government Draft, *Art. 78;* Government Report, point 245.1, page 112; Senate Debate, Amtliches Bulletin 1985, page 149, 151; House Debate, Amtliches Bulletin 1986, page 1343, 1350.
Swiss substantive law: Art. 275 CC.

1. See Art. 22, 23 subs. 1, 24.

Art. 81

3. Third
Party
Claims

The Swiss court that has jurisdiction pursuant to Articles 79 and 80 also decides:
(a) claims of authorities that have granted advances for child support;[1]
(b) claims of the mother for support and reimbursement of costs caused by the birth.

Bilateral treaty: With Iran: See Art. 33.
Legislative history: Experts Draft, *Art. 80;* Experts Report, page 171; Government Draft, *Art. 79;* Government Report, point 245.1, page 112; Senate Debate, Amtliches Bulletin 1985, page 151; House Debate, Amtliches Bulletin 1986, page 1343, 1350; Senate Debate, Amtliches Bulletin 2987, page 185.
Swiss substantive law: See Art. 29.

1. Advances on alimony out of public funds are made in a number of cantons. Foreign authorities that have made advances also have standing to recover them in Switzerland.

Art. 82

1. The relationship between parent and child is governed by the law at the child's habitual residence.

2. If, however, neither parent is domiciled in the country of the child's habitual residence, but the parents and the child are citizens of the same country,[1] the law of the country of their common citizenship[2] applies.

3. The provisions of this Statute on name (Art. 33 and 37 to 40), protection of minors (Art. 85) and inheritance law (Art. 90 to 95) are reserved.

> *Bilateral treaty:* With Iran: See Art. 33.
> *Legislative history:* Experts Draft, *Art. 81;* Experts Report, page 161; Government Draft, *Art. 80;* Government Report, point 245.2, page 113; Lausanne Colloque, page 180, 199; Senate Debate, Amtliches Bulletin 1985, page 149, 151; House Debate, Amtliches Bulletin 1986, page 1343, 1350.
> *Support obligation:* See Art. 83.
> *Jurisdiction:* See Art. 79.
> *Foreign decisions:* See Art. 84.

> 1. See Art. 22, 23 subs. 2, Art. 24.

> 2. See Art. 68.
>   Switzerland is a member of the Hague Convention of October 2, 1973 on the law applicable to maintenance obligations.

Art. 83

1. For support obligations between parents and child the Hague Convention of October 2, 1973, on the Law Applicable to Maintenance Obligations applies.

2. Inasmuch as the Convention does not regulate the claims of the mother for support and reimbursement of the costs caused by the birth, it applies by analogy.

> *Multilateral treaty:* For all countries: (Hague) Convention du 2 octobre 1973 sur la loi applicable aux obligations alimentaires, 1977, SR 0.211.213.01. With Austria, Belgium, Federal Republic of Germany, Japan, Liechtenstein, Spain:

(Hague) Convention du 24 octobre 1956 sur la loi applicable aux obligations alimentaires envers les enfants, 1964, SR 0.211.221.431.
Bilateral treaty: With Iran: See Art. 33.
Legislative history: Experts Draft, *Art. 82;* Experts Report, page 162; Fribourg Colloque, page 6, 17, 18; Government Draft, *Art. 81;* Government Report, point 245.2, page 114; Lausanne Colloque, page 202, 207; Senate Debate, Amtliches Bulletin 1985, page 151; House Debate, Amtliches Bulletin 1986, page 1343, 1350; Senate Debate, Amtliches Bulletin 1987, page 185; House Debate, Amtliches Bulletin 1987, page 1068; Senate Debate, Amtliches Bulletin 1987, page 506, 507.
Swiss substantive law: Art. 272, 276 et seq. CC.

Art. 84

III. Foreign
Decisions

1. Foreign decisions concerning the relationship between parent and child are recognized in Switzerland if they were rendered in the country of the child's habitual residence or in the country of the defendant parent's domicile or habitual residence.

2. The provisions of this Statute on name (Art. 39), protection of minors (Art. 85) and inheritance law (Art. 96) are reserved.

Multilateral treaties: With Austria, Belgium, Czechoslovakia, Denmark, Finland, France, Hungary, Italy, Liechtenstein, Luxemburg, Netherlands, Norway, Portugal, Spain, Sweden, Turkey, United Kingdom: (Hague) Convention du 2 octobre 1973 concernant la reconnaissance et l'exécution de décisions relatives aux obligations alimentaires, 1976, SR 0.211.213.02. With Austria, Belgium, Denmark, (Federal Republic of) Germany, Hungary, Liechtenstein, Spain, and Surinam: (Hague) Convention du 15 avril 1958 concernant la reconnaissance et l'exécution des décisions en matière d'obligations alimentaires envers les enfants, 1964, SR 0.211.221.432. With 37 countries: (New York) Convention du 20 juin 1956 sur le recouvrement des aliments à l'étranger, 1977, SR 0.274.15. With Austria, France, Luxemburg, Portugal and Spain: Convention européenne du 20 mai 1980 sur la reconnaissance et l'exécution des décisions en matière de garde des enfants et le rétablissement de la garde des enfants, 1983, SR 0.211.230.01.
Bilateral treaties: With Austria, Belgium, Czechoslovakia, (Federal Republic of) Germany, Italy, Liechtenstein, Spain and Sweden: Art. 25. With Iran: See Art. 33.
Legislative history: Experts Draft, *Art. 83;* Experts Report, page 163; Fribourg Colloque, page 6; Government Draft, *Art. 82;* Government Report, point 245.3, page 114; Lausanne Colloque, page 215; Senate Debate, Amtliches Bulletin 1985, page 149, 151; House Debate, Amtliches Bulletin 1986, page 1343, 1350.
Jurisdiction: See Art. 29.
Applicable law: See Art. 82.

Fifth Chapter: Guardianship and Other Protective Measures

Art. 85

1. The protection of minors, the jurisdiction of the Swiss judicial or administrative authorities, the applicable law, and the recognition of foreign decisions or measures are subject to the Hague Convention of October 5, 1961 on jurisdiction of authorities and applicable law in the area of protection of minors.

2. The convention applies by analogy[1] to majors, to persons who are minors only under Swiss law, and to persons who do not have their habitual residence[2] in one of the countries party to the Convention.

3. Jurisdiction lies with the Swiss judicial or administrative authorities if this is necessary[3] to protect a person or its assets.

Multilateral treaties: With Austria, France, (Federal Republic of) Germany, Luxemburg, Netherlands, Portugal and Turkey: (Hague) Convention du 5 octobre 1961 concernant la compétence des autorités et la loi applicable en matière de protection des mineurs, SR 0.211.231.01, reservation on Art. 15 withdrawn. With Canada, France and Portugal: (Hague international kidnapping) Convention du 25 octobre 1980 sur les aspects civils de l'enlèvement international d'enfants (avec annexe), SR 0.211.230.02. With Austria, France, Luxemburg, Portugal and Spain: Convention européenne du 20 mai 1980 sur la reconnaissance et l'exécution des décisions en matière de garde des enfants et le rétablissement de la garde des enfants, SR 0.211.230.01.
Bilateral treaties: See Art. 84. With *Austria:* Convention du 15 mars 1927 entre la Suisse et l'Autriche relative à la reconnaissance et à l'exécution de décisions judiciaires, Art. 7, SR 0.276.191.631; Convention du 16 décembre 1960 entre la Confédération suisse et la République d'Autriche relative à la reconnaissance et à l'exécution de décisions judiciaires, Art. 10, SR 0.276.191.632. With *France:* Convention du 15 juin 1869 entre la Suisse et la France sur la compétence judiciaire et l'exécution des jugements en matière civile (avec protocole explicatif), Art. 10, SR 0.276.193.491. With *(Federal Republic of) Germany:* Déclaration du 26 juin 1914 entre la Suisse et l'Allemagne concernant la correspondance en matière de tutelle, SR 0.211.231.022. With *Iran:* Convention d'établissement du 25 avril 1934 entre la Confédération suisse et l'Empire de Perse (Iran) (avec annexe), Art. 8, para 3, 4, SR 0.142.114.362. With *Italy:* Accord du 16 novembre 1966 entre la Confédération suisse et la République italienne sur la dispense de légalisation, l'échange des actes de l'état civil et la présentation des certificats requis pour contracter mariage, Art. 8 to 10, SR 0.211.112.445.4.
Previous law: Art. 10 to 18, 29, 30, 33 NAG, repealed; BGE 87 II 132.
Legislative history: Experts Draft, *Art. 84 and 85;* Experts Report, page 164; Fribourg Colloque, page 6, 17, 18, 29, 65; Government Draft, *Art. 83;* Government Report, point 251, page 115; Lausanne Colloque, page 204, 207, 214; Senate Debate, Amtliches Bulletin, 1985, page 149, 152; House Debate, Amtliches Bulletin, 1986, page 1344, 1350; Senate Debate, Amtliches Bulletin 1987, page 185; House Debate, Amtliches Bulletin, 1987, page 1068.
Swiss substantive law: Art. 296 et seq., 360 et seq. CC.

1. Applies by analogy (E), s'applique par analogie (F), gilt sinngemäss (G), si applica par analogia (I).

2. Habitual residence is used here in the sense of the Hague Convention, not in the sense of Art. 20.

3. Necessary (E), exige (F), unerlässlich (G), esige (I).

Sixth Chapter: Inheritance Law

Art. 86

I.
Jurisdiction
1. General
Rule

1. For probate proceedings[1] and inheritance litigation,[2] jurisdiction lies with the Swiss judicial or administrative authorities at the last domicile of the decedent.

2. Exception is made for jurisdiction of a country claiming exclusive jurisdiction over immovable property in its territory.

Bilateral treaties: With *Iran:* See Art. 33; With *Italy:* Convention d'établissement et consulaire du 22 juillet 1868 entre la Suisse et l'Italie (avec déclaration), Art. 17, SR 0.142.114.541; Protocole du 1er mai 1869 concernant l'exécution des conventions conclues et signées à Berne et à Florence entre la Suisse et l'Italie le 22 juillet 1868 SR 0.142.114.541.1 Art. IV. With the *United States:* Traité du 25 novembre 1850 conclu entre la Confédération suisse et les Etats-Unis d'Amérique du Nord, Art. VI, SR 0.142.113.361, and Nussbaum, American-Swiss Private International Law, 2d ed., page 61.
Previous law: Art. 23, 28 NAG, repealed in Appendix to PIL Statute.
Legislative history: Experts Draft, *Art. 87;* Experts Report, page 175; Fribourg Colloque, page 6, 36; Government Draft, *Art. 84;* Government Report, point 261.1, page 118; point 162.1, page 120; Lausanne Colloque, page 112, 116, 120, 133 Senate Debate, Amtliches Bulletin 1985, page 152; House Debate, Amtliches Bulletin 1986, page 1350.
Applicable law: See Art. 90, 91.
Foreign decisions, measures, certificates and rights: See Art. 96.
Swiss substantive law: Art. 451 et seq., 519, 522, 534, 537, 551 CC.

1. Probate proceedings (E), règlement de la succession (F), Nachlassverfahren (G), procedimento successorio (I)
The same German word is used for composition in bankruptcy law, a totally unrelated matter.

2. Inheritance litigation (E), litiges successoraux (F), erbrechtliche Streitigkeiten (G), controversie ereditarie (I).

Art. 87

2.
Jurisdiction
at Place of
Citizenship

1. If the decedent was a Swiss citizen last domiciled abroad, jurisdiction lies with the Swiss judicial or administrative authorities at the place of citizenship[1] to the extent[2] to which foreign authorities do not deal with the estate.

2. These Swiss authorities always have jurisdiction if a Swiss citizen last domiciled abroad has, by will or successorial pact,[3] subjected his assets situated in Switzerland, or his entire estate, to Swiss jurisdiction or Swiss law.[4] Article 82 subsection 2 is reserved.

Bilateral treaty: With Iran: See Art. 33.
Previous law: Art. 23 NAG, repealed in Appendix to PIL Statute.
Legislative history: Experts Draft, *Art. 88;* Experts Report, page 177; Fribourg Colloque, page 6, 36, 40; Government Draft, *Art. 85;* Government Report, point 216.2, page 64; point 262.2, page 121; Lausanne Colloque, page 116, 121, 141, 143; Senate Debate, Amtliches Bulletin 1985, page 152; House Debate, Amtliches Bulletin 1986, page 1350, 1351; Senate Debate, Amtliches Bulletin 1987, page 185.
Swiss substantive law: Art. 498 et seq. CC. A successorial pact, Art. 512 CC, is a disposition for cause of death by way of a contract made by public deed between the decedent and his heirs or legatees. It can be modified only by contrary agreement.

1. See Art. 22, 23 subs. 1, Art. 24.

2. To the extent (E), dans la mesure (F), soweit (G), semprechè (I). Here the translation follows the French and German text.

3. Will or successorial pact (E), testament ou un pacte successoral (F), letztwillige Verfügung oder Erbvertrag (G), testamento o contratto successorio (I). Art. 512 CC.

4. Swiss jurisdiction or Swiss law (E), compétence ou droit suisse (F), schweizerische Zuständigkeit oder schweizerisches Recht (G), competenza o diritto svizzeri (I), professio iuris (L).

Art. 88

3.
Jurisdiction
at Place of
Assets[1]

1. If the decedent was a foreigner[2] last domiciled abroad, jurisdiction for the assets in Switzerland lies with the Swiss judicial or administrative authorities at the place of the assets to the extent[3] to which foreign authorities[4] do not deal with them.

2. If the assets are at more than one place, jurisdiction lies with the Swiss judicial or administrative authority first seized.[5]

Bilateral treaty: With Iran: See Art. 33.
Previous law: Art. 28 NAG, repealed in Appendix to PIL Statute.
Legislative history: Experts Draft, *Art. 89;* Experts Report, page 178; Government Draft, *Art. 86;* Government Report, point 262.3, page 122; Lausanne Colloque, page 122, 145; Senate Debate, Amtliches Bulletin 1985, page 152; House Debate, Amtliches Bulletin 1986, page 1350, 1351; Senate Debate, Amtliches Bulletin 1987, page 186.

1. Jurisdiction at place of assets (E), for du lieu de situation (F), Zuständigkeit am Ort der gelegenen Sache (G), foro del luogo di situazione (I), forum rei sitae (L).

2. See Art. 22, 23 subs. 1, Art. 24.

3. See Art. 87.

4. Foreign authorities. These are any authorities whose decisions, measures, certificates would be recognized under Art. 96.

5. Seized (E), saisi (F), angerufen (G), adito (I).

Art. 89

4.
Conservatory
Measures[1]

If a decedent last domiciled abroad leaves assets in Switzerland, the Swiss authorities at the place of the assets take the conservatory measures[1] necessary for their protection.[2]

Bilateral treaty: With Iran: See Art. 33.
Legislative history: Experts Draft, *Art. 90;* Experts Report, page 178; Government Draft, *Art. 87;* Government Report, point 216.2, page 64; point 262.3, page 122; Lausanne Colloque, page 142, 145; Senate Debate, Amtliches Bulletin 1985, page 152; House Debate, Amtliches Bulletin 1986, page 1350, 1351, Senate Debate, Amtliches Bulletin, 1987, page 186.
Swiss substantive law: Art. 551 CC.

1. Conservatory measures (E), mesures conservatoires (F), sichernde Massnahmen (G), provvedimenti conservativi (I). Examples of measures: Official seizure, inventory, sealing. Measures are taken according to Swiss law. Which measures are taken differs from canton to canton. In some cantons, an inventory is drawn for cantonal inheritance tax law purposes.

2. Art. 153 expresses a similar idea.

II.
Applicable
Law
1. Last
Domicile in
Switzerland

1. The estate of a person last domiciled in Switzerland is governed by Swiss law.

2. A foreigner[1] may, however, by will or successorial pact,[2] subject his estate to the law of one of his countries of citizenship.[3] If, at the time of death, he no longer was a citizen of that country, or if he had become a Swiss citizen, the choice of law lapses.[4]

Bilateral treaties: With *France:* Convention du 15 juin 1869 entre la Suisse et la France sur la compétence judiciaire et l'exécution des jugements en matière civile (avec protocole explicatif) Art. 5 SR 0.276.193.491. With *Greece:* Convention d'établissement et de protection juridique du 1 décembre 1927 entre la Suisse et la Grèce Art. 10 SR 0.142.113.721. With *Iran:* Convention d'établissement du 25 avril 1934 entre la Confédération suisse et l'Empire de Perse (Iran) (avec annexe), para 4, Art. 8, SR 0.142.114.362. With *Italy:* Convention d'établissement et consulaire du 22 juillet 1868 entre la Suisse et l'Italie (avec déclaration) Art. 17 SR 0.142.114.541. Protocole du 1 mai 1869 concernant l'exécution des conventions conclues et signées à Berne et à Florence entre la Suisse et l'Italie le 22 juillet 1868, Art. IV SR 0.142.114.541.1. With the *United Kingdom*: Traité d'amitié, de commerce et d'établissement réciproque du 6 septembre 1855 entre la Confédération suisse et Sa Majesté la Reine du Royaume-Uni de la Grande Bretagne et d'Irlande Art. IV SR 0.142.113.671. With the *United States:* Traité du 25 novembre 1850 conclu entre la Confédération suisse et les Etats-Unis d'Amérique du Nord, Art. V and VI SR 0.142.113.361.

Previous law: Art. 22 NAG, repealed in Appendix to PIL Statute; BGE 102 II 136.

Legislative history: Experts Draft, *Art. 91;* Experts Report, page 180; Fribourg Colloque page 37, 38, 40, 41, 42, 65; Government Draft, *Art. 88;* Government Report, point 263, 263.1, page 123; Lausanne Colloque, page 110, 133, 135, 139, 153, 156; Senate Debate, Amtliches Bulletin, 1985, page 152; House Debate, Amtliches Bulletin, 1986, page 1350, 1351.

Jurisdiction: See Art. 86.

Foreign decisions, measures, contracts and rights: See Art 96.

1. See Art. 22, 23 subs. 2, Art. 24. A Swiss cannot subject his succession to the law of another country of citizenship, see Art. 23 subs. 2.

2. See Art. 87. The form of professio iuris is not covered by the Statute. Art. 116 might apply by analogy, or favor testamenti might provide a less stringent standard.

3. There is no preference for the country of citizenship with which the individual has the closest connection. Renvoi is excluded, see Art. 23.

4. Choice of law lapses (E), choix est caduc (F), Unterstellung fällt dahin (G), disposizione è inefficace (I).

Art. 91

2. Last Domicile Abroad

1. The estate of a person last domiciled abroad is governed by the law determined by the conflict of laws rules[1] of the country of domicile.

2. Inasmuch as Article 87 grants jurisdiction to the Swiss judicial or administrative authorities at the place of citizenship, the succession of a Swiss citizen last domiciled abroad is subject to Swiss law, unless the decedent by will or successorial pact[2] expressly reserved the law at his last domicile.[3]

> *Bilateral treaty:* With Iran: See Art. 33.
> *Previous law:* Art. 28 NAG, repealed in Appendix to PIL Statute.
> *Legislative history:* Experts Draft, *Art. 92;* Experts Report, page 180; Fribourg Colloque, page 38, 42; Government Draft, *Art. 89;* Government Report, point 216.2, page 64; point 263.2, page 124; Lausanne Colloque, page 142, 143, 145; Senate Debate, Amtliches Bulletin 1985, page 152; House Debate, Amtliches Bulletin 1986, page 1350, 1352; Senate Debate, Amtliches Bulletin, 1987, page 186; House Debate, Amtliches Bulletin, 1987, page 1068; Senate Debate, Amtliches Bulletin, 1987, page 507.

1. Conflict of laws rules (E), les règles de droit international privé (F), Kollisionsrecht (G), norme di diritto internazionale privato (I).

2. See Art. 87.

3. The choice is only between Swiss law and the law of the country of domicile.

Art. 92

3. Scope of the Law on Succession and Distribution of the Estate

1. The law governing the estate determines which assets are in the estate[1] and who is entitled to it and to what extent, who bears the liabilities of the estate, which remedies and measures are available and under which conditions.

2. Individual measures are carried out according to the law at the place of the authority having jurisdiction. That law governs especially conservatory measures and the distribution of the estate, including the execution of the will.

Bilateral treaty: With Iran: See Art. 33.
Legislative history: Experts Draft, *Art. 93 and 94;* Experts Report, page 187; Fribourg Colloque, page 37, 40, 70; Government Draft, *Art. 90;* Government Report, point 263.5, page 127; Lausanne Colloque, page 146; Senate Debate, Amtliches Bulletin 1985, page 153; House Debate, Amtliches Bulletin 1986, page 1350, 1352; Senate Debate, Amtliches Bulletin 1987, page 186; House Debate, Amtliches Bulletin, 1987, page 1069; Senate Debate, Amtliches Bulletin 1987, page 507.
Swiss substantive law: Art. 457, 537 et seq., 517, 518, 560, 602 CC.

1. Estate (E), succession (F), Nachlass (G), successione (I).

Art. 93

4. Form

1. For the form of wills the Hague Convention of October 5, 1961 on the Law Applicable to the Form of Wills applies.

2. This Convention applies by analogy to the form of other dispositions for cause of death.[1]

Multilateral treaty: For all countries: (Hague) Convention du 5 octobre 1961 sur les conflits de loi en matière de forme des dispositions testamentaires, SR 0.211.312.1.
Bilateral treaty: With Iran: See Art. 33.
Legislative history: Experts Draft, *Art. 95;* Experts Report, page 191; Fribourg Colloque, page 6; Government Draft, *Art. 91;* Government Report, point 264, page 128; Lausanne Colloque, page 149; Senate Debate, Amtliches Bulletin 1985, page 153; House Debate, Amtliches Bulletin 1986, page 1350, 1352; Senate Debate, Amtliches Bulletin 1987, page 186; House Debate, Amtliches Bulletin 1987, page 1069; Senate Debate, Amtliches Bulletin 1987, page 506, 507.
Swiss substantive law: Art. 498 et seq. CC.

1. Dispositions for cause of death (E), dispositions pour cause de mort (F), Verfügungen von Todes wegen (G), disposizione a causa di morte (I).
   This includes successorial pact, see Art. 87.

Art. 94

5. Capacity to Dispose[1] for Cause of Death

A person may dispose[1] for cause of death if he, at the time of disposal, had the capacity to dispose under the law[2] of the country of his domicile, habitual residence, or one of his citizenships.[3]

Bilateral treaty: With Iran: See Art. 31.
Previous law: Art. 7 subs. 4 NAG, repealed in Appendix to PIL Statute.
Legislative history: Experts Draft, *Art. 96;* Experts Report, page 192; Government Draft, *Art. 92;* Government Report, point 215.6, page 62; point 264, page 129; Senate Debate, Amtliches Bulletin 1985, page 153; House Debate, Amtliches Bulletin 1986, page 1350, 1352.
Swiss substantive law: Art. 467 CC: 18 years.

1. See Art. 93.

2. Under the law of one of his citizenships (E), en vertu du droit d'un de ses Etats nationaux (F), nach dem Recht eines ihrer Heimatstaaten (G), giusta un suo diritto nazionale (I).

3. Favor testamenti.

Art. 95

6.
Successorial
Pacts and
Mutual
Dispositions
for Cause of
Death

1. A successorial pact is governed by the law of the decedent's domicile at the time of conclusion.

2. If a decedent in the pact subjects his entire estate to the law of his country of citizenship,[1] that law applies instead of the law of the country of his domicile.

3. Mutual[2] dispositions for cause of death[3] must comply with the law of the domicile of each of the disposers or with the law of the country of common citizenship[1] chosen by them.

4. The provisions of this Statute on form and capacity are reserved (Art. 93 and 94).

Bilateral treaty: With Iran: See Art. 33.
Previous law: Art. 25 NAG, repealed in Appendix to PIL Statute.
Legislative history: Experts Draft, *Art. 97, 98;* Experts Report, page 192; Government Draft, *Art. 93;* Government Report, point 264.1, page 130; Lausanne Colloque, page 149; Senate Debate, Amtliches Bulletin 1985, page 153; House Debate, Amtliches Bulletin 1986, page 1350, 1352; Senate Debate, Amtliches Bulletin 1987, page 186.
Swiss substantive law: Art. 512 CC.

1. See Art. 90.

2. Mutual (E), réciproque (F), gegenseitig (G), reciproche (I). This includes correspective wills made by spouses.

3. See Art. 93.

Art. 96

III. Foreign
Decisions,
Measures,
Certificates[1]
and Rights

1. Foreign decisions, measures, and certificates concerning the estate as well as rights arising from probate proceedings abroad are recognized in Switzerland:

(a) if they were rendered, issued, or established in the country of the decedent's last domicile,[2] or in the country whose law he has chosen, or if they are recognized in one of these countries, or

(b) if they concern immovable property, and were rendered, issued, or established in the country in which the immovable property is situated, or if they are recognized there.

2. If a country claims exclusive jurisdiction over the decedent's immovable property situated in its territory, only that country's decisions, measures and documents are recognized.

3. Conservatory measures taken in the country in which the assets of the decedent are located are recognized in Switzerland.

Multilateral treaty: It is expected that Switzerland will join the Hague Convention of October 2, 1973 Schweizerisches Jahrbuch für internationales Recht 1972, p. 61.

Bilateral treaties: With Austria, Belgium, Czechoslovakia, France, (Federal Republic of) Germany, Italy, Liechtenstein and Sweden: See Art. 25. With Iran: See Art. 33.

Legislative history: Experts Draft, *Art. 99;* Experts Report, page 193; Fribourg Colloque, page 37; Government Draft, *Art. 94;* Government Report, point 265, page 130; Lausanne Colloque, page 144, 149; Senate Debate, Amtliches Bulletin 1985, page 152, 153; House Debate, Amtliches Bulletin 1986, page 1350, 1352; Senate Debate, Amtliches Bulletin 1957, page 186.

Jurisdiction: See Art. 86.

Applicable law: See Art. 90, 91.

1. Certificates (E), documents (F), Urkunden (G), documenti (I).

2. Last domicile (E), dernier domicile (F), letzter Wohnsitz (G), ultimo domicilio (I). See Art. 20.

Seventh Chapter: Real Rights[1]

Art. 97

I.
Jurisdiction
1.
Immovable
Property

Lawsuits on real rights in immovable property[1] in Switzerland are subject to the exclusive jurisdiction of the courts at the site.[2]

Previous law: Para. 6 Zurich ZPO; BGE 102 II 143.
Legislative history: Experts Draft, *Art. 100;* Experts Report, page 197; Fribourg Colloque, page 6; Government Draft, *Art. 95;* Government Report, point 272, page 132; Lausanne Colloque, page 228; Senate Debate, Amtliches Bulletin 1985, page 154; House Debate, Amtliches Bulletin 1985, page 1350, 1352.
Applicable law: See Art. 99, 119.
Jurisdiction on contracts concerning immovables: See Art. 112, 113.
Foreign decisions: See Art. 108.
Swiss substantive law: Art. 641 et seq., 655 et seq., 730 CC.

1. Lawsuits on real rights in immovable property (E), actions réelles immobilières (F), Klagen betreffend dingliche Rechte an Grundstücken (G), azioni concernenti diritti reali su fondi (I). 'Real rights' includes ownership, encumbrances and mortgages.

2. Courts at the site (E), tribunaux de lieu de situation des immeubles (F), Gerichte am Ort der gelegenen Sache (G), tribunali del luogo di situazione (I), forum rei sitae (L).

Art. 98

2. Movable
Goods

1. Lawsuits on real rights in movable goods[1] are subject to the jurisdiction of the Swiss courts at the defendant's domicile, or, if there is none, at his habitual residence.

2. If the defendant has neither his domicile nor his habitual residence in Switzerland, jurisdiction lies with the Swiss courts at the location of the goods.[2]

Legislative history: Experts Draft, *Art. 100;* Experts Report, page 197; Government Draft, *Art. 96;* Government Report, point 272, page 132; Senate Debate, Amtliches Bulletin, page 154; House Debate, Amtliches Bulletin, page 1353.
Applicable law: see Art. 100, 118.
Jurisdiction on contracts: see Art. 112.
Foreign decisions: see Art. 108.
Swiss substantive law: see Art. 713 et seq., 745, 884 CC.

1. Lawsuits on real rights in movable goods (E), actions réelles mobilières (F), Klagen betreffend dingliche Rechte an beweglichen Sachen (G), azioni concernenti diritti reali su cose mobili (I). 'Real rights' include title and pledges.

2. Location of the goods (E), lieu de la situation des biens (F), Ort der gelegenen Sache (G), luogo di situazione della cosa (I).

Art. 99

II.
Applicable
Law
1.
Immovable
Property

1. Real Rights in immovable property are governed by the law of the site.[1]

2. For claims arising from nuisance from immovable property, the provisions of this Statute on unlawful acts apply (Art. 138).

> *Previous law:* Art. 28 NAG, repealed.
> *Legislative history:* Experts Draft, *Art. 101;* Experts Report, page 197; Fribourg Colloque, page 85; Government Draft, *Art. 98;* Government Report, point 273, 273.1, page 133; Senate Debate, Amtliches Bulletin 1985, page 154; House Debate, Amtliches Bulletin 1986, page 1353.
> *Jurisdiction:* See Art. 97.
> *Means of transportation:* See Art. 107.
> *Applicable law to contracts concerning immovables:* See Art. 119.
> *Foreign decisions:* See Art. 108.
> *Swiss substantive law:* Art. 679, 684 CC; 'Lex Friedrich', Acquisition d'immeubles par des personnes domiciliées à l'étranger, SR 211.412.4 (Non-literal translation by Swiss-American Chamber of Commerce, 1985).

1. See Art. 97.

Art. 100

2. Movable
Goods:
(a) General
Rule

1. Acquisition and loss of real rights in movable goods are governed by the law of the country of location at the time of the event giving rise to the acquisition or loss.

2. The scope and exercise of real rights in movable goods is governed by the law at the location of the goods.[1]

Legislative history: Experts Draft, *Art. 102;* Experts Report, page 198; Government Draft, *Art. 99;* Government Report, point 273.2, page 133; Senate Debate, Amtliches Bulletin 1985, page 155; House Debate, Amtliches Bulletin 1986, page 1353; Festschrift Moser, page 29.
Jurisdiction: See Art. 98.
Means of transportation: See Art. 107.
Applicable law to contracts concerning movables: See Art. 118.
Foreign decisions: See Art. 108.
Swiss substantive law: Art. 714, 746, 884, 919 et seq. Code civil suisse du 10 décembre 1907, SR 210. Cattle: Ordonnance du 30 octobre 1917 sur l'engagement du bétail, SR 211.423.1.

1. See Art. 98.

Art. 101

(b) Goods in Transit[1]

Acquisition and loss by legal transaction of real rights in goods in transit[1] are governed by the law of the country of destination.[2]

Legislative history: Experts Draft, *Art. 103;* Experts Report, page 200; Fribourg Colloque, page 76; Government Draft, *Art. 100;* Government Report, point 273.3, page 134; Senate Debate, Amtliches Bulletin 1985, page 155; House Debate, Amtliches Bulletin 1986, page 1353.

1. Goods in transit (E), biens en transit (F), Sachen im Transit (G), cose in transito (I), res in transitu (L).

2. Law of the country of destination (E), droit de l'Etat de destination (F), Recht des Bestimmungsstaates (G), diritto dello Stato di destinazione (I), lex loci destinationis (L).

Art. 102

(c) Goods Entering Switzerland[1]

1. If movable goods enter Switzerland, and if an acquisition or loss of a real right in them has not yet occurred abroad, the events that occurred abroad are deemed to have occurred in Switzerland.

2. If movable goods enter Switzerland, and if a retention of title[2] has been validly created in them abroad without meeting the prerequisites of Swiss law, it remains valid in Switzerland for three months.

3. The existence of such a right created abroad may not be invoked against a third person in good faith.

Previous law: BGE 106 II 197.

Legislative history: Experts Draft, *Art. 104;* Experts Report, page 201; Fribourg Colloque, page 76; Government Draft, *Art. 101;* Government Report, point 273.4, page 135; Lausanne Colloque, page 281; Senate Debate, Amtliches Bulletin 1985, page 155; House Debate, Amtliches Bulletin 1986, page 1353; Festschrift Moser, page 30 to 46, 52, Senate Debate, Amtliches Bulletin 1987, page 187.

Swiss substantive law: Art. 715 CC; Eigentumsvorbehaltsregisterverordnung, Ordonnance du 19 décembre 1910 concernant l'inscription des pactes de réserve de propriété, SR 211.413.1.

1. Goods entering Switzerland (E), biens transportés en Suisse (F), Sachen, die in die Schweiz gelangen (G), cose che giungono in Svizzera (I).

2. Retention of title (E), réserve de propriété (F), Eigentumsvorbehalt (G), riserva di propretà (I).

Art. 103

(d)
Retention of
Title[1] on
Exports

The retention of title[1] in movable goods for export is governed by the law of the country of destination of the goods.[2]

Legislative history: Experts Draft, *Art. 105;* Experts Report, page 202; Government Draft, *Art. 102;* Government Report, point 273.5, page 135; Lausanne Colloque, page 282; Senate Debate, Amtliches Bulletin 1985, page 155; House Debate, Amtliches Bulletin 1986, page 1353; Festschrift Moser, page 31, 33, 46, 48, 50.

Swiss substantive law: Art. 715 CC; Eigentumsvorbehaltsregisterverordnung, Ordonnance du 19 décembre 1910 concernant l'inscription des pactes de réserve de propriété, SR 211.413.1.

1. See Art. 102.

2. See Art. 101.

Art. 104

(e) Choice of
Applicable
Law

1. The parties may subject the acquisition and loss of rights in movable goods to the law of the country of dispatch[1] or destination[2] of the goods, or to the law governing the underlying legal transaction.

2. This choice of law cannot be invoked against third parties.

Legislative history: Experts Draft, *Art. 106;* Experts Report, page 203; Fribourg Colloque, page 7; Government Draft, *Art. 103;* Government Report, point 273.6, page 136; Lausanne Colloque, page 282; Senate Debate, Amtliches Bulletin 1985, page 155; House Debate, Amtliches Bulletin 1986, page 1353; Festschrift Moser, page 30, 47, 51.

1. Law of the country of dispatch (E), droit de l'Etat de l'expédition (F), Recht des Abgangsstaates (G), diritto dello Stato di partenza (I), lex loci expeditionis (L).

2. See Art. 101.

Art. 105

3. Special
Rules
(a) Pledge of
Claims,[1]
Securities[2]
and Other
Rights

1. The pledge of claims,[1] securities,[2] and other rights is governed by the law chosen by the parties. The choice of law cannot be invoked against third parties.

2. If no choice of law has been made, the pledge of claims and securities is governed by the law of the pledgee's habitual residence; the pledge of other rights is governed by the law applicable to them.

3. Against the debtor the only law that can be invoked is the law governing the pledged right.

Multilateral treaties: See Art. 107.
Legislative history: Experts Draft, *Art. 105;* Experts Report, page 205; Government Draft, *Art. 105;* Government Report, point 273.8, page 138; Senate Debate, Amtliches Bulletin 1985, page 155; House Debate, Amtliches Bulletin 1986, page 1353; Senate Debate, Amtliches Bulletin 1987, page 187.
Swiss substantive law: Art. 899 CC.

1. Claims (E), créances (F), Forderungen (G), crediti (I).

2. Securities (E), papiers-valeurs (F), Wertpapiere (G), titoli di credito (cartevalori) (I).

Art. 106

1. The law designated by a document of title determines whether the document represents the goods. If the document does not designate a law, the law of the country in which the issuer of the document has his business establishment applies.

2. If the document represents the goods, the real rights in the document and in the goods are determined by the law that governs the document as a movable good.

3. If several parties claim real rights in the goods, some directly, and others based on a document of title, the law governing the goods themselves decides which one prevails.

Multilateral treaty: With some 40 countries: Convention internationale du 25 août 1924 pour l'unification de certaines règles en matière de connaissement (avec protocole de signature), SR 0.747.354.11.
Legislative history: Experts Draft, *Art. 108;* Experts Report, page 207; Government Draft, *Art. 106;* Government Report, 273.9, page 140; Senate Debate, Amtliches Bulletin 1985, page 155; House Debate, Amtliches Bulletin 1986, page 1353; Senate Debate, Amtliches Bulletin 1987, page 187; House Debate, Amtliches Bulletin 1987, page 1069.
Swiss substantive law: Art. 925 CC.

1. Document of title (E), titre représentatif de marchandises (F), Warenpapiere (G), titoli rapresentanti merci (I). Examples: Warehouse receipt, bill of lading.

Art. 107

The provisions of other federal statutes[1] on real rights in ships, aircraft, and other means of transportation[2] are reserved.

Multilateral treaties: Ships: With some 20 countries: Convention internationale du 10 avril 1926 pour l'unification de certaines règles relatives aux privilèges et hypothèques maritimes (avec protocole de signature), SR 0.747.322.2. *Aircraft:* With some 110 countries: Convention du 7 décembre 1944 relative à l'aviation civile internationale, SR 0.748.0; With some 40 countries: Convention du 19 juin 1948 relative à la reconnaissance internationale des droits sur aéronef, SR 0.748.217.1.
Legislative history: Experts Draft, *Art. 109;* Experts Report, page 208; Fribourg Colloque, page 208; Government Draft, *Art. 107;* Government Report, point 273.10, page 141; Senate Debate, Amtliches Bulletin 1985, page 155; House Debate, Amtliches Bulletin 1986, page 1353, 1354.

Swiss substantive law: Ships: Loi fédérale du 28 septembre 1923 sur le registre des bateaux, SR 747.11, Loi fédérale du 23 septembre 1953 sur la navigation maritime sous pavillon suisse, SR 747.30. *Aircraft:* Loi fédérale du 7 octobre 1959 sur le registre des aéronefs, SR 748.217.1; Loi fédérale du 21 décembre 1948 sur la navigation aérienne LNA), SR 748.0, (Translated in Air Laws and Treaties of the World, 1965); Ordonnance du Département fédéral des transports, des communications et de l'énergie du 8 juillet 1985 concernant l'admission et l'entretien des aéronefs (OAE), SR 748.215.1.

1. Provisions of other federal statutes (E), dispositions d'autres lois (F), Bestimmungen anderer Gesetze (G), disposizioni di altre leggi federali (I). Here, the translation follows the Italian text which is based on the notion that conflict of laws is now exclusively federal.

2. Means of transportation (E), moyens de transport (F), Transportmittel (G), mezzi di trasporto (I).

Art. 108

III. Foreign Decisions

1. Foreign decisions on real rights in immovable property are recognized in Switzerland if they were rendered in the country of the site of the property or are recognized there.

2. Foreign decisions on real rights in movable goods are recognized in Switzerland if:
(a) they were rendered in the country of the defendant's domicile;[1]
(b) they were rendered in the country of the location of the goods, provided that the defendant had his habitual residence[1] there; or
(c) they were rendered in the country where the agreed place of jurisdiction is.

Swiss Federal Constitution: Art. 59.
Bilateral treaties: See Art. 25.
Legislative history: Experts Draft, *Art. 110;* Experts Report, page 208; Government Draft, *Art. 108;* Government Report, point 274, page 141; Senate Debate, Amtliches Bulletin 1985, page 155; House Debate, Amtliches Bulletin 1986, page 1353, 1354; House Debate, Amtliches Bulletin 1987, page 187.
Jurisdiction: See Art. 97, 98.
Applicable law: See Art. 99, 100.

1. See Art. 20.

Eighth Chapter: Intellectual Property[1]

Art. 109

I.
Jurisdiction

1. Lawsuits on intellectual property rights[1] are subject to the jurisdiction of the Swiss courts at defendant's domicile[2] or, if there is none, at the place where protection is sought; lawsuits on the validity or the registration of intellectual property rights abroad are excepted.

2. If several defendants are subject to Swiss jurisdiction, and if the lawsuits are substantially based on the same facts and law, each judge has jurisdiction over all defendants; the judge seized first has exclusive jurisdiction.

3. If the defendant is not domiciled[2] in Switzerland, jurisdiction for lawsuits on validity or registration of intellectual property rights in Switzerland lies with the Swiss courts at the seat[3] of the registered agent or, if there is none, at the seat of the Swiss registration authority.

Swiss Federal Constitution: Art. 59.
Previous law: Copyright: Art. 20 subs. 2 URG, Loi fédérale du 7 décembre 1922 concernant le droit d'auteur sur les oeuvres littéraires et artistiques, SR 231.1, (translated in 'Copyright Laws and Treaties of the World', 1956). In revision. *Design:* Art. 14 subs. 3 MMG, repealed, Loi fédérale du 30 mars 1900 sur les dessins et modèles industriels, SR 232.12, (translated in 'Design Laws and Treaties of the World', 1960). *Patents:* Art. 75 PatG, Loi fédérale du 25 juin 1954 sur les brevets d'invention, SR 232.14, (translated in 54 Patent and Trademark Review 1956, page 279, and in 'Industrial Property', 1978). *Trademarks:* Art. 30 MschG, repealed, Loi fédérale du 26 septembre 1890 concernant la protection des marques de fabrique et de commerce, des indications de provenance et des mentions de récompenses industrielles, SR 232.11, (translated in Ruege und Graham 'Trademark Laws of the World', 1922). *Vegetable strains:* Art. 41 subs. 2, Loi fédérale du 20 mars 1975 sur la protection des obtentions végétales, SR 232.16, repealed.
Legislative history: Experts Report, page 196; Government Draft, *Art. 97, 127;* Government Report, point 27, 271, page 132; point 273.7, page 138; point 284.12 page 159; Senate Draft, *Art. 108a;* Senate Debate, Amtliches Bulletin 1985, page 114, 154, 155, 156; House Debate, Amtliches Bulletin 1986, page 1354; Festschrift Moser, page 60, 61; Senate Debate, Amtliches Bulletin 1987, page 187.
Applicable law: See Art. 110.
Foreign decisions: See Art. 111.
Swiss substantive law: Copyright: Urheberrechtsgesetz, Loi fédérale du 7 décembre 1922 concernant le droit d'auteur sur les oeuvres littéraires et artistiques, SR 231.1, (translated in 'Copyright Laws and Treaties of the World', 1956). In revision. *Design:* Mustergesetz, Loi fédérale du 30 mars 1900 sur les dessins et modèles industriels, SR 232.12, (translated in 'Design Laws and Treaties of the World' 1960). *Patents:* Patentgesetz, Loi fédérale du 25 juin 1954

sur les brevets d'invention, SR 232.14, (translated in 54 Patent and Trademark Review 1956, page 279, and in Industrial Property 1978). *Trademarks:* Markenschutzgesetz, Loi fédérale du 26 septembre 1890 concernant la protection des marques de fabrique et de commerce, des indications de provenance et des mentions de récompenses industrielles, SR 232.11, (translated in Ruege and Graham 'Trademark Laws of the World' 1922).

1. Intellectual property (E), propriété intellectuelle (F), Immaterialgüterrecht (G), diritti immateriali (I).

2. See Art. 20.

3. Seat (E), siège commercial (F), Geschäftssitz (G), sede commerciale (I). See Art. 20 and 21.

Art. 110

II.
Applicable
Law

1. Rights in intellectual property are governed by the law of the country for which protection of those rights is sought.

2. For claims of violation of rights in intellectual property, the parties may agree, at any time after the damage occured, that the law at the place of the court[1] applies.

3. Contracts on rights in intellectual property are subject to the provisions of this Statute on the law applicable to contracts (Art. 122).

Multilateral treaties: Copyright: With some 70 countries each: Convention de Berne (1886) du 13 novembre 1908 revisée pour la protection des oeuvres littéraires et artistiques (texte de Berlin), SR 0.231.11; and later conventions, last Convention de Berne pour la protection des oeuvres littéraires et artistiques, revisée à Stockholm le 14 juillet 1967 (avec protocole relatif aux pays en voie de développement), SR 0.231.14; (Geneva), Convention universelle du 6 septembre 1952 sur le droit d'auteur, SR 0.231.0. *Design:* With some 20 countries: Arrangement de La Haye concernant le dépôt international des dessins ou modèles industriels (1925), revisé à Londres le 2 juin 1934, SR 0.232.121.1. *Patents:* With some 90 countries: Convention d'Union de Paris pour la protection de la propriété industrielle (1893) revisée à La Haye le 6 novembre 1925, SR 0.232.01; and later conventions, last Convention de Paris pour la protection de la propriété industrielle, revisée à Stockholm le 14 juillet 1967, SR 0.232.04. *Trademarks:* with some 20 countries: Arrangement de Madrid (1891) concernant l'enregistrement international des marques, revisé à Stockholm le 14 juillet 1967, SR 0.232.112.3. *Vegetable strains:* With some 10

countries: Convention internationale du 2 décembre 1961 pour la protection des obtentions végétales (avec annexe), SR 0.232.161.
Legislative history: Experts Report, page 196; Government Draft, *Art.104;* Government Report, point 273.7, page 138; Senate Draft, *Art. 108b;* Senate Debate, Amtliches Bulletin 1985, page 155, 157; House Debate, Amtliches Bulletin 1986, page 1354; Festschrift Moser, page 62.
Jurisdiction: See Art. 109.
Foreign decisions: See Art. 111.

1. Law at the place of the court (E), droit du for (F), Recht am Gerichtsort (G), diritto del foro (I), lex fori (L).

Art. 111

III. Foreign Decisions

1. Foreign decisions on rights in intellectual property are recognized in Switzerland if:
(a) they were rendered in the country of defendant's domicile,[1] or
(b) they were rendered in the country for which protection of those rights was sought, provided that defendant was not domiciled[1] in Switzerland.

2. Foreign decisions on validity or registration of rights in intellectual property are recognized only if they were rendered in the country for which protection of those rights is sought, or if they are recognized there.

Swiss Federal Constitution: Art. 59.
Bilateral treaties: See Art. 25.
Legislative history: Experts Report, page 196; Government Draft, *Art. 108;* Government Report, point 274, page 141; Senate Draft, *Art. 108c;* Senate Debate, Amtliches Bulletin 1985, page 155, 157; House Debate, Amtliches Bulletin 1986, page 1354.
Jurisdiction: See Art. 109.
Applicable law: See Art. 110.

1. See Art. 20.

Ninth Chapter: Obligations[1]

First Section: Contracts

Art. 112

1. Lawsuits in contract are subject to the jurisdiction of the Swiss courts at defendant's domicile[2] or, if there is none, at his habitual residence.[2]

2. Lawsuits based on the activity of a business establishment[2] in Switzerland are also subject to the jurisdiction of the courts at the place of the business establishment.[2]

Swiss Federal Constitution: Art. 59.
Previous law: SchKG; Cantonal, e.g. Para. 2 Zurich ZPO. See Art. 109.
Legislative history: Experts Draft, *Art. 111;* Experts Report, page 211; Fribourg Colloque, page 6, 44, 49; Government Draft, *Art. 109;* Government Report, point 282, 282.1, 282.11, page 143; Senate Debate, Amtliches Bulletin 1985, page 157; House Debate, Amtliches Bulletin 1986, page 1355, 1356; Festschrift Moser, page 97.
Applicable law: See Art. 116 to 126.
Foreign decisions: See Art. 149.
Swiss substantive law: Art. 1 et seq. CO.

1. Obligations (E), droit des obligations (F), Obligatiouenrecht (G), diritto delle obbligazioni (I). In Swiss substantive law, this includes contracts, torts, unjust enrichment and agency without a mandate, all covered principally by the Swiss Federal Code of Obligations. The PIL Statute has no provisions on bills and notes. This is covered by Art. 1086 et seq. and 1138 et seq. CO which reproduce for the most part private international law and substantive law provisions of the Geneva Conventions of 1930 and 1931, SR 0.221.554.2 and SR 0.221.555.2.

2. See Art. 20 and 21.

Art. 113

If the defendant has neither his domicile,[1] nor his habitual residence,[1] nor a business establishment[1] in Switzerland, but performance of the contract is due in Switzerland, the lawsuit may be brought before the Swiss court at the place of performance of the contract.[2]

Legislative history: Experts Draft, *Art. 112;* Experts Report, page 212; Fribourg Colloque, page 6; Government Draft, *Art. 110;* Government Report, point 217.2, page 66; point 282.12, page 143; Senate Debate, Amtliches Bulletin 1985, page 158; House Debate, Amtliches Bulletin 1986, page 1355, 1356; Festschrift Moser, page 97.
Swiss substantive law: Art. 74 CO.

1. See Art. 20, 21, 112.

2. Court at the place of performance of the contract (E), tribunal du lieu d'exécution (F), Gericht am Erfüllungsort (G), tribunale del luogo di adempimento (I).

Art. 114

3. Contracts with Consumers[1]

1. For lawsuits of a consumer based on contracts for which the prerequisites of Article 120 subsection 1 are fulfilled jurisdiction lies, at the option of the consumer,[2] with the Swiss courts:
(a) at the domicile[3] of the consumer or his habitual residence,[3] or
(b) at the domicile[3] or, if there is none, at the habitual residence,[3] of the marketer.[4]

2. A consumer may not waive in advance the jurisdiction at his domicile[3] or his habitual residence.[3]

Swiss Federal Constitution: Art. 59, 31 sexies.
Legislative history: Experts Draft, *Art. 113;* Experts Report, page 212; Government Draft, *Art. 111;* Government Report, point 217, page 66, point 282.12, page 144; Senate Debate, Amtliches Bulletin 1985, page 158; House Debate, Amtliches Bulletin 1986, page 1284, 1286, 1288, 1290, 1355, 1356; Festschrift Moser, page 98, Senate Debate, Amtliches Bulletin 1987, page 187; House Debate, Amtliches Bulletin 1987, page 1069; Senate Debate, Amtliches Bulletin 1987, page 507.

1. Contracts with consumers (E), contrats conclus avec des consommateurs (F), Verträge mit Konsumenten (G), contratti con consumatori (I).

2. At the option of the consumer (E), au choix du consommateur (F), nach Wahl des Konsumenten (G), a scelta del consumatore (I).

3. See Art. 20, 21.

4. Marketer (E), fournisseur (F), Anbieter (G), fornitore (I).

Art. 115

4.
Employment
Contracts

1. Lawsuits on employment contracts are subject to the jurisdiction of the Swiss courts at the defendant's domicile,[1] or at the place where he habitually performs his work.[2]

2. For lawsuits by an employee, jurisdiction also lies with the Swiss courts at the employee's domicile[1] or habitual residence.[1]

Swiss Federal Constitution: Art. 59.
Legislative history: Experts Draft, *Art. 114;* Experts Report, page 213; Fribourg Colloque, page 48, 80, 86; Government Draft, *Art. 112;* Government Report, point 282.12, page 144; Senate Debate, Amtliches Bulletin 1985, page 161; House Debate, Amtliches Bulletin 1986, page 1355, 1356; Festschrift Moser, page 99.
Swiss substantive law: Art. 319 et seq., Art. 343 subs. 1 CO.

1. See Art. 20, 21.

2. Place where the employee performs his work (E), lieu dans lequel le travailleur accomplit son travail (F), Ort, wo der Arbeitnehmer seine Arbeit verrichtet (G), luogo in cui il lavoratore compie il suo lavoro (I).

Art. 116

II.
Applicable
Law
1. In
General
(a) Choice of
Applicable
Law

1. Contracts[1] are governed by the law chosen by the parties.

2. The choice of law[2] must be explicit or be clearly evident[3] from the agreement[3] or from the circumstances. Moreover,[4] it is governed by the chosen law.

3. The choice of law[2] can be made or altered at any time. If made or altered after the conclusion of the contract, it takes effect retroactively[5] from the time of the conclusion of the contract. The rights of third parties are reserved.

Treaties: See Art. 118. *Bills and notes:* (Geneva) Convention du 7 juin 1930 destinée à régler certains conflits de lois en matière de lettres de change et de billets à ordre (avec protocole), 1931, SR 0.221.554.2; Convention du 19 mars 1931 destinée à régler certains conflits de lois en matière de chèques (avec protocole), SR 0.221.555.2.
Previous law: Art. 418b subs. 2 CO, repealed; BGE 79 II 295, 91 II 44, 102 II 143.
Legislative history: Experts Draft, *Art. 118;* Experts Report, page 215; Fribourg

Colloque, page 5, 44, 46, 49, 50, 51; Government Draft, *Art. 113;* Government Report, point 282.2, 282.21, page 145; Senate Debate, Amtliches Bulletin 1985, page 162; House Debate, Amtliches Bulletin 1986, page 1355, 1356; Festschrift Moser, page 67, 68, 74, 76, 77, 102. Art. 8 subs. 1 of European Contract Treaty of 1980.

Common provisions on obligations: Art. 143 to 148.

Jurisdiction: See Art. 112.

Foreign decisions: See Art 149.

Swiss substantive law: Multilateral treaties for uniform substantive law: *Sales:* See Art. 118.

Air transportation: With more than 100 countries: (Warsaw) Convention du 12 octobre 1929 pour l'unification de certaines règles relatives au transport aérien international (avec protocole additionnel), SR 0.748.410; and later additional treaties, last Convention du 18 septembre 1961, complémentaire à la convention de Varsovie, pour l'unification de certaines règles relatives au transport aérien international effectué par une personne autre que le transporteur contractuel, SR 0.748.410.2.

Sea transportation: (Brussels) Convention internationale du 29 avril 1961 pour l'unification de certaines règles en matière de transport de passagers par mer (avec protocole), SR 0.747.355.1. *Rail Transportation:* With some 25 countries: (COTIF) Convention du 9 mai 1980 relative aux transports internationaux ferroviaires (COTIF) (avec protocole), SR 0.742.403.1.

Road transportation: With some 20 countries: (CMR) Convention du 19 mai 1956 relative au contrat de transport international de marchandises par route (CMR) (avec protocole de signature), SR 0.741.611. Art. 1 et seq. CO Translation by Swiss-American Chamber of Commerce (1977).

The *law of bills and notes* follows the (Geneva) Convention du 7 juin 1930 portant loi uniforme sur les lettres de change et billets à ordre (avec annexes et protocole), SR 0.221.554.1; Convention du 7 juin 1930 relative au droit de timbre en matière de lettres de change et de billets à ordre (avec protocole), SR 0.221.554.3; Acte final de la Conférence de Genève pour l'unification du droit en matière de lettres de change et de billets à ordre, du 7 juin 1930, SR 0.221.554.4; Convention du 19 mars 1931 portant loi uniforme sur les chèques (avec annexes et protocole), SR 0.221.555.1; Convention du 19 mars 1931 relative au droit de timbre en matière de chèques (avec protocole), SR 0.221.555.3; Acte final de la Conférence de Genève pour l'unification du droit en matière de chèques, du 19 mars 1931, SR 0.221.555.4.

1. Contracts (E), contrat (F), Vertrag (G), contratto (I). The Statute appears silent on whether the parties may split up their contract and subject different parts to different laws (dépéçage).

2. Choice of law is excluded by Art. 120. Restricted choice of law: See Art. 121 subs. 3, 122 subs. 4.

3. Clearly evident (E), de façon certaine (F), eindeutig (G), univocamente (I). This is to exclude hypothetical choice of law, qui elegit iudicem elegit ius, determination of the proper law of the contract on the basis of language and other factors. However, acceptance through silence, see Art. 123, is not impossible.

4. Moreover (E), en outre (F), im übrigen (G), per altro (I). Here, the translation follows the French text.

5. Retroactively (E), rétroagir (F), zurückwirken (G), retroattivamente (I).

113

Art. 117

1. If no law has been chosen, a contract is governed by the law of the country most closely connected with it.

2. The closest connection is presumed to exist with the country where the party which must make the characteristic performance[1] has its habitual residence,[2] or, if the contract is based on a business activity, has its business establishment.[2]

3. The characteristic perfomance[1] is, in particular:[3]
(a) in contracts to pass title,[4] the performance of the transferor;
(b) in contracts to grant the use of a thing or a right,[5] the performance of the party that grants the use;
(c) in mandates, construction, and similar contracts for services,[6] the service;
(d) in contracts for storage, the performance of the keeper;[7]
(e) in guarantee and surety contracts,[8] the performance of the guarantor or surety.

> *Previous law:* Art. 418b subs. 2 CO, repealed in Appendix to PIL Statute; BGE 78 II 74.
> *Legislative history:* Experts Draft, *Art. 120 and 121;* Experts Report, page 219; Fribourg Colloque, page 45, 46, 51, 81; Government Draft, *Art. 114;* Government Report, point 282.23, page 147; Lausanne Colloque, page 276; Senate Debate, Amtliches Bulletin 1985 page 162; House Debate, Amtliches Bulletin 1986, page 1355, 1356; Festschrift Moser, page 79 to 89, 94.
> *Contracts to sell movable goods:* See Art. 118.
> *Contracts concerning immovables:* See Art. 119.
> *Contracts with consumers:* See Art. 120.
> *Swiss substantive law:* Art. 184 et seq. CO.

1. Characteristic performance (E), prestation caractéristique (F), charakteristische Leistung (G), prestazione caracteristica (I). This is the performance of the party that is required principally to do other things than to pay money.

2. See Art. 20, 21.

3. Case law: In sole distributorship agreements the performance of the sole distributor, BGE 100 II 450; in insurance contracts the performance of the insurer, BGE 71 II 287; Art. 492 CO, Translation: Foreign Tax Law Association (1958).

4. Contracts to pass title (E), contrats d'aliénation (F), Veräusserungsverträge (G), contratti di alienazione (I).

5. Contracts to grant the use of a thing or a right (E), contrats portant sur l'usage d'une chose ou d'un droit (F), Gebrauchsüberlassungsverträge (G), contratti di cessione d'uso (I). This includes rental (leases), lending, and (surprisingly) loan, Art. 253 et seq. CO.

6. Contracts for services (E), contrats de prestation de service (F), Dienstleistungsverträge (G), contratti di prestazione di servizi (I).
Employment contracts: See Art. 121.
Licensing agreements: See Art. 122.
Swiss substantive law: Art. 319 et seq. CO.

7. Keeper (E), dépositaire (F), Verwahrer (G), depositario (I).

8. Guarantee and surety contracts (E), contrats de garantie ou de cautionnement (F), Garantie- und Bürgschaftsverträge (G), contratti di garanzia o fideiussione (I).
Swiss substantive law: Art. 472 CO.

Art. 118

2. In Particular (a) Contracts to Sell Movable Goods

1. For contracts to sell movable goods the Hague Convention of June 15, 1955 on the Law Applicable to the International Sales of Goods applies[1].

2. Article 120 is excepted.

> *Multilateral treaty:* For all countries: (Hague) Convention du 15 juin 1955 sur la loi applicable aux ventes à caractère international d'objets mobiliers corporels, SR. 0.221.211.4.
> *Legislative history:* Experts Draft, *Art. 121;* Experts Report, page 221; Government Draft, *Art. 115;* Government Report, point 282.24, page 149; Senate Debate, Amtliches Bulletin 1985, page 162; House Debate, Amtliches Bulletin 1986, page 1355, 1356; Festschrift Moser, page 89, 95, Senate Debate, Amtliches Bulletin 1987, page 189; House Debate, Amtliches Bulletin 1987, page 1069; Senate Debate, Amtliches Bulletin 1987, page 507.
> *Contracts with consumers:* See Art. 120.
> *Swiss substantive law: Treaty:* Switzerland will probably join the Vienna Convention on International Sales. In international cases, as there defined, the Vienna Convention will then apply rather than the Swiss Federal Code of Obligations. *Statute:* Art. 1 et seq., 184 et seq. CO.

1. Convention du 15 juin 1955 sur la loi applicable aux ventes à caractère international d'objets mobiliers corporels, SR 0.221.211.4. There are no special rules for sales at a trade fair, auction or stock exchange.

Art. 119

1. Contracts on immovable property or its use are governed by the law of the country of the site of the property.[1] A choice of law is permitted.

2. The form of the contract is governed by the law of the country where the immovable property is situated, unless that law permits the application of a different law. For immovable property in Switzerland, the form is governed by Swiss law.[2]

Previous law: BGE 102 II 143.
Legislative history: Experts Draft, *Art. 123, 125;* Experts Report, page 225, 227; Fribourg Colloque, page 45, 47; Government Draft, *Art. 116;* Government Report, point 282.24, page 149; Senate Debate, Amtliches Bulletin 1985, page 162; House Debate, Amtliches Bulletin 1986, page 1355, 1356; Festschrift Moser, page 68, 90, 95, 103, 104, Senate Debate, Amtliches Bulletin 1987, page 169.
Contract for rent of movables: See Art. 117 Subs. 3 lit b.
Swiss substantive law: Art. 216, 730 CO; Lex Friedrich, Loi fédérale du 16 décembre 1983 sur l'acquisition d'immeubles par des personnes à l'étranger (LFAIE), SR 211.412.41, (non-literal translation by Swiss-American Chamber of Commerce, 1985). Rent (lease) of immovables: Art. 253 et seq. CO, and Bundesbeschluss of June 30, 1972 on Massnahmen gegen Missbräuche im Mietwesen, SR 221.213.1.

1. Law of the country of the site of the property (E), le droit du lieu de leur situation (F), Recht des Staates, in dem sich das Grundstück befindet (G), diritto dello Stato di situazione (I), lex rei sitae, lex situs (L).

2. This means that in most cases a public (notarized) deed is required to transfer title or a limited right in the immovable property.

Art. 120

1. Contracts for goods and services for the current personal or family consumption or use of a consumer[1] not connected with the professional or business activity of the consumer are governed by the law of the country in which the consumer has his habitual residence:[2]
(a) if the marketer[3] received the order in that country;
(b) if in that country an offer or advertisement preceded the making of the contract and the consumer performed in that country the legal actions required to make the contract, or

(c) if the marketer[3] prompted the consumer to go abroad and make his order there.

2. A choice of law is excluded.

Swiss Federal Constitution: Art. 31 sexies.
Legislative history: Experts Draft, *Art. 122;* Experts Report, page 222, 224; Fribourg Colloque, page 47; Government Draft, *Art. 117;* Government Report, point 282.25, page 150; Senate Debate, Amtliches Bulletin 1985, page 162; House Debate, Amtliches Bulletin 1986, page 1288, 1290, 1355, 1357; Festschrift Moser, page 73, 75, 90 to 92, 95, 105; Senate Debate, Amtliches Bulletin, 1987, page 188; House Debate, Amtliches Bulletin 1987, page 1069; Senate Debate, Amtliches Bulletin 1987, page 507.
Jurisdiction: See Art. 114.
Swiss substantive law: Consumer Protection Statute in preparation. The expression, 'Consumer Contracts' was avoided because the contracts as such are of the current type; what makes them different is one party.

1. Contracts with consumers (E), contrats conclus avec des consommateurs (F), Verträge mit Konsumenten (G), contratti con consumatori (I).

2. See Art. 20.

3. See Art. 114.

Art. 121

(d)
Employment
Contracts

1. An employment contract is governed by the law of the country where the employee habitually performs his work.[1]

2. If the employee habitually performs his work[1] in more than one country, the employment contract is governed by the law of the country of the employer's business establishment[2] or, if there is none, of the employer's domicile[2] or habitual residence.[2]

3. The parties may subject the employment contract to the law of the country of the employee's habitual residence[2] or of the employer's business establishment,[2] domicile,[2] or habitual residence.[2]

Legislative history: Experts Draft, *Art. 122;* Experts Report, page 222; Fribourg Colloque, page 47, 50, 51, 87; Government Draft, *Art. 118;* Government Report, point 282.26, page 152, Senate Debate, Amtliches Bulletin 1985, page 163; House Debate, Amtliches Bulletin 1986, page 1355, 1357; Festschrift Moser, page 73, 74, 92, 95.
Jurisdiction: See Art. 115.
Employee inventions: See Art. 122.
Swiss substantive law: Art. 319 et seq., 361 and 362 CO.

1. See Art. 115.

2. See Art. 20.

Art. 122

(e) Contracts on Intellectual Property

1. Contracts on rights in intellectual property are governed by the law of the country where the transferor or licensor has his habitual residence.[1]

2. A choice of law is permitted.

3. Contracts between employers and employees on rights in intellectual property created within the scope of employment are subject to the law governing the employment contract.[2]

Previous law: BGE 101 II 293.
Legislative history: Experts Report, page 221; Government Draft, *Art. 119;* Government Report, point 282.27, page 153; Senate Debate, Amtliches Bulletin 1985, page 163; House Debate, Amtliches Bulletin 1986, page 1355, 1357; Festschrift Moser, page 60, 65, 72, 93, 95, Senate Debate, Amtliches Bulletin 1987, page 190; House Debate, Amtliches Bulletin 1987, page 1069.
Swiss substantive law: Sale of an intellectual property right is governed by Art. 187 CO. The license contract is an innominate contract.

1. Switzerland grants more licenses than it receives.

2. Despite the wording of subs. 3, an employment contract can provide compensation for the employee's invention in advance. See Art. 121.

Art. 123

3. Common
Provisions
(a) Silence
in Response
to an Offer

If a party does not answer an offer[1] to make a contract, it may invoke the law of its habitual residence for the effects of silence.[2]

Legislative history: Experts Draft, *Art. 124;* Experts Report, page 226; Fribourg Colloque, page 47, 80; Government Draft, *Art. 120;* Government Report, point 282.3, page 155, point 282.22, page 147; Senate Debate, Amtliches Bulletin 1985, page 163; House Debate, Amtliches Bulletin 1986, page 1355, 1357; Festschrift Moser, page 77, 101.

1. Party does not answer an offer (E), partie ne répond pas à l'offre (F), Partei schweigt auf einen Antrag (G), parte non risponde a una proposta (I).

2. Silence (E), silence (F), Schweigen (G), silenzio (I). "Silence" stands for all inaction.

Art. 124

(b) Form

1. A contract is valid as to its form if it conforms to the law governing the contract or to the law at the place where it is concluded.[1]

2. If, at the time of conclusion of the contract, the parties are in different countries, it is sufficient for it to conform to the law of one of these countries.

3. If, for the protection of a party, the law governing the contract prescribes the fulfillment of a form, the form is goverened by that law unless it permits the application of a different law.

Previous law: BGE 111 II 178 et seq.
Legislative history: Experts Draft, *Art. 125;* Experts Report, page 226; Fribourg Colloque, page 48, 84; Government Draft, *Art. 121;* Government Report, point 282.3, page 155; Senate Debate, Amtliches Bulletin 1985, page 163; House Debate, Amtliches Bulletin 1986, page 1355, 1357; Festschrift Moser, page 103 to 106; Senate Debate, Amtliches Bulletin 1987, page 190.
Form of contract on immovable property: See Art. 119.
Swiss substantive law: Art. 11 et seq. CO. Generally, Swiss law allows contracts to be made consensually without the application of a form. Exceptions: Rail transportation contract is a real contract. Assignment, Bürgschaft, promise to make gift, termination of apartment lease, and generally real estate transactions are subject to stringent forms. 'Bürgschaft': Art. 493 CO, but see BGE 111 II 178 et seq.

1. Law at the place where it is concluded (E), droit du lieu de conclusion (F), Recht am Abschlussort (G), diritto del luogo di stipulazione (I), lex loci contractus, locus regit actum quoad formam (L).

Art. 125

(c)
Performance
and
Inspection
Modalities

The modalities of performance and the inspections are governed by the law of the country where they in fact take place.

Previous law: BGE 101 II 83.
Legislative history: Experts Draft, *Art. 126;* Experts Report, page 228; Fribourg Colloque, page 48; Government Draft, *Art, 122;* Government Report, point 282.3, page 156; Senate Debate, Amtliches Bulletin 1985, page 164; House Debate, Amtliches Bulletin 1986, page 1355, 1357; Festschrift Moser, page 106; Senate Debate, Amtliches Bulletin 1987, page 190.
Swiss substantive law: Art. 108 et seq. CO.

Art. 126

(d) Agency

1. If agency is based on a legal transaction[1] the relationship between principal and agent[2] is governed by the law applicable to their contract.[3]

2. The conditions under which an act of an agent binds the principal to a third party are governed by the law of the country in which the agent has his business establishment or, if there is none or none is discernable by the third party, in which the agent principally acts in the particular case.

3. If the agent is in an employment relationship with the principal and if he has no business establishment[4] of his own, the location of his business establishment is at the seat[5] of the principal.

4. The law made applicable by subsection 2 above also applies to the relationship between an unauthorized agent[6] and a third party.

120

Previous law: Art. 418b subs. 2 CO, repealed; BGE 88 II 195, 95 II 442.
Legislative history: Experts Draft, *Art. 127;* Experts Report, page 229; Government Draft, *Art. 123;* Government Report, point 282.4, page 156; Senate Debate, Amtliches Bulletin 1985, page 164; House Debate, Amtliches Bulletin 1986, page 1355, 1358; Festschrift Moser, page 68, 107, 108; Senate Debate, Amtliches Bulletin 1987, page 190.
Power of representation of companies: See Art. 158.
Swiss substantive law: Art. 32 et seq., 394 et seq., CO.

1. Agency based on a legal transaction (E), représentation repose sur un contrat (F), rechtsgeschäftliche Vertretung (G), rappresentanza negoziale (I).

2. Agent (E), représentant (F), Vertreter (G), rappresentante (I).

3. Normally mandate, see Art. 117 subs. 3 lit. c.

4. See Art. 21.

5. See Art. 19, 21

6. Unauthorized agent (E), représentant sans pouvoir (F), nicht ermächtigter Vertreter (G), rappresentante non autorizzato (I), falsus procurator (L).

Second Section: Unjust Enrichment[1]

Art. 127

I.
Jurisdiction

Lawsuits in unjust enrichment[1] are subject to the jurisdiction of the Swiss courts at the domicile of the defendant or, if he has none, at the place of his habitual residence or business establishment.

Swiss Federal Constitution: Art. 59, Appendix I.
Legislative history: Experts Draft, *Art. 128;* Experts Report, page 231; Government Draft, *Art. 124;* Government Report, point 283, 283.1, page 157; Senate Debate, Amtliches Bulletin 1986, page 164; House Debate, Amtliches Bulletin 1987, page 1355, 1358.
Applicable law: See Art. 128.
Foreign decisions: See Art. 149.
Swiss substantive law: Art. 62 et seq. CO.

1. Unjust enrichment (E), enrichissement illégitime (F), ungerechtfertigte Bereicherung (G), indebito arricchimento (I). Unjust enrichment has a function that is merely subsidiary to both contracts (Art. 112 et seq.) and unlawful acts (Art. 129 et seq.).

Art. 128

II.
Applicable
Law

1. Claims based on unjust enrichment[1] are governed by the law applicable to the existing or reputed legal relationship[2] on which the enrichment is based.

2. If there is no such legal relationship, claims in unjust enrichment are governed by the law of the country in which the enrichment took place. The parties may agree that the law at the place of the court[3] applies.

Previous law: BGE 78 II 385, 93 II 373.
Legislative history: Experts Draft, *Art. 128;* Experts Report, page 231; Government Draft, *Art, 125;* Government Report, point 283.2, page 157, Senate Debate, Amtliches Bulletin 1985, page 164; House Debate, Amtliches Bulletin 1986, page 1355, 1358; Senate Debate, Amtliches Bulletin 1987, page 190.
Jurisdiction: See Art. 127.
Foreign decisions: See Art. 149.
Swiss substantive law: Art. 62 CO. The statute of limitations on unjust enrichment claims under Swiss substantive law is one year from knowledge of the claim, and in any event ten years from the enrichment, Art. 67 CO.

1. Under Swiss concepts, the statute of limitations is governed by the same law.

2. Reputed legal relationship (E), rapport judidique supposé (F), vermeintliches Rechtsverhältnis (G), rapporto giuridico presunto (I).

3. Lex fori.

Third Section: Unlawful Acts[1]

Art. 129

I.
Jurisdiction
1. General
Rule

1. Lawsuits based on unlawful acts[1] are subject to the jurisdiction of the Swiss courts at the domicile[2] of the defendant or, if he has none, at the place of his habitual residence[2] or business establishment.[2]

2. If the defendant has neither his domicile,[2] nor his habitual residence,[2] nor his business establishment[2] in Switzerland, jurisdiction lies with the Swiss court where the act occurred or where it had its effect.

3. If several defendants are subject to Swiss jurisdiction, and if the lawsuits are substantially based on the same facts and law, each judge has jurisdiction over all defendants; the judge seized first has exclusive jurisdiction.

> *Swiss Federal Constitution:* Art. 59, Appendix I.
> *Multilateral treaty:* On jurisdiction collision at sea: Convention internationale du 10 mai 1952 pour l'unification de certaines règles relatives à la compétence civile en matière d'abordage, SR 0.747.313.24.
> *Legislative history:* Experts Draft, *Art. 115;* Experts Report, page 213; Fribourg Colloque, page 59, 60, 81; Government Draft, *Art. 126;* Government Report, point 284, 284.1, 284.11, page 158; Senate Debate, Amtliches Bulletin 1985, page 164; House Debate, Amtliches Bulletin 1986, page 1355, 1358; Festschrift Moser, page 244; Senate Debate, Amtliches Bulletin 1987, page 190.

1. Unlawful acts (E), actes illicites (F), unerlaubte Handlungen (G), atti illeciti (I).

2. See Art. 20.

Art. 130

2. In Particular

1. For damage caused by a nuclear plant or shipment, jurisdiction lies with the Swiss courts at the place where the damaging event[1] occurred.

2. If this place cannot be ascertained, jurisdiction lies as follows:
(a) if the operator[2] of a nuclear plant is liable, with the Swiss courts at the site of the plant;
(b) if the holder of a transportation permit is liable, with the Swiss courts at the holder's domicile[3] or of his elected domicile.[4]

> *Previous law:* BGE 99 II 315.
> *Legislative history:* Government Draft, *Art. 127;* Government Report, point 284.12, page 159; Senate Debate, Amtliches Bulletin 1985, page 164; House Debate, Amtliches Bulletin 1986, page 1355, 1358; Senate Debate, Amtliches Bulletin 1987, page 190.
> *Swiss substantive law: Treaties:* Switzerland is not a party to the Paris and Brussels Conventions.
> *Statute:* Kernenergiehaftpflichtgesetz, Loi fédérale du 18 mars 1983 sur la responsabilité civile en matière nucléaire (LRCN), SR 732.44.

1. Damaging event (E), événement dommageable (F), schädigendes Ereignis (G), evento dannoso (I).

2. Operator (E), l'exploitant (F), Inhaber (G), esercente (I).

3. See Art. 20.

4. The holder of the transportation permit must elect a domicile in Switzerland pursuant to Art. 3. Kernenergiehaftpflichtgesetz, Loi fédérale du 18 mars 1983 sur la responsabilité civile en matière nucléaire (LRCN), SR 732.44.

Art. 131

3. Direct Claim[1]

For lawsuits based on a right to claim directly from a liability insurer[1] jurisdiction lies with the Swiss courts at the place of business establishment[2] of the insurer, or at the place where the act occurred or where it had its effect.

> *Legislative history:* Experts Draft, *Art. 116;* Experts Report, page 213; Government Draft, *Art. 128;* Government Report, point 284.12, page 159; Senate Debate, Amtliches Bulletin 1985, page 164; House Debate, Amtliches Bulletin 1985, page 1355, 1358.
> *Swiss substantive law:* See Art. 60 VVG, Loi fédérale du 2 avril 1908 sur le contrat d'assurance, SR 221.229.1.

1. Right to claim directly from a liability insurer (E), l'action directe contre l'assureur de la responsabilité (F), unmittelbares Forderungsrecht gegen den Haftpflichtversicherer (G), diritto di credito diretto nei confronti dell'assicuratore della responsabilità (I).

2. See Art. 20.

Art. 132

II. Applicable Law
1. In General
(a) Choice of Applicable Law

The parties may always[1] agree after the damaging event that the law of the place of the court[2] applies.

> *Legislative history:* Experts Draft, *Art. 130;* Experts Report, page 236, 237; Fribourg Colloque, page 55; Government Draft, *129 subs. 4;* Government Report, point 284.221, page 161; Senate Draft, *Art. 128a;* Senate Debate, Amtliches Bulletin 1985, page 165; House Debate, Amtliches Bulletin 1986, page 1355, 1358; Final Text, *Art. 132;* Festschrift Moser, page 123.
> *Jurisdiction:* See Art. 129.
> *Foreign decisions:* See Art. 149.

1. This is possible even in Art. 135, 138 and 139.

2. Law at the place of the court (E), droit du for (F), Recht am Gerichtsort (G), diritto del foro (I), lex fori (L). Whether the parties could also choose a different law is not clear.

Art. 133

(b) No Applicable Law Chosen

1. If the damaging and the damaged parties[1] have their habitual residences[3] in the same country, claims based on unlawful acts are governed by the law of that country.

2. If the damaging and the damaged party do not have their habitual residences[3] in the same country, the law of the country where the unlawful act was committed[2] is applicable. If the effect did not occur in the country where the unlawful act was committed, the law of the country where the effect occurred is applicable if the damaging party should have expected the effect to occur in that country.

3. Notwithstanding subsections 1 and 2, claims based on an unlawful act violating an existing legal relationship between the damaging and the damaged party are governed by the law that applies to the pre-exisiting legal relationship.[5]

Treaty: With International Atomic Energy Organization: Accord du 6 septembre 1978 entre la Confédération suisse et l'Agence internationale de l'énergie atomique relatif à l'application de garanties dans le cadre du traité sur la non-prolifération des armes nucléaires, Art. 16, SR 0.515.031.
Previous law: BGE 87 II 113; 92 II 257.
Legislative history: Experts Draft, *Art. 129, 130, 131;* Experts Report, page 233, 238; Fribourg Colloque, page 7, 53, 55, 56, 58, 59, 61, 62, 76, 77, 81, 86; Government Draft, *Art. 129,* subs. 1 to 3; Government Report, point 284.21, page 160; Senate Debate, Amtliches Bulletin 1985, page 165; House Debate, Amtliches Bulletin 1986, page 1356, 1358; Festschrift Moser, page 147, 149; Senate Debate, Amtliches Bulletin 1987, page 190; Final Text, *Art. 133;* Festschrift Moser, page 124 to 127.

1. Damaging and damaged parties (E), auteur et lésé (F), Schädiger und Geschädigter (G) danneggiatore e danneggiato (I).

2. Law of the country where the unlawful act was committed (E), droit de l'Etat dans lequel l'acte illicite a été commis (F), Recht des Staates in dem die unerlaubte Handlung begangen worden ist (G), diritto dello Stato in cui l'atto è stato commesso (I), lex loci delicti commissi (L).

3. See Art. 20.

4. Accessory determination of applicable law.

5. Pre-existing legal relationship (E), rapport juridique existant (F), vor-bestehendes Rechtsverhältnis (G), rapporto giurdico esistente (I).

Art. 134

2. In
Particular
(a) Traffic
Accidents

For claims based on traffic accidents the Hague Convention of May 4, 1971 on the Law Applicable to Traffic Accidents applies.

Multilateral treaty: With seven countries: (Hague) Convention du 4 mai 1971 sur la loi applicable en matière d'accidents de la circulation routière, 1987 SR 0.741.31, declared universally applicable by Art. 134 PIL Statute.
Previous law: Art. 85 Federal Statute on Road Traffic, repealed in annex to the PIL Statute.
Legislative history: Experts Draft, *Art. 132;* Experts Report, page 241; Fribourg Colloque, page 6, 54, 62, 81; Government Draft, *Art. 130;* Government Report, point 284.31, page 164; Senate Debate, Amtliches Bulletin 1985, page 165; House Debate, Amtliches Bulletin 1986, page 1356, 1358; Senate Debate, Amtliches Bulletin 1987, page 190; House Debate, Amtliches Bulletin 1987, page 1069; Senate Debate, Amtliches Bulletin 1987, page 509; Final Text, *Art. 134;* Festschrift Moser, page 123.
Right to direct claim: See Art. 131.
Swiss substantive law: SVG, Loi fédérale du 19 décembre 1958 sur la circulation routière, SR 741.01.

Art. 135

(b) Products
Liability[1]

1. Claims[2] based on a defect or defective description of a product are governed at the option of the damaged party:[3]
  (a) by the law of the country where the damaging party has his business establishment[4] or, if he has none, his habitual residence,[4] or
  (b) by the law of the country where the product was acquired, unless the damaging party proves that it came to market in that country without his assent.

2. If claims based on a defect or defective description of a product are governed by foreign law, no damages can be awarded in Switzerland beyond those that would be awarded under Swiss law for such a damage.[5]

> *Legislative history:* Experts Draft, *Art. 133;* Experts Report, page 243; Fribourg Colloque, page 54, 55, 56, 58, 59, 60, 81; Government Draft, *Art. 131;* Government Report, point 284.32, page 165; Senate Debate, Amtliches Bulletin 1985, page 165; House Debate, Amtliches Bulletin 1986, page 1356, 1358; Final Text, *Art. 135;* Festschrift Moser, page 131 to 142.
> *Choice of applicable law:* See Art. 132.
> *Swiss substantive law:* Art. 41 CO.

1. Products liability (E), responsabilité du fait d'un produit (F), Produktemängel (G), vizi di un prodotto (I).

2. The person answerable in products liability cases is not specified. Privity of contract may not be required by the applicable law.

3. Favor laesi.

4. In case of corporate plaintiffs or defendants, the seat or the place of the business establishment are meant, see Art. 20.

5. For such a damage (E), pour un tel dommage (F), für einen solchen Schaden (G), in simili casi (I). Here, the translation follows the French and German text.

Art. 136

(c) Unfair Competition[1]

1. Claims of unfair competition[1] are governed by the law of the country in whose market the unfair act has its effect.

2. If the unlawful act is directed exclusively against operational interests[2] of the damaged party, the applicable law will be that of the country in which the establishment concerned[3] is located.

3. Article 133 subsection 3 is reserved.

> *Legislative history:* Experts Draft, *Art. 134;* Experts Report, page 244; Fribourg Colloque, page 54, 56, 61; Government Draft, *Art. 132;* Government Report, point 284.33, page 166; Senate Debate, Amtliches Bulletin 1985, page 166; House Debate, Amtliches Bulletin 1986, page 1356, 1358; Festschrift Moser, page 143, 144, 154, 157.

Swiss substantive law: UWG, Loi fédérale du 30 septembre 1943 sur la concurrence déloyale, SR 241.

1. Unfair competition (E), concurrence déloyale (F), unlauterer Wettbewerb (G), concorrenza sleale (I).

2. Operational interests (E), intérêts d'entreprise (F), betriebliche Interessen (G), interessi aziendali (I). Operational interests are violated in case of sabotage, economic espionage, inducement to breach of contract. Public law provisions on business hours, special sales regulations, display of prices may become applicable through Art. 19.

3. Concerned (E), lésé (F), betroffen (G), interessata (I).

Art. 137

(d) Restraint of Competition[1]

1. Claims of restraint of competition[1] are governed by the law of the country in whose market the restraint directly[2] affects the damaged party.

2. If claims of restraint of competition are governed by foreign law, no damages can be awarded in Switzerland beyond those that would be awarded under Swiss law in case of an unlawful restraint of competition.[1]

Previous law: BGE 93 II 196.
Legislation history: Experts Draft, *Art. 135;* Experts Reports, page 246; Fribourg Colloque, page 60, 81; Government Draft, *Art. 133;* Government Report, point 284.34, page 167; Senate Debate, Amtliches Bulletin 1985, page 166; House Debate, Amtliches Bulletin 1986, page 1356, 1358; Festschrift Moser, page 143, 152, 160 to 177.
Swiss substantive law: See Kartellgesetz; Loi fédérale du 20 décembre 1985 sur les cartels et organisations analogues (Loi sur les cartels), SR 251. (Translated by Swiss-American Chamber of Commerce 1986; OECD Guide to Legislation on Restrictive Business Practices, Schluep in World Law of Competition, Unit B, Vol. 6, SW 11–15, para. 1.02; Schürmann Pocket Edition) Swiss law does not provide for treble damages.

1. Restraint of competition (E), entrave à la concurrence (F), Wettbewerbsbehinderung (G), ostacoli alla concorrenza (I).

2. Directly (E), directement (F), unmittelbar (G), direttamente (I).

128

Art. 138

(e) Nuisance   Claims based on a damaging nuisance[1] from an immovable property are governed, at the option of the damaged party,[2] by the law of the country where the immovable property is situated or by the law of the country where the effect occurs.

Legislative history: Experts Draft, *Art. 137;* Experts Report, page 248; Fribourg Colloque, page 58; Government Draft, *Art. 134;* Government Report, point 284.35, page 168; Senate Debate, Amtliches Bulletin 1985, page 166; House Debate, Amtliches Bulletin 1986, page 1356, 1358; Senate Debate, Amtliches Bulletin 1987, House Debate, Amtliches Bulletin 1987, page 1069; Senate Debate, Amtliches Bulletin 1987, page 509.
Choice of applicable law: See Art. 132.
Jurisdiction of the Swiss courts: See Art. 129.
Jurisdiction for nuclear liability: See Art. 130.
Swiss substantive law: See Art. 679, 684 CC.
Water: Gewässerschutzgesetz, Loi fédéral du 8 octobre 1971 sur la protection des eaux contre la pollution (Loi sur la protection des eaux), SR 814.20 (translated by WHO in 24 International Digest of Health Legislation 1973, 2, 403 et seq.).

1. Damaging nuisance (E), immissions dommageables (F), schädingender Einwirkungen (G), immissioni nocive (I).

2. Favor laesi.

Art. 139

(f) Violation of the Right of Personality[1]   *1.* Claims of violations of the right of personality[1] by media, especially by press, radio, television or other means of public information, are governed at the option of the damaged party:[2]
- (a) by the law of the country of the damaged party's habitual residence,[3] if the damaging party[4] should have expected[5] the effect to occur in that country;
- (b) by the law of the country of the damaging party's business establishment[3] or habitual residence;[3] or
- (c) by the law of the country where the damaging act has its effect, if the damaging party should have expected the effect to occur in that country.

2. The right to present an opposing view[6] in recurrent media[7] is governed exclusively by the law of the country where the periodical was published, or the radio or television broadcast was made.

Legislative history: Experts Draft, *Art. 136;* Experts Report, page 247, 248; Fribourg Colloque, page 54, 56, 61; Government Draft, *Art. 135;* Government Report, point 22, 221, page 69, point 284.36, page 168; Senate Debate, Amtliches Bulletin 1985, page 166; House Debate, Amtliches Bulletin 1986, page 1356, 1359; Senate Debate, Amtliches Bulletin 1987, page 191.
Choice of applicable law: See Art. 132.
Swiss substantive law: Art. 28 et seq. CC.

1. Right of personality (E), personnalité (F), Persönlichkeit (G), personalità (I), see Art. 34 subs. 2.

2. Favor laesi.

3. See Art. 20.

4. Damaging party (E), auteur du dommage (F), Urheber (G), l'autore della lesione (I). In the French and Italian texts, by 'auteur', 'autore' the publisher is meant, not the author of the libelous etc. text.

5. Should have expected (E), ait dû s'attendre (F), rechnen musste (G), dovesse presumere (I).

6. Right to present an opposing view (E), droit de réponse à l'encontre (F), Gegendarstellungsrecht (G), diritto di risposta (I).

7. Recurrent media (E), médias à caractère périodique (F), periodisch erscheinende Medien (G), mezzi di communicazione sociale periodici (I).

Art. 140

3. Special Provisions (a) More than One Person Liable

If more than one person has participated in an unlawful act, for each of them the applicable law is determined separately and regardless of the nature of the participation.

Legislative history: Experts Draft, *Art. 138;* Experts Report, page 249; Fribourg Colloque, page 58; Government Draft, *Art. 136;* Government Report, point 284.4, page 169; Senate Debate, Amtliches Bulletin 1985, page 166; House Debate, Amtliches Bulletin 1986, page 1356, 1359; Festschrift Moser, page 108; Senate Debate, Amtliches Bulletin 1987, page 191.

Art. 141

(b) Direct
Claim

The damaged party may avail itself of its claim[1] directly against a liability insurer if the law governing the unlawful act or the law governing the insurance contract so provides.

Legislative history: Experts Draft, *Art. 139;* Experts Report, page 249; Fribourg Colloque, page 58; Government Draft, *Art. 137;* Government Report, point 284.4, page 169; Senate Debate, Amtliches Bulletin 1985, page 166; House Debate, Amtliches Bulletin 1986, page 1356, 1359; Festschrift Moser, page 113. *Swiss substantive law:* Art. 60 VVG, Loi fédérale du 2 avril 1908 sur le contrat d'assurance, SR 221.229.1.

1. May avail itself of its claim (E), peut diriger l'action (F), kann Anspruch geltend machen (G), può far valere la sua pretesa (I). Here, the translation follows the Italian text.

Art. 142

4. Scope of
Application

1. The law governing the unlawful act[1] determines in particular the capacity to commit an unlawful act, the conditions for and the scope of liability,[2] and the liable person.

2. Regulations on safety and conduct[3] at the place of the act must be taken into account.

Legislative history: Experts Draft, *Art. 140;* Experts Report, page 249, 250; Fribourg Colloque, page 58, 60; Government Draft, *Art. 138;* Government Report, point 284.4, page 169; Senate Debate, Amtliches Bulletin 1985, page 166; House Debate, Amtliches Bulletin 1986, page 1356, 1359; Festschrift Moser, page 109.

1. Unlawful act (E), l'acte illicite (F), unerlaubte Handlung (G), l'atto illecito (I).

2. Scope of liability (E), étendue de la responsabilité (F), Umfang der Haftung (G), le condizioni e l'estensione della responsabilità (I). The chapter covers not only damages, but all remedies against unlawful acts, including claims for desistment, reinstatement of original state, presentation of an opposing view, publication of judgment.

3. Regulations on safety and conduct (E), règles de sécurité et de comportement (F), Sicherheits- und Verhaltungsvorschriften (G), norme di sicurezza e di condotta (I).

131

Fourth Section: Common Provisions

Art. 143

I. Plurality
of Debtors
1. Claims
against
More than
One Debtor

If a creditor has a claim against more than one debtor, the legal consequences arising from this[1] are governed by the law that governs the legal relationship between the creditor and the debtor from whom the creditor claims.

> *Legislative history:* Experts Draft, *Art. 141;* Experts Report, page 251; Fribourg Colloque, page 45, 82; Government Draft, *Art. 139;* Government Report, point 285.2, page 170; Senate Debate, Amtliches Bulletin 1985, page 167; House Debate, Amtliches Bulletin 1986, page 1356, 1359; Festschrift Moser, page 109. *Swiss substantive law:* Art. 50 CO.

> 1. This article deals with the question whether several debtors are answerable jointly, by quota, or subsidiarily to each other, and in which order. If the several laws applicable do not coincide on these questions, adjustment will become necessary.

Art. 144

2. Recovery
Among
Debtors[1]

1. A debtor can recover from another debtor, either directly or through subrogation into the legal position of the creditor, only to the extent permitted by the laws governing both debts.

2. The implementation of recovery[2] is governed by law applicable to the debt of the person against whom recovery is taken. Questions only concerning the relationship between the creditor and the person who is taking recovery are subject to the law governing the debt of the person taking recovery.

3. The right of recovery of an institution that fulfills a public function[3] is determined by the law governing that institution. Permissibility and implementation of recovery are regulated by subsections 1 and 2 above.

> *Previous law:* BGE 88 II 430, 98 II 231, 107 II 489.
> *Legislative history:* Experts Draft, *Art. 142;* Experts Report, page 251; Fribourg Colloque, page 45, 82; Government Draft, *Art. 140;* Government Report, point 285.2, page 170; Senate Debate, Amtliches Bulletin 1985, page 167; House Debate, Amtliches Bulletin 1986, page 1356, 1359; Festschrift Moser, page 109, 110, 111; Senate Debate, Amtliches Bulletin 1987, page 191.

Swiss substantive law: Art. 50, 51 CO; Art. 41 UVG, Loi fédéral du 20 mars 1981 sur l'assurance-accidents (LAA), SR 832.20.

1. Recovery among debtors (E), recours entre codébiteurs (F), Rückgriff zwischen Schuldnern (G), regresso tra debitori (I).

2. Implementation of recovery (E), l'exercice du recours (F), Durchführung des Rückgriffs (G), l'esercizio del regresso (I).

3. Public function (E), tâche publique (F), öffentliche Aufgabe (G), compiti pubblici (I). Example: Schweizerische Unfallversicherungsanstalt SUVA.

Art. 145

II. Transfer of Claims
1. By Contractual Assignment

1. The contractual assignment[1] of a claim[2] is governed by the law chosen by the parties or, if none was chosen, by the law applicable to the claim. The choice of law has no effect on the debtor without his assent.

2. For the assignment of a claim of an employee, the choice of law is only valid to the extent permitted for the employment contract by Article 121 subsection 3.

3. The form of assignment is exclusively subject to the law governing the contract to assign.

4. Questions only concerning the relationship between assignor and assignee are subject to the law governing the legal relationship on which the assignment is based.

Previous law: 74 II 87; 87 II 392.
Legislative history: Experts Draft, *Art. 143;* Experts Report, page 254; Fribourg Colloque, page 50, 82; Government Draft, *Art. 141;* Government Report, point 285.3, page 172; Senate Debate, Amtliches Bulletin 1985, page 167; House Debate, Amtliches Bulletin 1986, page 1356, 1359; Festschrift Moser, page 111.
Swiss substantive law: Art. 164 et seq. CO.

1. Contractual assignment (E), cession contractuelle (F), Abtretung durch Vertrag (G), cessione contrattuale (I).

2. Claim (E), créance (F), Forderung (G), credito (I).

Art. 146

2. By
Operation
of Law

1. The transfer of a claim by operation of law is subject to the law governing the underlying legal relationship between the old and the new creditor or, if there is none, to the law governing the claim.

2. The provisions of the law governing the claim which protect the debtor are reserved.

Legislative history: Experts Draft, *Art. 144;* Experts Report, page 255; Government Draft, *Art. 142;* Government Report, point 285.3, page 172; Senate Debate, Amtliches Bulletin 1985, page 167; House Debate, Amtliches Bulletin 1986, page 1356, 1359; Festschrift Moser, page 112.
Swiss substantive law: Art. 166 CO.

Art. 147

III.
Currency[1]

1. A currency[1] is defined by the law of the issuing country.

2. The effects of a currency on the amount of a debt[2] are determined by the law governing the debt.

3. The currency in which payment must be made[3] is determined by the law of the country where payment must be made.

Legislative history: Experts Draft, *Art. 146;* Experts Report, page 257; Government Draft, *Art. 143;* Government Report, point 285.4, page 173; Senate Debate, Amtliches Bulletin 1985, page 167; House Debate, Amtliches Bulletin 1986, page 1356, 1359; Festschrift Moser, page 113, 114.
Swiss substantive law: Art. 84 CO; BG über das Münzwesen, SR 941.1

1. Currency (E), monnaie (F), Währung (G), moneta (I).

2. Amount of a debt (E), ampleur d'une dette (F), Höhe einer Schuld (G), ammontare di un debito (I).

3. Must be made (E), doit être effectué (F), zu zahlen ist (G), deve avvenire (I).

Art. 148

1. The statute of limitations[1] to and the extinction of a claim are governed by the law applicable to the claim.

2. In case of set-off, the extinction is subject to the law governing the claim whose extinction is intended by the set-off.

3. Novation, waiver and set-off agreements[2] are governed by the provisions of this Statute on the law applicable to the contracts (Articles 116 et seq.).

Previous law: BGE 81 II 175 189; 63 II 384.
Legislative history: Experts Draft, *Art. 147;* Experts Report, page 258, 259; Government Draft, *Art. 144;* Government Report, point 285.5, page 174; Senate Debate, Amtliches Bulletin 1985, page 167; House Debate, Amtliches Bulletin 1986, page 1356, 1359; Festschrift Moser, page 115.
Swiss substantive law: Art. 127 et seq. CO.

1. Statute of limitations (E), prescription (F), Verjährung (G), prescrizione (I).

2. Set-off agreements (E), contrat de compensation (F), Verrechnungsvertrag (G), contratto di compensazione (I).

Fifth Section: Foreign Decisions

Art. 149

1. Foreign decisions concerning claims under the law of obligations are recognized in Switzerland:
(a) if rendered in the country of the defendant's domicile;[1] or
(b) if rendered in the country of the defendant's habitual residence,[1] provided the claims are connected with the activities there.

2. A foreign decision is also recognized:[2]
(a) if it concerns a contractual obligation, was rendered in the country of performance of that obligation, and the defendant was not domiciled[1] in Switzerland;
(b) if it concerns claims arising from a contract with consumers, was rendered at the domicile[1] or habitual residence[1] of the consumer, and the conditions of Article 120 subsection 1 are met;

(c) if it concerns an employment contract, was rendered either at the place of the employer's operation or at the place of work, and the employee was not domiciled[1] in Switzerland;

(d) if it concerns claims arising from the operation of a business establishment[1] and was rendered at the seat of that establishment;[1]

(e) if it concerns claims of unjust enrichment, was rendered at the place of the act or effect, and the defendant was not domiciled[1] in Switzerland; or

(f) if it concerns claims for unlawful acts, was rendered at the place of the act or effect, and the defendant was not domiciled[1] in Switzerland.

Swiss Federal Constitution: Art. 59, Appendix I.
Multilateral treaties: See Art. 110, 107, 134.
Bilateral treaties: See Art. 23.
Legislative history: Experts Draft, *Art. 148;* Experts Report, page 259 to 261; Fribourg Colloque, page 7, 44, 68; Government Draft, *Art. 145;* Government Report, point 286, page 175; Senate Debate, Amtliches Bulletin 1985, page 167; House Debate, Amtliches Bulletin 1986, page 1288, 1356, 1359; Festschrift Moser, page 116, 117; Senate Debate, Amtliches Bulletin 1987, page 188; House Debate, Amtliches Bulletin 1987, page 1069.
Jurisdiction: See Art. 112, 127, 129.
Applicable law: See Art. 116, 128, 132.

1. See Art. 20

2. Further, see Art. 26, in particular letter c.

Note on the Swiss Private International Law of Bills and Notes

The Swiss private international law of bills and notes/negotiable instruments remains outside the scope of the PIL Statute. See Art. 1086 to 1095 and 1138 to 1142 CO, corresponding to the Geneva Convention on Drafts SR 0.215.551.2 and the Geneva Convention on Checks, SR 0.211.555.2.

Tenth Chapter: Companies

Art. 150

<table>
<tr><td>I.
Definitions[1]</td><td>

1. As used in this Statute, the term companies means organized bodies of persons and organized units of assets.[2]

2. Partnerships that have not provided themselves[3] with an organization are subject to the law governing contracts (Art. 116 et seq.).
</td></tr>
</table>

> *Bilateral treaties:* With *Federal Republic of Germany:* On Board of Directors of Border Water Power Plants, Accord du 6 décembre 1955 entre la Confédération suisse et la République fédérale d'Allemagne au sujet du règlement de questions concernant les conseils d'administration des sociétés anonymes constituées en République fédérale d'Allemagne en vue d'exploiter les usines hydroélectriques frontières du Rhin, 1957, SR 0.221.333.213.6. With *Greece:* Convention d'éstablissement et de protection juridique du 1 décembre 1927 entre la Suisse et la Grèce, Art. 11, para. 1, SR 0.142.113.721. With *Iran:* See Art. 33. With *Soviet Union:* Traité de commerce du 17 mars 1948 entre la Confédération suisse et l'Union des Républiques soviétiques socialistes, 1948, Art. 10, SR 0.946.297.721. With *Yugoslavia:* Traité de commerce du 27 septembre 1948 entre la Confédération suisse et la République fédérative populaire de Yougoslavie, 1948, Art. 10, SR 0.946.298.181. For further commercial treaties, see Commerce extérieur, SR 0.946.
>
> *Previous law:* Art. 935 subs. 2, 952 subs. 2 CO; Art. 14 final title CO, repealed in Annex to the PIL Statute; SchKG; cantonal civil procedure.
>
> *Legislative history:* Experts Draft, *Art. 149;* Experts Report, page 262, 263; Government Draft, *Art. 146;* Government Report, point 292, page 176; Lausanne Colloque, page 227; Senate Debate, Amtliches Bulletin 1985, page 168; House Debate, Amtliches Bulletin 1986, page 1359; Festschrift Moser, page 182; Senate Debate, Amtliches Bulletin 1987, page 191.
>
> *Swiss substantive law:* Art. 52 et seq., 60 et seq., 80 et seq. CC and Art. 530 et seq., 552 et seq. CO.

1. Definitions (E), notions (F), Begriffe (G), definizioni (I).

2. Trust is unknown in Swiss substantive law.

3. Provided themselves (E), dotées (F), sich gegeben (G), che si son dotate (I).

Art. 151

1. Disputes in company law,[1] and lawsuits against the company, the members of the company, or the persons liable in company law are subject to the jurisdiction of the Swiss courts at the seat of the company.[2]

2. Lawsuits against a member of a company or a person liable in company law are also subject to the jurisdiction of the Swiss courts at the defendant's domicile[3] or, if he has none, his habitual residence.[3]

3. Lawsuits for responsibility arising from the public issue of shares and bonds[4] are also subject to the jurisdiction of the Swiss courts at the place of issue. This jurisdiction cannot be waived by a choice of jurisdiction.

> *Swiss Federal Constitution:* Art. 59, Appendix I.
> *Legislative history:* Experts Draft, *Art. 150;* Experts Report, page 264; Government Draft, *Art. 147;* Government Report, point 293, page 177; Senate Debate, Amtliches Bulletin 1985, page 168; House Debate, Amtliches Bulletin 1986, page 1359; Festschrift Moser, page 181.
> *Applicable law:* See Art. 154.
> *Foreign decisions:* See Art. 165.
> *Swiss substantive law:* Art. 752, 761 CO; Ordonnance du 7 décembre 1949 sur la communauté des créanciers dans les emprunts par obligations, SR. 221.522.1.
>
> 1. Company law (E), droit des sociétés (F), gesellschaftsrechtlich (G), diritto societario (I).
>
> 2. Company (E), société (F), Gesellschaft (G), società (I).
>
> 3. See Art. 20.
>
> 4. Shares and bonds (E), titres de participation et d'emprunts (F), Beteiligungspapiere und Anleihen (G), titoli di partecipazione e di prestiti (I), see Art. 156.

Art. 152

For lawsuits against persons liable under Article 159 and against the foreign company on whose behalf they act, jurisdiction lies:
(a) with the Swiss courts at the defendant's domicile[1] or, if he has none, his habitual residence; or

(b) with the Swiss courts at the place where the company is in fact administered.

Legislative history: Experts Draft, *Art. 157;* Experts Report, page 265; Government Draft, *Art. 148;* Government Report, point 293, page 178; Senate Debate, Amtliches Bulletin 1985, page 168; House Debate, Amtliches Bulletin 1986, page 1359, 1360; Senate Debate, Amtliches Bulletin 1987, page 191, House Debate, Amtliches Bulletin 1987, page 1069.
Swiss substantive law: Art. 761 CO.

1. See Art. 20.

Art. 153

3. Protective Measures

For measures to protect the assets in Switzerland of companies having their seat[1] abroad, jurisdiction lies with the Swiss judicial or administrative authorities at the place of the assets to be protected.

Legislative history: House Debate, *Art.148a;* House Debate, Amtliches Bulletin 1985, page 1360; Senate Debate, Amtliches Bulletin 1986, page 191; Festschrift Moser, page 181.
Swiss substantive law: Art. 61, Loi fédérale du 8 octobre sur l'approvisionnement économique du pays (loi sur l'approvisionnement du pays [LAP]), SR 531.

1. See Art. 21.

Art. 154

III. Applicable Law
1. General Rule

1. Companies[1] are subject to the law of the country according to which they are organized if they meet its provisions on publicity or registration or, if no such provisions exist, if they organize themselves according to the law of that country.

2. If a company does not meet these conditions, it is governed by the law of the country where it is in fact administered.[2]

139

Previous law: BGE 94 I 80, 95 II 448, but 99 II 160, 102, Ia 410 and 105 III 110.
Bilateral treaties: With *Federal Republic of Germany* on Board of Directors of Border Water Power Plants: Accord du 6 décembre 1955 entre la Confédération suisse et la République fédérale d'Allemagne au sujet du règlement de questions concernant les conseils d'administration des sociétes anonymes constituées in République fédérale d'Allemagne en vue d'exploiter les usines hydroélectriques frontières du Rhin, 1957, SR 0.221.333.213.6: With *Greece*: Convention d'établissement et de protection juridique du 1 décembre 1927 entre la Suisse et la Grèce, Art. 11, para. 1, SR 0.142.113.721. With *Iran*: see Art. 33. With *Soviet Union*: Traité de commerce du 17 mars 1948 entre la Confédération suisse et l'Union des Républiques soviétiques socialistes, 1948, Art. 10, SR 0.946.297.721. For further bilateral treaties, see Commerce extérieur, SR 0.946. *Legislative history:* Experts Draft, *Art. 152;* Experts Report, page 268; Government Draft, *Art. 149;* Government Report, point 294, 294.1, page 179; Senate Debate, Amtliches Bulletin 1985, page 168; House Debate, Amtliches Bulletin 1986, page 1359, 1360; Festschrift Moser, page 67, 184; Senate Debate, Amtliches Bulletin 1987, page 191, final; House Debate, Amtliches Bulletin 1987, page 1069.
Jurisdiction: See Art. 151.
Foreign decisions: See Art. 165.
Swiss substantive law: Art. 38 et seq., Handelsregisterverordnung, Ordonnance du 7 juin 1937 sur le registre du commerce, SR 221.411. The question whether a company is foreign or Swiss may be relevant for certain internal Swiss public law purposes such as 'Lex Friedrich', Loi fédérale du 16 décembre 1983 sur l'acquisition d'immeubles par des personnes à l'étranger (LFAIE), 1984, SR 211.412.41, see BGE 104 Ib 12, or Art. 6 of the Accord du 2 mai 1968 entre la Confédération suisse et la République de l'Equateur relatif à la protection et à l'encouragement des investissements, 1969, Art. 149, SR 0.975.232.7. Even though for conflict of laws purposes, Switzerland follows the theory of incorporation, internal Swiss law is influenced by the theory of reale Verbandspersönlichkeit.

1. Public law entities are subject to the public law that has created them. Switzerland is also the seat of a number of international organisations established by international treaty, for instance the Bank for International Settlement in Basel, Convention du 20 janvier 1930 concernat la Banque des règlements internationaux (avec Charte constitutive de la Banque), SR 0.192.122.971.

2. Administered (E), administrée (F), verwaltet (G), amministrata (I). Contrast 'managed' in Art. 159.

Art. 155

2. Scope Except for Articles 156 to 161, the law applicable to the company[1] governs in particular:
(a) its legal nature;
(b) formation and dissolution;

140

(c) capacity to have rights and to act;

(e) its organization;

(f) its internal relations, in particular those between the company and its members;

(g) the liability for violations of company law;

(h) the liability for its debts;

(i) the power of representation of persons acting on its behalf on the basis of its organization.[2]

Previous law: BGE 80 II 53, 110 II 188.

Legislative history: Experts Draft, *Art. 153;* Experts Report, page 270; Government Draft, *Art. 150;* Government Report, point page 150; Senate Debate, Amtliches Bulletin 1985, page 168; House Debate, Amtliches Bulletin 1986, page 1359, 1360; Festschrift Moser, page 184; Senate Debate, Amtliches Bulletin 1987, page 191.

Swiss substantive law: Art. 52 et seq. CC. For Swiss/German corporations operating border water power plants, Accord du 6 décembre 1955 entre la Confédération suisse et la République fédérale d'Allemagne au sujet du règlement de questions concernant les conseils d'administration des sociétés anonymes constituées en République fédérale d'Allemagne en vue d'exploiter les usines hydroélectriques frontières du Rhin, 1957, SR 0.221.333.213.6.

1. Law applicable to the company (E), le droit applicable à la société (F), das auf die Gesellschaft anwendbare Recht (G), il diritto applicabile alla società (I), lex societatis (L).

2. On the basis of organization (E), conformément à son organisation (F), aufgrund ihrer Organisation (G), in virtù della sua organizzazione (I). Here, the translation follows the German and Italian texts.

Art. 156

IV. Special Rules
1. Claims from Public Issue of Shares or Bonds

Claims arising from the public issue of shares or bonds[1] by means of a prospectus, circular letter, or similar publication may be asserted under the law governing the company[2] or under the law of the country of issue.[3]

Legislative history: Government Draft, *Art. 151;* Government Report, point 294.4, 294.41, page 181; Senate Debate, Amtliches Bulletin 1985, page 168; House Debate, Amtliches Bulletin 1986, page 1359, 1360; Festschrift Moser, page 188; Senate Debate, Amtliches Bulletin 1987, page 192.

Swiss substantive law: Art. 752 CO.

1. See Art. 151.

2. See Art. 154.

3. Law of the country of issue (E), le droit de l'Etat d'émission (F), Recht des Staates in dem die Ausgabe erfolgt ist (G), diritto dello stato di emissione (I).

Art. 157

2. Protection of Name and Business Designation[1]

1. The protection of a name or business designation of a company registered in the Swiss Register of Commerce against violation in Switzerland is governed by Swiss law.

2. If a company is not registered in the Swiss Register of Commerce,[2] the protection of its name or business designation is governed by the law applicable to unfair competition (Art. 136) or to violations of the right of personality (Art. 132, 133 and 139).

Previous law: Art. 30; Loi fédérale du 26 septembre 1980 concernant la protection des marques de fabrique et de commerce, des indications de provenance et des mentions de récompenses industrielles, SR 232.11; BGE 80 II 171, 83 II 321, 90 II 315, 91 II 117, 92 II 305.
Legislative history: Experts Draft, *Art. 155;* Experts Report, point 294.42, page 181; Government Draft, *Art. 152;* Government Report, point 294.42, page 181; Senate Debate, Amtliches Bulletin 1985, page 169; House Debate, Amtliches Bulletin 1986, page 1359, 1360; Festschrift Moser, page 187.
Swiss substantive law: Art. 927, 944 CO.

1. Protection of name and business designation (E), protection du nom et de la raison sociale (F), Namens – und Firmenschutz (G), protezione del nome e della ditta (I).

2. The registers of commerce are actually kept by the cantons and in some cases their subdivisions (districts). A Swiss Federal Register of Commerce exists. All Swiss registrations appear in the private yearly publication, Schweizerisches Ragionenbuch.

Art. 158

A company may not invoke those limitations of the power of representation of an officer[1] or an agent[2] that are unknown to the law of the country in which the other party has its business establishment[3] or habitual residence,[3] unless the other party knew or should have known of the limitation.

Previous law: BGE 95 II 442.

Legislative history: Experts Draft, *Art. 156;* Experts Report, page 273; Government Draft, *Art. 153;* Government Report, point 294.43, page 182; Senate Debate, Amtliches Bulletin 1985, page 169; House Debate, Amtliches Bulletin 1986, page 1359, 1360; Festschrift Moser, page 187; Senate Debate, Amtliches Bulletin 1987, page 192.

Swiss substantive law: Art. 718, 933 CO. Many Swiss companies enter their officers in the Register of Commerce with joint signing power by two only and also provide for joint bank signatures.

1. Limitations of the power of representation of an officer (E), restrictions du pouvoir de représentation d'un organe (F), Beschränkung der Vertretungsbefugnis eines Organs (G), limitazione del potere di rappresentanza di un organo (I). Here, the translation follows the French and Italian texts.

2. Agent (E), représentant (F), Vertreter (G), rappresentante (I).
An agent is a person *distinct* from the company: a company acts *through* it's officers.

3. See Art. 20.

Art. 159

If the business of a company organized under foreign law is managed[2] in Switzerland or from Switzerland, the liability of the persons acting on its behalf is governed by Swiss law.

Previous law: BGE 108 II 398.

Legislative history: Experts Draft, *Art. 157;* Experts Report, page 274; Government Draft, *Art. 154;* Government Report, point 294.44, page 183; Senate Debate, Amtliches Bulletin 1985, page 169; House Debate, Amtliches Bulletin 1986, page 1359, 1360; Festschrift Moser, page 188, 189; Senate Debate, Amtliches Bulletin 1987, page 192.

1. Liability for foreign companies (E), responsabilité pour une société étrangère (F), Haftung für ausländische Gesellschaften (G), responsabilità per società straniere (I).

2. Business managed (E), activités exercées (F), Geschäfte ausgeführt (G), affari gestiti (I). Contrast 'administered' in Art. 154.

Art. 160

1. A company with a seat abroad may have a branch office[1] in Switzerland. This branch office is subject to Swiss law.

2. The power to act on behalf of such a branch office is governed by Swiss law. At least one of the persons empowered to act on behalf of the branch office must be domiciled[2] in Switzerland and registered in the Register of Commerce.

3. The Federal Council[3] issues detailed regulations on the obligation to register in the Register of Commerce.

Legislative history: Experts Draft, *Art. 158;* Experts Report, page 275; Government Draft, *Art. 155;* Government Report, point 295, page 183; Senate Debate, Amtliches Bulletin 1985, page 169; House Debate, Amtliches Bulletin 1986, page 1359, 1360; Festschrift Moser, page 184.
Swiss substantive law: Art. 935 subs. 2, and 952 subs. 2 CO, Art. 75 subs. 1 and 3 Handelsregisterverordnung. Ordonnance du 7 juin 1937 sur le registre du commerce, SR 221.411 (translated by American Chamber of Commerce in Switzerland, 1974).

1. Branch office (E), succursale (F), Zweigniederlassung (G), succursale (I).

2. Here, domicile is probably understood as in Swiss domestic law.

3. The federal government. The regulations are mentioned above.

Art. 161

1. If permitted by the foreign law, a foreign company may subject
itself to Swiss law without liquidation and re-establishment, if it
meets the conditions of the foreign law, and if adaptation to a form of
organization of Swiss law is possible.

2. The Federal Council[1] may permit a company to subject itself to
Swiss law without regard to the foreign law, particularly if required
by important Swiss interests.

> *Previous law:* Art. 14 final title CO, repealed by Appendix to the PIL Statute.
> *Legislative history:* Experts Draft, *Art. 159;* Experts Report, page 276; Govern-
> ment Draft, *Art. 156;* Government Report, point 296, page 184; Senate Debate,
> Amtliches Bulletin 1985, page 169; House Debate, Amtliches Bulletin 1986,
> page 1359, 1360; Festschrift Moser, page 185; Senate Debate, Amtliches
> Bulletin 1987, page 192.
> *Swiss substantive law:* Art. 50 Handelsregisterverordnung, Ordonnance du 7
> juin 1937 sur le registre du commerce, SR 221.411 (translated by Swiss-
> American Chamber of Commerce, 1974).

1. The federal government.

Art. 162

1. A company required to register under Swiss law[1] is governed by
Swiss law as soon as it proves that it has moved the center of its
activities to Switzerland and has adapted itself to Swiss law.

2. A company not required to register under Swiss law is governed
by Swiss law as soon as the intent to be subject to Swiss law is clearly
evident, a sufficient connection with Switzerland exists, and it has
adapted itself to Swiss law.

3. Before registration, a company with a capital[2] must prove by an
audit report made by an auditor hereto licensed by the Federal
Council[3] that, under Swiss law, its registered capital is covered.

> *Legislative history:* Experts Draft, *Art. 159;* Experts Report, page 276; Govern-
> ment Draft, *Art. 156;* Government Report, point 296, page 184; Senate Debate,
> Art. *156a;* Senate Debate, Amtliches Bulletin 1985, page 169; House Debate,
> Amtliches Bulletin 1986, page 1359, 1361.

1. Under Swiss law, there are: Share corporations; Limited partnerships with shares; Limited liability companies; Cooperative companies; General or collective partnerships, unless purpose is not commercial; Limited partnerships, unless purpose is not commercial; Foundations, except family and ecclesiastical foundations; Membership associations which conduct business.

2. Under Swiss law these are the first three in above note 1.

3. The federal government.

Art. 163

VII. Transfer of Company from Switzerland to Foreign Country
1. General Rule

1. A Swiss company may subject itself to foreign law without liquidation and re-establishment if it proves:

(a) that the conditions of Swiss law are met;

(b) that it continues to exist under foreign law; and

(c) that it has by public notice informed its creditors of the impending change of applicable law and invited them to announce their claims.

2. The provisions on provisional measures of protection in case of international conflicts pursuant to Article 61 of the Federal Statute of October 8, 1982 on Economic National Defense[1] are reserved.

Legislative history: Experts Draft, *Art. 160;* Experts Report, page 278; Government Draft, *Art. 157;* Government Report, point 296, page 185; Senate Debate, Amtliches Bulletin 1985, page 170; House Debate, Amtliches Bulletin 1986, page 1359, 1361; Senate Debate, Amtliches Bulletin 1987, page 192.
Swiss substantive law: Art. 50, 51. Handelsregisterverordnung, Ordonnance du 7 juin 1937 sur le registre du commerce, SR 221.411 (translated by Swiss-American Chamber of Commerce, 1974); Loi fédéral du 8 octobre 1982 sur l'approvisionnement économique du pays (loi sur l'approvisionnement du pays [LAP]), SR 531.01; Arrêté du Conseil fédéral du 12 avril 1957 protégeant par des mesures conservatoires les personnes morales, sociétés de personnes et raissons individualles, 1957, SR 531.54. Examples of legislation on the receiving side: Canadian province of New Brunswick Foreign Resident Corporation Act, 1963, State of Delaware, General Corporation Law, 1981, section 389.

1. Economic national defense (E), du pays approvisionnement économique (F), wirtschaftliche Landesversorgung (G), approvvigionamento economico del paese (I).

Art. 164

2. Company
Debts

1. A company registered in the Swiss Register of Commerce may be deleted from it only if a credible case is made that the creditors are satisfied or their claims are secured, or if the creditors agree[1] to the deletion of the company from the Register.

2. Until the creditors are satisfied or their claims are secured, the company is subject to execution of debt in Switzerland.

Legislative history: Experts Draft, *Art. 160;* Experts Report, page 278; Government Draft, *Art. 157;* Government Report, point 296, page 185; Senate Draft, *Art. 157a;* Senate Debate, Amtliches Bulletin 1985, page 170; House Debate, Amtliches Bulletin 1986, page 1359, 1361.

1. Agree (E), consentent à (F), einverstanden (G), acconsentano (I). The consent must be expressed in writing.

Art. 165

VIII.
Foreign
Decisions

1. Foreign decisions on claims in company law are recognized in Switzerland if rendered in the country:
(a) in which the company has its seat,[1] or if the decisions are recognized there and the defendant did not have his domicile[2] in Switzerland;[3]
(b) in which the defendant has his domicile or habitual residence.[2]

2. Foreign decisions on claims arising from the public issue of shares or bonds by means of a prospectus, circular letter, or similar publication are recognized in Switzerland if they were rendered in the country where the issue was made, and the defendant did not have his domicile[2] in Switzerland.

Swiss Federal Constitution: Art. 59, Appendix I.
Legislative history: Experts Draft, *Art. 161;* Experts Report, page 279; Government Draft, *Art. 158;* Government Report, point 297, page 186 with Berichtigung, dated January 3, 1983; Senate Debate, Amtliches Bulletin 1985, page 170; House Debate, Amtliches Bulletin 1986, page 1359, 1361; Festschrift Moser, page 190; Senate Debate, Amtliches Bulletin 1987, page 192; House Debate, Amtliches Bulletin 1987, page 1069, Senate Debate, Amtliches Bulletin 1987, page 509.

Jurisdiction: See Art. 151.
Applicable law: See Art. 154, 156.

1. See Art. 21.

2. See Art. 20.

3. In which the company has its seat, or if the decisions are recognized there and the defendant did not have his domicile in Switzerland (E), lorsqu'elles ont été rendues ou qu'elles sont reconnes dans l'Etat du siège de la société et que le défendeur n'était pas domicilé en Suisse (F), in dem die Gesellschaft ihren Sitz hat, oder wenn sie dort anerkannt werden und der Beklagte seinen Wohnsitz nicht in der Schweiz hatte (G), sono state pronunciate o vengano riconosciute nello Stato di sede della società e il convenuto non era domiciliato in Svizzera (I). Here, the translation follows the German text.

Eleventh Chapter: Bankruptcy and Composition

Art. 166

I.
Recognition

1. A foreign bankruptcy decree that was issued in the country of the debtor's domicile[1] is recognized upon a motion by the foreign receiver in bankruptcy[2] or by one of the creditors:
(a) if the decree is enforceable in the country where it was issued;
(b) if no grounds for denial under Article 25 exist; and
(c) if the country where the decree was issued grants reciprocity.

2. If the debtor has a branch office in Switzerland, a procedure pursuant to Article 50 subsection 1 of the Federal Statute on Execution of Debts and Bankruptcy is permitted until the schedule of claims[3] takes force of law pursuant to Article 172 of this Statute.

> *Previous law:* Territoriality of bankruptcy. BGE 40 III 123, 57 III 113, 37 III 587, 40 III 365, 102 III 71, 90 III 83, 100 Ia 18, 102 III 71, 54 III 25, 111 III 38.
> *Bilateral treaties:* With *France:* Convention du 15 juin 1869 entre la Suisse et la France sur la compétence judiciaire et l'exécution des jugements en matière civile (avec protocole explicatif), Art. 6 to 9, SR 0.276.193.491; With *Württemberg*, 1825/1826, Zürcher Gesetzessammlung 1981 Nr. 283.1; With *Bavaria*, 1834, Zürcher Gesetzessammlung 1981 Nr. 283.2.
> *Legislative history:* Experts Draft, *Art. 162;* Experts Report, page 282; Government Draft, *Art. 159;* Government Report, point 210.3, page 188; Lausanne Colloque, page 234; Senate Debate, Amtliches Bulletin 1985, page 171; House Debate, Amtliches Bulletin 1986, page 1361.
> *Prosecution of attachment:* See Art. 4.
> *Swiss substantive law:* SchKG.

148

1. In the country of the debtor's domicile (E), dans l'Etat du domicile du débiteur (F), am Wohnsitz des Schuldners (G), nello stato di domicilio del debitore (I). The French and Italian texts are correct. See Art. 20.

2. Receiver in bankruptcy (E), l'administration de la faillite (F), Konkursverwaltung (G), amministrazione del fallimento (I).

3. Schedule of claims (E), état de collocation (F), Kollokationsplan (G), graduatoria (I).

Art. 167

II. Procedure
1.
Jurisdiction

1. A motion for recognition of a foreign bankruptcy decree must be brought before the competent court at the location of the assets in Switzerland. Article 29 applies by analogy.[1]

2. If assets are located in several places, the court first seized has jurisdiction.

3. Claims[2] of the debtor in bankruptcy are deemed to located at the domicile of his debtor.

Legislative history: Experts Draft, *Art. 163;* Experts Report, page 284; Government Draft, *Art. 160;* Government Report, point 210.4, page 190; Senate Debate, Amtliches Bulletin 1985, page 171; House Debate, Amtliches Bulletin 1986, page 1361.

1. By analogy (E), par analogie (F), sinngemäss (G), per analogia (I).

2. Claims (E), créances (F), Forderungen, (G), crediti (I). Not only money claims.

Art. 168

2.
Conservatory
Measures[1]

As soon as a motion to recognize a foreign bankruptcy decree has been made, the court may, upon petition of the movant, order conservatory measures pursuant to Articles 162 to 165 and 170 of the Federal Statute on Execution of Debts and Bankruptcy.

149

Legislative history: Experts Draft, *Art. 164;* Experts Report, page 284; Government Draft, *Art. 161;* Government Report, point 210.4, page 191; Lausanne Colloque, page 236; Senate Debate, Amtliches Bulletin 1985, page 171; House Debate, Amtliches Bulletin 1986, page 1361; Senate Debate, Amtliches Bulletin, page 192.
Swiss substantive law: Art. 162 to 165 SchKG.

1. Conservatory measures (E), mesures conservatoires (F), sichernde Massnahmen (G), provvedimenti conservativi (I).

Art. 169

3.
Publication

1. The decision on the recognition of the foreign bankruptcy decree is published.[1]

2. The recognition is communicated to the Office of Execution of Debts, the Office of Bankruptcy, the Land Register, and the Register of Commerce at the location of the assets, as well as, depending on the case, to the Office for Intellectual Property. The same applies for closing, suspension and revocation of bankruptcy.

Legislative history: Experts Draft, *Art. 165;* Experts Report, page 284; Government Draft, *Art. 162;* Government Report, point 210.4, page 191; Senate Debate, Amtliches Bulletin 1985, page 172; House Debate, Amtliches Bulletin 1986, page 1361; Senate Debate, Amtliches Bulletin, page 192.

1. Published (E), publiée (F), veröffentlicht (G), pubblicata (I). In Schweizerisches Handelsamtsblatt, Feuille officielle suisse du commerce, Foglio ufficiale svizzero di commercio.

Art. 170

III. Legal
Conse-
quences
1. In
General

1. Unless otherwise provided by this Statute, the recognition of a foreign bankruptcy decree leads to the debtor's assets in Switzerland becoming subject to the consequences of Swiss law.[1]

2. The time limits under Swiss law start to run with the publication of the decision on recognition.

3. Neither an assembly nor a committee of creditors is formed.

> *Legislative history:* Experts Draft, *Art. 166;* Experts Report, page 284; Government Draft, *Art. 163;* Government Report, point 210.5, page 191; Senate Debate, Amtliches Bulletin 1985, page 172; House Debate, Amtliches Bulletin 1986, page 1361; Senate Debate, Amtliches Bulletin 1987, page 192.
> *Swiss substantive law:* Art. 221 to 234, 247, 197 SchKG.

1. The competent bankruptcy office draws up an inventory of assets, issues a call to the creditors in Schweizerisches Handelsamtsblatt and prepares the schedule of claims. The competent bankruptcy offices may be gathered from Neues Schweizerisches Ortslexikon, frequently published.

Art. 171

2. Undue Preference

Lawsuits for avoidance of undue preference[1] are governed by Articles 285 to 292 of the Federal Statute on Execution of Debts and Bankruptcy. They can also be brought by a foreign receiver in bankruptcy or one of the creditors in bankruptcy hereto empowered.[2]

> *Legislative history:* Experts Draft, *Art. 166;* Experts Report, page 284; Fribourg Colloque, page 59; Government Draft, *Art. 164;* Government Report, point 210.5, page 191; Senate Debate, Amtliches Bulletin 1985, page 172; House Debate, Amtliches Bulletin 1986, page 1361, 1362.
> *Swiss substantive law:* Art. 285 to 292 SchKG.

1. Lawsuits for avoidance of undue preference (E), action révocatoire (F), Anfechtungsklage (G), l'azione revocatoria (I), actio Pauliana (L).

2. Empowered (E), qui en ont le droit (F), berechtigt (G), leggitimato (I). Here, the translation follows the Italian text.

Art. 172

3. Schedule of Claims[1]

1. In the schedule of claims[1] only the following are entered:
(a) claims secured by pledge pursuant to Article 219 of the Federal Statute on Execution of Debts and Bankruptcy; and
(b) claims not secured by pledge pursuant to Article 219 subsection 4 (first to fourth class) of the Federal Statute on Execution of Debts and Bankruptcy, if the creditors are domiciled[2] in Switzerland.

2. Only creditors of subsection 1 may bring a lawsuit on the schedule of claims[3] pursuant to Article 250 of the Federal Statute on Execution of Debts and Bankruptcy.

3. If a creditor has been partly satisfied in a foreign proceeding connected with the bankruptcy, that amount must be credited after deduction of the costs towards the dividend in the Swiss bankruptcy proceedings.

Previous law: BGE 30 I 438, 42 III 472.
Legislative history: Experts Draft, Art. 167 and 168; Experts Report, page 285; Government Draft, Art. 165; Government Report, point 210.5, page 192; Lausanne Colloque, page 236; Senate Debate, Amtliches Bulletin 1985, page 172; House Debate, Amtliches Bulletin 1986, page 1288, 1291, 1361, 1362; Senate Debate, Amtliches Bulletin 1987, page 192; House Debate, Amtliches Bulletin 1987, page 1069.
Swiss substantive law: Art. 219, 247 SchKG.

1. Schedule of claims (E), collocation (F), Kollokationsplan (G), graduatoria (I).

2. It is not clear whether in the Swiss private law sense or in the sense of Art. 20 of the PIL Statute.

3. Lawsuit on the schedule of claims (E), action en contestation de l'état de collocation (F), Kollokationsklage (G), azione di impugnazione della graduatoria (I).

Art. 173

4.
Distribution
(a)
Recognition
of Foreign
Schedules
of Claims

1. Upon satisfaction of the creditors pursuant to Article 172 subsection 1, the balance is made available to the foreign receiver or to the empowered creditors in bankruptcy.

2. This balance may be made available only after the foreign schedule of claims has been recognized.

3. For the recognition of a foreign schedule of claims, jurisdiction lies with the Swiss court that has recognized the foreign decree in bankruptcy. It examines in particular whether the claims of creditors domiciled[1] in Switzerland have been taken into account adequately in the foreign schedule of claims. These creditors must be heard.

Legislative history: Experts Draft, *Art. 169, 162;* Experts Report, page 282; Government Draft, *Art. 166;* Government Report, point 210.5, page 192; Senate Debate, Amtliches Bulletin 1985, page 172; House Debate, Amtliches Bulletin 1986, page 1361, 1363.
Swiss substantive law: Art. 219 SchKG.

1. It is not clear whether in the sense of Swiss private law or in the sense of Art. 20 of the PIL Statute.

Art. 174

(b) Non-recognition of Foreign Schedules of Claims

1. If the foreign schedule of claims is not recognized,[1] the balance must be distributed to the creditors domiciled[2] in Switzerland in the fifth class of Article 219 subsection 4 of the Federal Statute on Execution of Debts and Bankruptcy.

2. The same applies if the schedule of claims is not submitted for recognition within the time limit set by the judge.

Legislative history: Experts Draft, *Art. 162;* Experts Report, page 282; Government Draft, *Art. 167;* Government Report, point 210.5, page 193; Lausanne Colloque, page 236; Senate Debate, Amtliches Bulletin 1985, page 172; House Debate, Amtliches Bulletin 1986, page 1361, 1363.
Swiss substantive law: Art. 219 SchKG.

1. For instance, for reasons of Ordre public. The decision to deny recognition has no res judicata effect. In particular, if the foreign schedule of claims is amended, it may be re-submitted for recognition.

2. See Art. 172.

Art. 175

IV. Recognition of Foreign Composition and Similar Proceedings[1]

A decree issued on the basis of a composition agreement or a similar proceeding by a foreign authority having jurisdiction is recognized in Switzerland. Articles 166 to 170 apply by analogy. The creditors domiciled in Switzerland must be heard.

Legislative history: Experts Draft, *Art. 170;* Experts Report, page 285; Government Draft, *Art. 168;* Government Report, 210.6, page 193; Lausanne Col-

loque, page 236; Senate Debate, Amtliches Bulletin 1985, page 173; House Debate, Amtliches Bulletin 1986, page 1361, 1363
Swiss substantive law: Art. 293 to 317 SchKG.

1. Recognition of foreign composition and similar proceedings (E), concordat et procédure analogue, reconnaissance (F), Anerkennung ausländischer Nachlassverträge und ähnlicher Verfahren (G), riconoscimento di concordati e di analoghi procedimenti stranieri (I). The same French word is used for inter-cantonal law-making treaties. There is no connection, of course.

Twelfth Chapter: International Arbitration*

Art. 176

I. Scope; Seat of the Arbitral Tribunal

1. The provisions of this chapter shall apply to all arbitrations if the seat[1] of the arbitral tribunal is in Switzerland and if, at the time of the conclusion of the arbitration agreement, at least one of the parties had neither its domicile[2] nor its habitual residence[2] in Switzerland.

2. The provisions of this chapter shall not apply where the parties have agreed in writing that the provisions of this chapter are excluded and that the cantonal provisions on arbitration[3] should apply exclusively.[4]

3. The seat of the arbitral tribunal shall be determined by the parties, or the arbitral institution designated by them,[5] or, failing both, by the arbitrators.[6]

*The translation of this chapter is the result of a joint effort with Dr. Robert Briner, Geneva/The Hague, and Dr. Marc Blessing, Zurich.
Previous law: Art. 1, 2, Concordat, now restricted to domestic arbitration, see Appendix III.
Legislative history: Experts Draft, *Art. 171;* Experts Report, page 293; Government Draft, *Art. 169;* Government Report, 2101.2, 2101.21, page 197; Lausanne Colloque, page 249; Senate Committee Draft, *Art. 169a;* Senate Debate, Amtliches Bulletin 1985, page 173, 176, 179, deleted; House Draft, *Art. 169;* House Debate, Amtliches Bulletin 1986, page 1284, 1286, 1288, 1290, 1363, 1365; Festschrift Moser, page 194; Senate Debate, Amtliches Bulletin 1987, page 193; House Debate, Amtliches Bulletin 1987, page 1070; Senate Debate, Amtliches Bulletin 1987, page 509.

1. Seat (E), siège (F), Sitz (G), sede (I).

2. See Art. 20.

3. Concordat in all but Lucerne and Thurgau.

4. The agreement must expressly exclude the PIL Statute.

5. See Art. 12 ICC Rules.

6. See Art. 189.

Art. 177

II.
Arbitrability[1]

1. Any dispute of financial interest[2] may be the subject of an arbitration.

2. A state, or an enterprise owned by, or an organisation controlled by a state, which is party to an arbitration agreement, cannot invoke its own law in order to contest its capacity to arbitrate or the arbitrability of a dispute covered by the arbitration agreement.

Previous law: Art. 5, Concordat, now restricted to domestic arbitration, see Appendix III.
Legislative history: Experts Draft, Art. *172;* Experts Report, page 293; Government Draft, *Art. 170;* Government Report, point 2101.22, page 197; Lausanne Colloque, page 117; Senate Debate, Amtliches Bulletin 1985, page 173; House Debate, Amtliches Bulletin 1986, page 1363, 1365; Festschrift Moser, page 199 to 201; Senate Debate, Amtliches Bulletin 1987, page 193; House Debate, Amtliches Bulletin 1987, page 1070; Senate Debate, Amtliches Bulletin 1987, page 509.

1. Arbitrability (E), arbitrabilité (F), Schiedsfähigkeit (G), compromettibilità (I).

2. See Art. 5.

Art. 178

III.
Arbitration
Agreement[1]

1. The arbitration agreement must be made in writing, by telegram, telex, telecopier or any other means of communication which permits it to be evidenced by a text.

155

2. Furthermore,[2] an arbitration agreement is valid if it conforms either to the law chosen by the parties, or to the law governing the subject matter of the dispute, in particular the main contract, or to Swiss law.

3. The validity of an arbitration agreement cannot be contested on the ground that the main contract is not valid or that the arbitration agreement concerns a dispute which had not yet arisen.

> *Multilateral treaty:* New York Convention Art. II.
> *Previous law:* Art. 4, 6, Concordat, now restricted to domestic arbitration; Art. 13 CO; BGE 110 II 54, 111 16 253.
> *Legislative history:* Experts Draft, *Art. 173;* Experts Report, page 296; Government Draft, *Art. 171;* Government Report, point 2101.24, page 200; Senate Debate, Amtliches Bulletin 1985, page 173, 179; House Debate, Amtliches Bulletin 1986, page 1363, 1365; Festschrift Moser, page 198, 201, 202; Senate Debate, Amtliches Bulletin 1987; House Debate, Amtliches Bulletin, 1987, page 1070; Senate Debate, Amtliches Bulletin 1987, page 509.
> *Capacity and representation:* See Art. 35, 126, 158.

> 1. Arbitration agreement (E), convention d'arbitrage (F), Schiedsvereinbarung (G), patto di arbitrato (I).

> 2. Furthermore (E), quant au fond (F), im übrigen (G), materialmente (I). Here the translation follows the German text.

Art. 179

IV. Arbitrators 1. Constitution of the Arbitral Tribunal[1]

1. The arbitrators shall be appointed, removed or replaced in accordance with the agreement of the parties.[2]

2. In the absence of such agreement, the judge where the tribunal has its seat[3] may be seized with the question; he shall apply, by analogy, the provisions of cantonal law on appointment, removal or replacement of arbitrators.[4]

3. When a judge has been designated as the authority for appointing an arbitrator, he shall make the appointment[5] unless a summary examination shows that no arbitration agreement exists between the parties.[6]

Previous law: Art. 10 et seq., Concordat, now restricted to domestic arbitration, see Appendix III; BGE 78 I 352, 88 I 100, 88 Ia 308, 93 I 345.
Legislative history: Experts Draft, *Art. 176 and 177;* Experts Report, page 300; Government Draft, *Art. 174;* Government Report, point 2101.26, page 202; Lausanne Colloque, page 174; Senate Debate, Amtliches Bulletin 1985, page 173; House Draft, *Art. 171a;* House Debate, Amtliches Bulletin 1986, page 1363, 1365; Festschrift Moser, page 206, 207; Senate Debate, Amtliches Bulletin 1987, page 194; House Debate, Amtliches Bulletin 1987, page 1070; Senate Debate, Amtliches Bulletin 1987, page 509.

1. Arbitrators. constitution of the arbitral tribunal (G), tribunal arbitral. constitution (F), Schiedsgericht. Bestellung (G), arbitri. costituzione del tribunale arbitrale (I). Here the translation follows the Italian text.

2. See Art. 2 ICC Rules.

3. To be defined by cantonal law.

4. See Art. 10 et seq. Concordat, Appendix III.

5. It is not clear whether the appointment decision is subject to constitutional complaint, and if so, how this will work in practice.

6. See Art. 178.

Art. 180

2. Challenge of an Arbitrator[1]

1. An arbitrator may be challenged:
(a) if he does not meet the qualifications agreed upon by the parties;
(b) if a ground for challenge exists under the rules of arbitration[2] agreed upon by the parties;[3]
(c) if circumstances exist that give rise to justifiable doubts as to his independence.[4]

2. No party may challenge an arbitrator nominated by it, or whom it was instrumental in appointing, except on a ground which came to that party's knowledge after such appointment. The ground for challenge must be notified to the arbitral tribunal and the other party without delay.

3. To the extent that the parties have not made provision for this challenge procedure,[5] the judge at the seat of the arbitral tribunal[6] shall make the final decision.[7]

Previous law: Art. 18 and 21 Concordat, now restricted to domestic arbitration; BGE 111 Ia 259.
Legislative history: Experts Draft, *Art. 177;* Experts Report, page 300; Amtliches Bulletin 1986, page 1363, 1366; House Draft, *Art.171c;* Festschrift Moser, page 208; Senate Debate, Amtliches Bulletin 1987, page 194; House Debate, Amtliches Bulletin 1987, page 1070; Senate Debate, Amtliches Bulletin 1987, page 510.

1. Challenge of an arbitrator (E), récusation des arbitres (F), Ablehnung eines Schiedsrichters (G), ricusa (I).

2. Rules of arbitration (E), règlement d'arbitrage (F), Verfahrensordnung (G), ordinamento procedurale arbitrale (I).

3. See Art. 2 subs. 7 and 8 ICC Rules.

4. Independence (E), indépendance (F), Unabhängigkeit (G), indipendenza (I). The word 'impartiality' was purposefully omitted.

5. See Art. 2 subs. 8 ICC Rules.

6. To be defined by cantonal law.

7. It is unclear whether the decision is 'final' in the sense that no constitutional complaint is possible.

Art. 181

V. Lis Pendens[1]

The arbitral proceedings shall be pending from the time when one of the parties seizes with a claim either the arbitrator or arbitrators designated in the arbitration agreement or, in the absence of such designation in the arbitration agreement, from the time when one of the parties initiates the procedure for the appointment of the arbitral tribunal.[2]

Previous law: Art. 13 Concordat, now restricted to domestic arbitration, see Appendix III.
Legislative history: Experts Draft, *Art. 174;* Experts Report, page 299; Government Draft, *Art. 172;* Government Report, point 2101.26, page 201; Senate Debate, Amtliches Bulletin 1985, page 174, 179; House Debate, Amtliches Bulletin 1986, page 1363, 1366; Festschrift Moser, page 210; Senate Debate, Amtliches Bulletin 1987, page 194.

1. Lis pendens (E), litispendance (F), Rechtshängigkeit (G), litispendenza (I), lis pendens (L).

2. See Art. 3 subs. 1 para. 2 ICC Rules.

Art. 182

1. The parties may, directly or by reference to rules of arbitration,[1] determine the arbitral procedure; they may also submit the arbitral procedure to a procedural law of their choice.

2. If the parties have not determined the procedure, the arbitral tribunal shall determine it to the extent necessary,[2] either directly or by reference to a statute[3] or to rules of arbitration.[1]

3. Regardless of the procedure chosen, the arbitral tribunal shall guarantee equal treatment of the parties and the right of both parties to be heard in adversarial proceedings.[4]

> *Previous law:* Art. 24, 25 Concordat, now restricted to domestic arbitration. *Legislative history:* Experts Draft, *Art. 175;* Experts Report, page 299; Government Draft, *Art. 173;* Government Report, point 2101.26, page 202; Senate Debate, Amtliches Bulletin 1985, page 174, 179; House Debate, Amtliches Bulletin 1986, page 1363, 1366; Festschrift Moser, page 210, 212; Senate Debate, Amtliches Bulletin 1987, page 194; House Debate, Amtliches Bulletin 1987, page 1071; Senate Debate, Amtliches Bulletin 1987, page 510.
>
> 1. See Art. 180. See Art. 14 and 15 ICC Rules, Articles 5 to 13 LCIA Rules.
>
> 2. To the extent necessary (E), au besoin (F), soweit nötig (G), per quanto necessario (I).
>
> 3. Such as the Zurich Code of Civil Procedure. The Swiss Federal Code of Civil Procedure is rarely used since it is designed for those (rare) cases where the Swiss Federal Supreme Court sits as a trial court in a civil matter.
>
> 4. Adversarial proceedings (E), procédure contradictoire (F), kontradiktorisches Verfahren (G), contraddittorio (I).

Art. 183

1. Unless the parties have otherwise agreed, the arbitral tribunal may, on motion of one party, order provisional or conservatory measures.

2. If the party concerned does not voluntarily comply with these measures, the arbitral tribunal may request the assistance of the competent state judge;[1] the judge shall apply his own law.[2]

3. The arbitral tribunal or the state judge[1] may make granting the provisional or conservatory measures subject to appropriate sureties.

> *Previous law:* Art. 16, 26, 27 Concordat, now restricted to domestic arbitration, see Appendix III.
> *Legislative history:* Experts Draft, *Art. 176 and 177;* Experts Report, page 300; Government Draft, *Art. 174;* Government Report, point 2101.26, page 202; Senate Debate, Amtliches Bulletin 1985, page 174, 175; House Draft, *Art. 173a, 179;* House Debate, Amtliches Bulletin 1986, page 1363, 1365; Festschrift Moser, page 211, 212; House Debate, Amtliches Bulletin 1987 page 1366; Senate Debate, Amtliches Bulletin 1987, page 195.

1. To be defined by cantonal law.

2. See Art. 8 subs. 5 ICC Rules.

Art. 184

3. Taking of Evidence[1]

1. The arbitral tribunal shall itself conduct the taking of evidence.[1]

2. If the assistance of the state judiciary authorities is necessary for the taking of evidence, the arbitral tribunal, or one party by agreement with the arbitral tribunal, may request the assistance of the state judge at the seat of the arbitral tribunal;[2] the judge shall apply his own law.

> *Previous law:* Art. 3, 26, 27 Concordat, now restricted to domestic arbitration, see Appendix III.
> *Legislative history:* Experts Draft, *Art. 175;* Experts Report, page 299; Government Draft, *Art. 174;* Government Repor, point 2101.26, page 202; Senate Debate, Amtliche Bulletin 1985, page 174, 175; House Draft, *Art. 173b;* House Debate, Amtliches Bulletin 1986, page 1363, 1367; Festschrift Moser, page 212; Senate Debate, Amtliches Bulletin 1987, page 195; House Debate, Amtliches Bulletin 1987, page 1070.

1. Taking of evidence (E), administration des preuves (F), Beweisaufnahme (G), assunzione delle prove (I). See ICC Rules Art. 14.

2. To be defined by cantonal law.

Art. 185

For any further judicial assistance the state judge at the seat of the arbitral tribunal[1] shall have jurisdiction.

Previous law: Art. 27 Concordat, now restricted to domestic arbitration, see Appendix III.
Legislative history: Experts Draft, *Art. 176;* Experts Report, page 300; Government Draft, *Art. 74;* Government Report, point 2101.26, page 202; Senate Debate, Amtliches Bulletin 1985, page 174, 179; Senate Draft, *Art. 173c;* Senate Debate, Amtliches Bulletin 1987, page 195; House Debate, Amtliches Bulletin 1987, page 1072;

1. To be defined by cantonal law.

Art. 186

1. The arbitral tribunal shall decide on its own jurisdiction.[1]

2. A plea of lack of jurisdiction must be raised prior to any defense on the merits.

3. As a rule, the arbitral tribunal shall decide on its jurisdiction by preliminary award.

Previous law: Art. 8, Concordat, now restricted to domestic arbitration, see Appendix III; BGE 108 Ia 308.
Legislative history: Experts Draft, *Art. 176 and 177;* Experts Report, page 300; Government Draft, *Art. 176;* Government Report, point 2101.26, page 202; Senate Debate, Amtliches Bulletin 1985, page 173, 179; House Draft, *Art. 174a;* House Debate, Amtliches Bulletin 1986, page 1363, 1367; Festschrift Moser, page 204, 205; Senate Debate, Amtliches Bulletin 1987, page 195.

1. See Art. 7, 8 subs. 3 and 4 ICC Rules.

Art. 187

VIII.
Decisions
on the
Merits
1. Applicable
Law*1.* The arbitral tribunal shall decide the case according to the rules of law[1] agreed upon by the parties[2] or, in the absence of a choice of law, by applying the rules of law with which the dispute has the closest connection.[3]

2. The parties may authorize the arbitral tribunal to decide the case ex aequo et bono.[4]

> *Previous law:* Art. 31 Concordat, now restricted to domestic arbitration, see Appendix III; BGE 107 I 63 6.
> *Legislative history:* Experts Draft, *Art. 175;* Experts Report, page 299; Fribourg Colloque, page 49; Government Draft, *Art. 175;* Government Report, point 2101.25, page 201; Senate Debate, Amtliches Bulletin 1985, page 173; House Debate, Amtliches Bulletin 1986, page 1363, 1367; Festschrift Moser, page 72, 212 to 218; Senate Debate, Amtliches Bulletin 1987, page 195.

> 1. Rules of law (E), règles de droit (F), Recht (G), diritto (I). Here, the translation follows the French text. Whether this includes alleged rules of law such as 'lex mercatoria' is not clear.

> 2. See Art. 14.

> 3. Compare Art. 28 Uncitral Model Law, Art. 13 subs. 3 to 5 ICC Rules.

> 4. Ex aequo et bono (L), en équité (F), nach Billigkeit (G), secondo equità (I).

Art. 188

2. Partial
AwardUnless the parties otherwise agree, the arbitral tribunal may render partial awards.[1]

> *Previous law:* Art. 32 Concordat, now restricted to domestic arbitration, see Appendix III.
> *Legislative history:* House Draft, *Art. 175a;* House Debate, Amtliches Bulletin 1986, page 1363, 1367; Festschrift Moser, page 219; Senate Debate, Amtliches Bulletin 1987, page 195.
> *Preliminary award on jurisdiction:* See Art. 186.

> 1. Partial award (E), sentence partielle (F), Teilentscheid (G), decisioni parziali (I).

Art. 189

1. The arbitral award shall be rendered in conformity with the rules of procedure and in the form agreed upon by the parties.[1]

2. In the absence of such an agreement, the arbitral award shall be made[2] by a majority, or, in default of a majority, by the chairman alone. The award shall be in writing, supported by reasons, dated and signed. The signature of the chairman is sufficient.

Previous law: Art. 31, 33, 34 Concordat, now restricted to domestic arbitration, see Appendix III
Legislative history: House Draft, *Art. 176a;* House Debate, Amtliches Bulletin 1986, page 1363, 1367; Festschrift Moser, page 219; Senate Debate, Amtliches Bulletin 1987, page 195.

1. Parties (E), parties (F), Parteien (G), parti (I).

2. All arbitrators must participate, except in the case of an obstructive arbitrator.

Art. 190

1. The award is final from its notification.[2]

2. The award may only be challenged:[3]
(a) When the sole arbitrator was not properly appointed or when the arbitral tribunal was not properly constituted;[4]
(b) When the arbitral tribunal wrongly accepted or declined jurisdiction;[5]
(c) When the arbitral tribunal's decision went beyond the questions submitted to it,[6] or failed to decide one of the items in the claim;
(d) When the principle of equality of the parties or the right of the parties to be heard[7] was breached;
(e) When the award is contrary to public policy.[8]

3. Where the tribunal decided on its constitution or on its jurisdiction in a preliminary award, challenge is possible only on the basis of the above subsections 2 (a) and 2 (b); the time limit runs from the notification[9] of the preliminary award.

Previous law: Art. 35, 36 to 43 Concordat, now restricted to domestic arbitration, see Appendix III.

Legislative history: Experts Draft, *Art. 178, 79;* Experts Report, page 300; Government Draft, *Art. 177;* Government Report, point 2101.27, page 202; Senate Debate, Amtliches Bulletin 1985, page 173, 179; House Draft, *Art. 177a;* House Debate, Amtliches Bulletin 1986, page 1363, 1368; Festschrift Moser, page 219 to 225; Senate Debate, Amtliches Bulletin 1987, page 195; House Debate, Amtliches Bulletin 1987, page 1072.

1. Action for annulment (E), recours (F), Anfechtung (G), impugnazione (I).

2. Notification (E), communication (F), Eröffnung (G), notificato che sia (I). Here, the translation follows the Italian text. Since the award will normally be 'made' in writing, see Art. 189, it is unclear whether it is possible to 'notify' an award before it is 'made'. If so, premature oral disclosure of the award may lead to problems.

3. Be challenged (E), recours (F), angefochten (G), impugnato (I). The time limit is 30 days from notification, see Art. 191 subs. 1 and the relevant portions of the Swiss General Statute on the Organisation of The Federal Judiciary. Reproduced in Appendix II

4. See Art. 179.

5. See Art. 186.

6. Beyond the questions submitted to it (E), au-delà des demandes dont il était saisi (F), Streitpunkte, die ihm nicht unterbreitet wurden (G), punti litigiosi che non gli erano stati sottoposti (I), ultra petita (L).

7. See Art. 182.

8. Probably in the sense of the New York Convention.

9. Notification (E), communication (F), Zustellung (G), notifiazione (I). Here, the translation follows the French and Italian texts.

Art. 191

2.
Competent
Authority

1. The action for annulment may only be brought before the Federal Supreme Court. The procedure applicable to the annulment is governed by the provisions of the Federal Statute on the Organization of the Federal Judiciary regarding the constitutional complaint.[1]

2. The parties may agree that the state judge at the seat of the arbitral tribunal decides in lieu of the Federal Supreme Court.[2] His decision is final. For this purpose the cantons designate a sole cantonal authority.[3]

> *Previous law:* Art. 36 to 43 Concordat, now restricted to domestic arbitration, see Appendix III.
> *Legislative history:* Experts Draft, *Art. 179;* Experts Report, page 301; Government Draft, *Art. 177;* Government Report, point 2101.27, page 203; Senate Draft, *Art. 177a;* Senate Debate, Amtliches Bulletin 1985, page 173, 174, 179; House Draft, *Art. 177a;* House Debate, Amtliches Bulletin 1986, page 1368; Festschrift Moser, page 225 to 227; Senate Debate, Amtliches Bulletin 1987, page 195; House Debate, Amtliches Bulletin 1987, page 1072; Senate Debate, Amtliches Bulletin 1987, page 510.

> 1. Constitutional complaint (E), recours de droit public (F), staatsrechtliche Beschwerde (G), ricorso di diritto pubblico (I). Time limit: 30 days, see Appendix II, Art. 84.

> 2. This probably means that no constitutional complaint is possible against such state judge decisions.

> 3. The cantons are expected to enact introductory statutes.

Art. 192

X. Waiver of Annulment[1]

1. If none of the parties have their domicile, their habitual residence, or a business establishment in Switzerland, they may, by an express statement in the arbitration agreement or by a subsequent written agreement, waive fully the action for annulment or they may limit it to one or several of the grounds listed in Art. 190, subsection 2.[2]

2. If the parties have waived fully the action for annulment and if the award is to be enforced in Switzerland, the New York Convention of June 10, 1958 on the Recognition and Enforcement of Foreign Arbitral Awards applies by analogy.[3]

> *Previous law:* Art. 36 to 43 Concordat, now restricted to domestic arbitration, see Appendix III.
> *Legislative history:* Experts Draft, *Art. 180;* Experts Report, page 301; Government Draft, *Art. 178;* Government Report, point 2101.27, page 203; Senate Debate, Amtliches Bulletin 1985, page 174, 179; House Debate, Amtliches Bulletin 1986, page 1363, 1369; Festschrift Moser, page 227 to 229.

1. Waiver of annulment (E), renonciation au recours (F), Verzicht auf Rechtsmittel (G), rinuncia all'impugnazione (I). Exclusion agreement.

2. A mere statement that the award shall be final or a reference to arbitration rules to that effect is probably insufficient.

3. See Art. 194.

Art. 193

XI. Deposit and Certificate of Enforceability[1]

1. Each party may at its own expense deposit a copy of the award with the Swiss court at the seat of the arbitral tribunal.

2. On request of a party, the court shall certify the enforceability of the award.

3. On request of a party, the arbitral tribunal shall certify that the award was rendered pursuant to the provisions of this Statute; such certificate has the same effect as the deposit of the award.

> *Previous law:* Art. 3, 35 Concordat, now restricted to domestic arbitration, see Appendix III.
> *Legislative history:* Experts Draft, *Art. 181;* Experts Report, page 302; Government Draft, *Art. 179;* Government Report, point 2101.27, page 203; Senate Debate, Amtliches Bulletin 1985, page 173, 179; House Debate, Amtliches Bulletin 1986, page 1363, 1369; Senate Debate, Amtliches Bulletin 1987, page 199; House Debate, Amtliches Bulletin 1987, page 1072.
>
> 1. Deposit and certificate of enforceability (E), dépôt et certificat de force exécutoire (F), Vollstreckbarkeitsbescheinigung (G), deposito e attestazione dell'esecutività (I).

Art. 194

XII. Foreign Arbitral Awards

The recognition and enforcement of a foreign arbitral award is governed by the New York Convention of June 10, 1958 on the Recognition and Enforcement of Foreign Arbitral Awards.

> *Multilateral treaties:* With some 70 countries: (New York) Convention du 10 juin 1958 pour la reconnaissance et l'exécution des sentences arbitrales étrangères,

1965, SR 0.277.12. Switzerland made the reservation, AS 1965 p. 793, which is now in effect dropped, that it would apply the New York Convention with respect to treaty countries only. With some 30 countries: (Geneva) Protocole du 24 septembre 1923 relatif aux clauses d'arbitrage, SR 0.277.11. With some 10 countries: (Geneva) Convention du 26 septembre 1927 pour l'exécution des sentences arbitrales étrangères, SR 0.277.111. With some 80 countries: (Washington) Convention du 18 mars 1965 pour le règlement des différends relatifs aux investissements entre Etats et ressortissants d'autres Etats, 1968, SR 0.975.1

Bilateral treaties: With Austria, Belgium, Czechoslovakia, France, (Federal Republic of) Germany, Italy, Liechtenstein, Spain, Sweden: see Art. 25. With Soviet Union and Yugoslavia: see Art. 154.

Previous law: Art. 4 NAG, repealed in Appendix to PIL Statute.

Legislative history: Experts Draft, *Art. 182;* Experts Report, page 302; Fribourg Colloque, page 6; Government Draft, *Art. 180;* Government Report, point 2101.29, page 204; Senate Debate, Amtliches Bulletin 1985, page 173, 179; House Debate, Amtliches Bulletin 1986, page 1369; Festschrift Moser, page 229; Senate Debate, Amtliches Bulletin 1987, page 199.

Thirteenth Chapter: Final Provisions

First Section: Abrogation and Amendment of Federal Law Presently in Force

Art. 195

Abrogation and amendment of federal law presently in force is provided for in the appendix which forms part of this Statute.

Legislative history: Experts Draft, *Art. 191;* Experts Report, page 309; Government Draft, *Art. 181;* Government Report, points 2102.1, page 204; Senate Debate, Amtliches Bulletin 1985, page 179; House Debate, Amtliches Bulletin 1986, page 1369.

See Appendix to the PIL Statute.

Second Section: Transitory Provisions[1]

Art. 196

I. Non-
retroactivit

1. The legal effects of factual situations or legal transactions[2] initiated and completed before the entry into force of this Statute[3] are governed by the previous law.

2. The legal effects of factual situations or legal transactions[2] initiated before the entry into force of this Statute,[3] but designed to continue,[4] are subject to the previous law, prior to that date. From the entry into force of this Statute[3] onwards these effects are governed by the new law.

> *Legislative history:* Experts Draft, *Art. 192;* Experts Report, page 309; Government Draft, *Art. 183;* Government Report, point 2101.2, page 207; Lausanne Colloque, page 131; Senate Debate, Amtliches Bulletin, 1985, page 183; House Debate, Amtliches Bulletin, 1986, page 1370; Festschrift Moser, page 198.
>
> 1. For the effect of the Transitory Provisions on international arbitrations, see Concordat, Note to, Art. 46.
>
> 2. Factual situations or legal transaction (E), faits ou actes juridiques (F), Sachverhalte oder Rechtsvorgänge (G), fatti o atti giuridici (I).
>
> 3. January 1, 1989.
>
> 4. Designed to continue (E), qui continuent de produire (F), auf Dauer angelegt (G), che perdurano (I). Here the translation follows the German text.

Art. 197

II.
Transitory
Law
1.
Jurisdiction

1. For lawsuits or petitions pending at the time of entry into force of this Statute[1] jurisdiction continues to lie with the Swiss judicial or administrative authorities seized, even though they no longer have jurisdiction according to this Statute.

2. Lawsuits and petitions that were rejected by Swiss courts or authorities for lack of jurisdiction before the entry into force of this Statute[1] may be brought again after the entry into force of this Statute[1] if pursuant to this Statute they have henceforth jurisdiction and the claim can still be asserted.

Legislative history: Experts Draft, *Art. 193;* Experts Report, page 309; Government Draft, *Art. 184;* Government Report, point 2102.2, page 207; Senate Debate, Amtliches Bulletin, 1985, page 183; House Debate, Amtliches Bulletin, 1986, page 1370; Festschrift Moser, page 198.
Applicable law: See Art. 198.
Recognition and enforcement of foreign decision: See Art. 199.

1. January 1, 1989.

Art. 198

2. Applicable Law

For lawsuits and petitions that are pending at the trial level at the time of entry into force of this Statute,[1] the applicable law is determined according to this Statute.

Legislative history: Experts Draft, *Art. 194;* Experts Report, page 309; Government Draft, *Art. 185;* Government Report, 2102.2, page 207; Senate Debate, Amtliches Bulletin, 1985, page 183; House Debate, Amtliches Bulletin 1986, page 1370; Festschrift Moser, page 198.
Jurisdiction: See Art. 197.
Recognition and enforcement: See Art. 199.

1. January 1, 1989.

Art. 199

3. Recognition and Enforcement of Foreign Decisions

For motions for recognition or enforcement of foreign decisions that are pending at the time of entry into force of this Statute[1], the conditions for recognition and enforcement are governed by this Statute.

Legislative history: Experts Draft, *Art. 195;* Experts Report, page 309; Government Draft, *Art. 186;* Government Report, point 2102.2, page 207; Senate Debate, Amtliches Bulletin, 1985, page 183; House Debate, Amtliches Bulletin 1986, page 1370; Festschrift Moser, page 198.
Jurisdiction: See Art. 197.
Applicable law: See Art. 198.

1. January 1, 1989.

Third Section: Referendum and Enactment

Art. 200

1. This Statute is subject to optional referendum.[1]

2. The Federal Council determines the date of coming into force.[2]

Legislative history: Experts Draft, *Art. 196;* Experts Report, page 309; Government Draft, *Art. 187;* Government Report, point 2102.3, page 207; Senate Debate, Amtliches Bulletin, 1985, page 183; House Debate, Amtliches Bulletin 1986, page 1370.

1. No referendum was demanded by the requisite 50,000 voters or eight cantons within the statutory deadline.

2. January 1, 1989.

Abrogation and Amendment of Federal Law Presently in Force

I. Abrogation of Federal Law Presently in Force[1]

The following are repealed:

(a) the Federal Statute of June 25, 1981, concerning the Civil Status of Residents and Sojourners;
(b) Article 418b, subsection 2, of the Code of Obligations;
(c) Article 14 of the Final and Transitional Provisions to the Code of Obligations;
(d) Article 85 of the Federal Statute on Road Traffic;
(e) Article 30 of the Federal Statute of September 26, 1890, concerning Protection of Business and Trade Designations, Designations of Origin of Goods and Commercial Marks;
(f) Article 14 subsection 3 of the Federal Statute of March 30, 1900, concerning Commercial Samples and Models;
(g) Article 41 subsection 2 of the Federal Statute on the Protection of Vegetable Strains of March 20, 1975.

II. Amendment of Federal Law Currently in Force[2]

1. Federal Statute on the Organization of the Federal Judiciary.[2]
Art. 43 Margin title and subs. 1
. . . .[3]

Art. 43 a
. . . .[3]

Art. 48 subs. 1 bis
. . . .[3]

Art. 49
. . . .[3]

Art. 50 subs. 1 bis
. . . .[3]

Art. 55 subs. 1 letter c
. . . .[3]

Art. 60 subs. 1 letter c
. . . .[3]

Art. 61 subs. 1
. . . .[3]

Art. 68 subs. 1 and 1 bis
. . . .[3]

Art. 85
. . . .[3]

2. Swiss Federal Statute of June 25, 1954 on Patents:
Art. 75, subs. 1. lit. b
(b) For actions brought by third parties against the application or titulary of a patent, the court at the domicile of the defendent.

3. Federal Code of Civil Prodedure:
Art. 2 subs. 2
2. An agreement on a place of jurisdiction in Switzerland is not binding upon the Swiss Federal Supreme Court; it may ex officio dismiss the lawsuit without prejudice. If one of the parties has its domicile, habitual residence or a business establishment in Switzerland, or, if pursuant to the Federal Statute on Private International Law of December 18, 1987, Swiss law is applicable to the dispute, the Swiss Federal Supreme Court must accept jurisdiction.

Senate, December 18, 1987	House, December 18, 1987
The Chairman: Masoni	The Chairman: Reichling
The Secretary: Huber	The Secretary: Anliker

1. *Legislative history:* Experts Draft, *Art. 191;* Experts Report, page 309; Government Draft, *Art. 181;* Government Report, points 2102.1, page 204; Senate Debate, Amtliches Bulletin 1985, page 179; House Debate, Amtliches Bulletin 1986, page 1369.

2. *Legislative history:* Experts Draft, *Art. 190;* Experts Report, page 306; Fribourg Colloque, page 4; 254, Government Draft, *Art. 182;* Government Report, point 2102.11, page 205; Senate Debate, Lausanne Colloque, page 241; Amtliches Bulletin 1985, page 179; House Debate, Amtliches Bulletin 1986, page 1369; Senate Debate, Amtliches Bulletin 1987, page 199; House Debate, Amtliches Bulletin 1987, page 1072; Senate Debate, Amtliches Bulletin 1987, page 510.

3. See Appendix II.

Appendices

Swiss Federal Constitution

of May 29, 1874, as amended[1]

Excerpts

. . .

Art. 3

The Cantons are sovereign insofar as their sovereignty is not limited by the Federal Constitution and, as such, exercise all rights which are not entrusted to the federal power.

Art. 4

All Swiss citizens are equal before the law. In Switzerland, there shall be no subjects, nor privileges of place, birth, person or family.

Men and women have equal rights. The law provides for equality, in particular in the areas of family, school, and work. Men and women have the right to equal pay for equivalent work.

. . .

Art. 7

[1]All separate alliances and all treaties of a political nature between Cantons are prohibited.

[2]The Cantons may, however, conclude agreements among themselves concerning matters of legislation, justice and administration, provided they bring such agreements to the notice of the federal authority, which is entitled to prevent the execution of the agreements if they contain anything contrary to the Confederation or to the rights of other Cantons. If this is not the case, the contracting Cantons may request the cooperation of the federal authorities for the execution of such agreements.

---

1. SR 101. Translated by Swiss Federal Department of Foreign Affairs (unofficial translation)

Art. 8

The Confederation alone has the right to declare war and to make peace, as well as to conclude alliances and treaties, especially customs and commercial treaties, with foreign states.

. . .

Art. 43

[1]Every citizen of a Canton is a Swiss citizen.

[2]In this capacity, he may take part in all federal elections and votes at his domicile after having duly proved his right to vote.

[3]No one may exercise political rights in more than one Canton.

[4]The established Swiss citizen shall enjoy at his domicile all the rights of the citizens of that Canton and, with these, all the rights of the citizens of that commune. However, sharing in property belonging in common to local citizens or to corporations and the right to vote in matters exclusively regarding local citizens are excepted unless cantonal legislation should provide otherwise.

[5]In cantonal and communal matters, he shall acquire the right to vote after having settled for three months.

[6]Cantonal laws on establishment and on the right of established citizens to vote in communal matters shall require the approval of the Federal Council.

. . .

Art. 46

[1]In matters of civil law, established persons shall, as a rule, be subject to the jurisdiction and legislation of their domicile.

[2]Federal legislation shall enact the provisions required to implement this principle and to prevent double taxation.

Art. 47

A federal law shall specify the difference between establishment and residence and at the same time lay down provisions regulating the political and civil rights of resident Swiss citizens.

. . .

Art. 54

[1]The right to marry is placed under the protection of the Confederation.

[2]This right may not be limited for religious or economic reasons nor on account of previous conduct or of other police considerations.

[3]A marriage which has been celebrated in a Canton or abroad according to the local legislation shall be recognized as valid within the whole territory of the Confederation.

[4]Through her marriage, the woman acquires the citizenship of her husband.

[5]Children born before marriage shall be legitimized by the subsequent marriage of their parents.

[6]No bride-admission fee or any other similar tax may be levied.

. . .

Art. 59

[1]The solvent debtor having a domicile in Switzerland must be sued, for personal debts, before the judge of his domicile; therefore, his property may not be seized or attached for personal claims outside the Canton in which he has his domicile.

[2]In the case of aliens, the pertinent provisions of international treaties remain reserved.

[3]Imprisonment for debts is abolished.

Art. 60

All Cantons are bound to afford all Swiss citizens the same treatment as their own citizens in the fields of legislation and of judicial proceedings.

Art. 61

Final judgments rendered in civil law cases in all Cantons shall be enforceable in the whole of Switzerland.

. . .

Art. 64

[1]The Confederation is entitled to legislate
on civil capacity,
on all legal matters relating to commerce and movable property
transactions (law of contracts and tort including commercial law and
law of bills of exchange),
on copyrights in literature and arts, on protection of inventions
suitable for industrial use, including designs and models,
on suits for debts and bankruptcy.
[2]The Confederation is also entitled to legislate in the other fields of
civil law.
[3]The organisation of the courts, procedure and jurisdiction shall
remain a matter for the Cantons as before.

. . .

Art. 85

The matters within the competence of the two Councils are in
particular the following:

. . .

5) Alliances and treaties with foreign states as well as approval of
treaties of Cantons among themselves or with foreign states. However, such treaties of the Cantons shall only be submitted to the
Federal Assembly if the Federal Council or another Canton raises an
objection to them.
6) Measures for the external security as well as for the preservation
of the independence and neutrality of Switzerland, declaration of war
and conclusion of peace.

. . .

Art. 102

[1]The powers and obligations of the Federal Council, within the
limits of this constitution, are in particular the following:

. . .

8) It shall watch over the external interest of the Confederation, particularly its international relations, and it shall be in charge of external affairs generally.

9) It shall watch over the external security of Switzerland and over the preservation of its independence and neutrality.

. . .

Swiss Federal Statute on the Organization of the Federal Judiciary

of December 16, 1943, as amended
last by the Appendix to the PIL Statute[1]

Excerpts

. . .

First Chapter: General Provisions

First Section: Organization of Federal Supreme Court

. . .

Article 4

Relatives

1. Relatives and spouses of relatives in direct line and up to the fourth grade in the lateral line, spouses of sisters and persons relative through adoption may not simultaneously exercise the function of a member, deputy member, or secretary of the Swiss Federal Supreme Court, a federal public prosecutor, the federal solicitor general or another representative of the Federal Prosecutor's Office.

2. The same incompatibility exists between the secretary of a federal investigating judge and that judge or the representative of the Federal Prosecutor's Office.

3. Those who through marriage enter into an incompatible relationship, thereby renounce their function.

. . .

1. These amendments are printed in *italics*. The text in italics is identical with the full text of the Appendix to the PIL Statute.

Second Section: Withdrawal and Challenge

Mandatory
Withdrawal

Article 22

1. A member or deputy member of the Swiss Federal Supreme Court, representatives of the Federal Prosecutor's Office, investigating judges, their secretaries or jury members may not exercise his function:

(a) in all matters in which he himself, his spouse, his betrothed, his and his spouse's relatives up to the degree mentioned in Art. 4, or the spouse of his sister or of a brother of his wife, or a person whose guardian or tutor he is or who is his relative through adoption, has a direct interest in the outcome of the dispute;

(b) in a matter in which he already acted in a different function, as a member of an administrative or judicial authority, as an officer of a court, as legal counsel, representative or lawyer of a party, as an expert or a witness;

2. Moreover, a member or a deputy member of the Swiss Federal Supreme Court or a member of the jury may not exercise his function, if the representative or lawyer of a party is his or his spouse's relative in direct line or up to the second grade in the lateral line.

Article 23

Grounds for
Challenge

1. A member or deputy member of the Swiss Federal Supreme Court, a representative of the Federal Prosecutor's Office, an investigating judge, their secretary or a member of the jury may be challenged by the parties or may himself withdraw:

(a) in matters of a legal person whose member he is;

(b) if between him and a party a special friendship or a personal enmity or a special duty or dependency relationship exists;

(c) if circumstances exist which make him appear prejudiced in the case.

. . .

181

Third Section: Common Procedural Provisions

Article 29

Party
Represen-
tatives.
Domicile for
Notices

1. Party representatives must place a written power of attorney into the record by legitimizing themselves; such a power may be requested at any time.

2. In civil and criminal matters only lawyers admitted to the bar and teachers of law at Swiss universities may act as representatives of parties before the Swiss Federal Supreme Court, save in the cases arising from cantons where the legal profession may be exercised freely.[1]

3. By way of exception, and subject to reciprocity, foreign lawyers are admitted as representatives.[2]

4. Parties domiciled abroad must indicate a domicile in Switzerland for notices. Notices to parties who have not complied with this requirement may be omitted or given by way of publication.

5. If a party is manifestly incapable of conducting its case by itself the Court may order it to appoint a representative. If within the deadline set the party does not comply, the Court appoints a representative at the party's expense.

. . .

1. Obsolete since there are no such cantons any longer.

2. In the last years, no such exceptions were granted.

Article 32

Deadlines
(a)
Computation

1. When deadlines are computed the day on which the deadline starts to run is not counted.

2. If the last day of a deadline is a Sunday or a holiday recognized by the applicable cantonal law the deadline runs on the following weekday.

3. A deadline is considered to have been observed if the action was taken within the deadline. A written submission must have reached or be handed over to the Swiss Postal Office, addressed to the authority to whom they must be made, at the latest on the last day of the deadline. If within the deadline the submission reaches the Swiss Federal Supreme Court directly, the deadline is deemed to have been observed even if the submission should have been made to the cantonal authority.

Article 33

(b)
Extension

1. Statutory deadlines may not be extended.

2. Judicial deadlines may be extended for sufficient and properly authenticated reasons if the request was submitted before the deadline ran.

Article 34

(c)
Interruption
of Deadline

1. Statutory and judicial deadlines do not run:
(a) on the seventh day before Easter through the seventh day after Easter;
(b) from the 15th of July to the 15th of August;
(c) from the 18th of December to the 1st of January.

2. This does not apply in criminal and enforcement of debt and bankruptcy matters.
. . .

Second Chapter: Civil Jurisdiction

First Section: The Swiss Federal Supreme Court as Trial Court
Second Section: The Swiss Federal Supreme Court on Appeals

Article 43

Grounds for
Apppeal
(a)
Federal
Law

1. On appeal a claim may be made that the challenged decision is based on a violation of federal law including the international treaties concluded by the Confederation. For the violation of constitutional rights of the citizens, the constitutional complaint is reserved.

183

2. Federal law is violated if a legal norm expressly stated in a federal provision or resulting therefrom was not applied or applied incorrectly.

3. Federal law is not violated by incorrect findings of facts unless these were made on basis of a violation of federal provisions on evidence.

4. An incorrect legal assessment is to be considered a violation of law.

Article 43a

(b) Foreign Law

1. *On appeal a claim may also be made that*:
   (a) *the challenged decision does not apply foreign law as required by the Swiss Private International Law*;
   (b) *the challenged decision unjustly finds that foreign law cannot be ascertained.*

2. *In case of civil disputes of non-financial interest the claim may also be made that the challenged decision applies the foreign law incorrectly.*

Article 44

Civil Matters of Non-financial Interest

. . .

Article 45

Civil Matters of Financial Interest, (a) Without Threshold Sum

. . .

Article 46

(b) With Threshold Sum

. . .

184

Article 47

(c)
Computation.
Counterclaim

. . .

Article 48

Decisions
Subject to
Appeal,
(a) Final
decisions

1. Appeal is possible, as a rule, only against decisions of last resort of the highest cantonal judicial or other decision-making authorities that may not be challenged by an ordinary cantonal judicial remedy.

1 bis
Cantonal decisions made pursuant to Art. 178 subs. 2 of the Federal Statute of December 18, 1987 on Private International Law are excepted.

. . .

Article 49

(b) Interim
Decisions on
Jurisdiction

1. Against separate preliminary or interim decisions on jurisdiction rendered by the authorities designated in Art. 48 subs. 1 and 2 appeal is possible for violation of federal provisions on subject matter jurisdiction, venue and international jurisdiction.

2. Final decisions made pursuant to Art. 191 subs. 2 of the Federal Statute of December 18, 1987 on Private International Law are excepted.

3. The constitutional complaint for violation of Art. 59 of the Swiss Federal Constitution is reserved.

Article 50

(c) Other
Interim
Decisions

1. Appeal against other separate interim or separate preliminary decisions, rendered by the authorities designated in Art. 48, subs. 1 and 2, is, by way of exception, possible if thereby a final decision can be reached immediately, and this results in considerable saving of

185

time or expense for an extended procedure for taking evidence, which justifies to call upon the Swiss Federal Supreme Court separately.

1 bis
Final decisions made pursuant to Art. 191 subs. 2 of the Federal Statute of December 18, 1987 on Private International law are excepted.

. . .

Article 54

Deadline for Appeal – Enforceability

1. An appeal must be filed within 30 days from the receipt of written notification of the decision (Art. 51 letter d) with the authority that rendered the decision. This deadline is not extended by filing an extraordinary cantonal judicial remedy or obtaining an order granting stay of execution.

2. Before the deadline has run for appeal and joining appeal, final decisions do not become enforceable, except to the extent this is required to file an extraordinary cantonal judicial remedy. By filing a permissible appeal or joining appeal enforcement is stayed to the extent of the motions.

. . .

Article 55

Appellate Brief

1. An appellate brief must designate the challenged decision and indicate the party against whom appeal is made, and include the following:
(a) In disputes of financial interest, if the dispute is not over a certain specified sum of money, the indication whether the amount in dispute is SFr. 15'000.-- or more or at least SFr. 8'000.-- or more, and the grounds which lead the appellant to contest a different finding of fact made below if there was one;
(b) The exact indication which items of the decision are challenged and which amendments are sought. It is not sufficient to simply refer to the motions made in the cantonal procedure. New motions are excluded.

(c) *The reasons for the motions. They shall state briefly which provisions of federal law are violated by the challenged decision, and how. Statements directed against findings of fact, new allegations of fact, defenses, denials, proofs, and comments on violations of cantonal law are excluded.*

(d) In case of a challenge of a finding of fact subject to assessment under federal law which was made by a cantonal authority and is claimed to be clearly based on oversight: The precise indication of the finding of fact and of the element of the record with which it conflicts.

. . .

Article 56

Notification.
Transfer of
the Record

. . .

Article 57

Extra-
ordinary
Cantonal
Remedies

. . .

Article 58

Interim
Orders

. . .

Article 59

Joining
Appeal

. . .

Article 60

Final
Disposition
in Summary,
Preliminary
Procedure

1. The Swiss Federal Supreme Court may, immediately or after having received the answer brief, unanimously and without public deliberation:

(a) decide not to hear the appeal

187

if it is inadmissible, or
if reasons of cantonal or foreign law are decisive in any event;

(b) take the measures foreseen in Art. 52;

(c) *reverse the challenged decision and remand the case to the cantonal authority for a new decision, if the dispute that it decided in full or in part under federal law should be decided exclusively under cantonal law.*

2. Once the deadline for joining appeal has similarly run, immediately or after having received the answer brief, the Swiss Federal Supreme Court may decide unanimously and without public deliberation to reject the appeal if it considers the appeal to be without any doubt unfounded.

3. The same provisions apply to joining appeal.

Art. 61

Answer

1. *The appellate brief is notified to the appellee. The appellee may within 30 days file a short answer. Article 55, subs. 1, letters a and d apply by analogy. New motions, allegations of facts, defenses, denials and proofs, and comments on the evidence and the violation of cantonal law are excluded.*
   . . .

Third Section: Action for Annulment before the Federal Supreme Court

Article 68

Grounds for
Annulment

1. *In civil matters that are not subject to appeal under Art. 44 to 46, an action for annulment may be brought against decisions of the cantonal authority of last resort:*

(a) *if instead of the applicable federal law, cantonal law was applied;*

(b) *if instead of the applicable federal law, foreign law was applied; or conversely.*

(c) *if foreign law other than that required by Swiss Private International Law was applied.*

(d) *if the foreign law applicable under the Swiss Private International Law was not or not properly ascertained;*

(e) *if provisions of federal law were violated, including international treaties concluded by the Confederation on subject matter jurisdiciton, venue and international jurisdiction. The constitutional complaint for violations of Art. 4 of the Federal Constitution is reserved.*

1 bis

Cantonal decisions made pursuant to Art. 191, subs. 2 of the Federal Statute of December 18, 1987 on Private International Law are excepted.

2. If independent decisions on jurisdiction were left unchallenged they may no longer be challenged together with the final decision.

Article 69

Deadline

1. The action for annulment must be filed within 30 days from the relevant notification under cantonal law with the authority which made the decision.

2. If, as a matter of course, written reasons for the decisions are subsequently supplied, the decision may still be challenged by action for annulment within 30 days of notification.

3. These deadlines are not extended by filing an extraordinary cantonal remedy, or by obtaining an order granting a stay of execution.

Article 70

Enforce-
ability

1. Action for annulment does not prevent enforceability.

2. On request the president of the Swiss Federal Supreme Court may stay execution of the challenged decision and make this depend on the posting of security.

Article 71

Brief

The brief in annulment must refer to the challenged decision and contain:
(a) The motions for relief by the complainant.

189

(b) Particulars of the content of the challenged decision unless it is attached in reasoned form. If a reasoned decision was made in writing, it must be attached; if it is not submitted within the last deadline set, the action for annulment is not heard.

(c) A short explanation of the alleged violation of law.

Article 72

Procedure   . . .

Article 73

Decision   . . .

Article 74

Additional   . . .
Provisions

Third Chapter: Enforcement of Debt and Bankruptcy Matters

Article 75

Cantonal   . . .
Supervisory
Authorities

Article 76

Supervisory   . . .
Procedure
(a) Record

Article 77

(b)   . . .
Notification
of Decisions

190

Article 78

Recourse to
the Supreme
Court
(a) Recipient

. . .

Article 79

(b) Recourse
Brief

. . .

Article 80

(c) Transfer
of Record

. . .

Article 81

(d)
Procedure
before
Supreme
Court

. . .

Article 82

Complaint to
Swiss
Federal
Supreme
Court for
Denial of
Justice

. . .

Fourth Chapter: Constitutional Law Matters before the Swiss Federal Supreme Court

Article 83

Constitution-
al Claims

The Swiss Federal Supreme Court decides:
(a) conflicts of jurisdiction between federal authorities on the one
    hand and cantonal authorities on the other;

(b) constitutional disputes between cantons if one of the cantons requests its decision;

(c) lawsuits filed by the Swiss Federal Council for granting citizenship to persons without citizenship pursuant to the Swiss Federal Statute of December 3, 1850 concerning persons without citizenship and citizenship disputes between municipalities of different cantons;

(d) disputes between authorities or different cantons on the application of the Swiss Federal Statute of June 25, 1891 concerning the civil law status of residents and sojourners.[1]

(e) disputes between guardianship authorities of different cantons on the rights and obligations of the guardianship authority of the place of citizenship and on the change of domicile of a person under guardianship.

[1]Abrogated by Appendix to PIL Statute. Letter d is accordingly obsolete.

Article 84

Constitutional Complaints (a) In General

1. Against cantonal enactments or decisions a complaint may be made to the Swiss Federal Supreme Court:

(a) For violation of constitutional rights of the citizen;

(b) For violation of concordats;

(c) For violation of international treaties, except for violation of civil or criminal provisions in international treaties by cantonal decisions;

(d) For violation of federal provisions on the subject matter jurisdiction and venue of authorities.

2. In all these cases, however, a complaint is admissible only if the alleged violation of the law cannot be challenged otherwise by lawsuit or judicial remedy to the Swiss Federal Supreme Court or another federal authority.

Article 85

(b) Special Cases

Further the Swiss Federal Supreme Court decides:

. . .

(c) *Actions for annulment of arbitral awards under Art. 190 et seq. of the Federal Statute on Private International Law.*

Article 86

Relationship with Cantonal Remedies

1. Complaints pursuant to Article 85 are admissible only against cantonal decisions of last resort.

2. Complaints for violation of constitutional rights of the citizens are admissible only when all cantonal judicial remedies have been exhausted; except in case of complaints because of violation of freedom to take domicile (Art. 45 of the Swiss Federal Constitution), the prohibition of double taxation (Art. 46, subs. 2 of the Swiss Federal Constitution), the guarantee of the constitutional judge (Art. 58 of the Swiss Federal Constitution), the guarantee of the judge at the domicile (Art. 59 of the Swiss Federal Constitution), the right of the citizens of other cantons to equal treatment with the citizens of the canton in legislation and judicial proceedings (Art. 60 of the Swiss Federal Constitution) and the right to judicial assistance (Art. 61 of the Swiss Federal Constitution).

3. The complainant may, however, also in these exceptional cases and in the cases of Art. 84 letter b), c) and d) first resort to the cantonal judicial remedies.

Article 87

Complaints because of Violation of Art. 4 of the Federal Constitution

The constitutional complaint because of violation of Art. 4 of the Swiss Federal Constitution is admissible only against final decisions of last resort, against interim decisions of last resort only if they lead to a disadvantage to the party concerned that can not be remedied.

Article 88

Standing

Citizen (private persons) and corporate bodies have standing to complain of violations of law which they have suffered through provisions or decisions that are generally applicable or that affect them personally.

Article 89

Deadline for Complaint

1. The complaint must be filed in with the Swiss Federal Supreme Court, in writing within 30 days after the provision or decision has been declared or notified effectively pursuant to cantonal law.

2. If, as a matter of course, written reasons for the decision are subsequently supplied, the complaint may still be filed within 30 days since notification of the reasoned version.

3. In case of complaints because of intercantonal conflict of jurisdiction the deadline for complaint begins to run only when in both cantons decisions were rendered against which constitutional complaint may be filed.

Article 90

Complaint Brief

1. The complaint brief must refer to the challenged decision and include:
(a) the motions of the complainant;
(b) the essential facts and a short statement which constitutional rights or which legal provisions were violated by the challenged provision or decision, and how.

2. If the complainant has access to a copy of the challenged decision he must attach it; if he fails to submit it, he is given a short deadline within which to comply, failing which the complaint is not heard.

Article 91

Instruction Procedure

. . .

Article 92

Summary Procedure

1. The Chamber, with three judges sitting, may without public deliberation before or after the exchange of written briefs unanimously decide not to hear a clearly inadmissible complaint or to reject a clearly unjustified complaint.

2. It may also, with three judges sitting, and without public deliberation, unanimously decide after the exchange of written briefs to accept a clearly justified complaint.

3. The decision must be summarily motivated.

Article 93

Exchange of
Briefs

. . .

Article 94

Provisional
Orders

The president of the Swiss Federal Supreme Court may after having received the complaint brief, upon motion of a party, take those provisional measures that are required to maintain an existing situation or provisionally secure endangered legal interests.

Article 95

Taking of
Evidence

. . .

Article 96

Relationship
with Other
Federal
Bodies

. . .

195

Swiss Intercantonal Concordat on Arbitration
of August 27, 1969, SR 279*

Chapter I. General Provisions

Scope

Art. 1[1]

1. This Concordat shall apply to any proceedings before an arbitral tribunal the seat of which is within one of the cantons party to this Concordat.[2]

2. The application of arbitration agreements and rules of private or public institutions is reserved insofar as they do not violate mandatory provisions of this Concordat.

3. The following provisions of this Concordat are mandatory: Art. 2 subs. 2 and 3, Art. 4 to 9, 12, 13, 18 to 21, 22 subs. 2, Art. 25, 26 to 29, 31 subs. 1, Art. 33, subs. 1, a to f, 2 and 3, and Art. 36 to 46.

> 1. If one of the parties is non-Swiss in the sense of Art. 176 of the PIL Statute, then the twelfth chapter of the PIL Statute (Art. 176 to 194) applies.
> This article applies to domestic arbitration in Concordat cantons only.
> 2. Two cantons are not (yet) members of the Concordat: Lucerne and Thurgau.
> In these cantons domestic arbitration is subject to separate cantonal legislation.

Seat of the Arbitral Tribunal[1]

Art. 2

1. The seat of the arbitral tribunal is at the place chosen by agreement between the parties or by a decision of the body designated by them, or if there is none, by decision of the arbitrators.

---

* This governs domestic arbitration in all cantons, except Lucerne and Thurgau.

Some provisions may be applicable by analogy in international arbitration pursuant to Art. 179 subs. 2 of the PIL Statute.

2. If neither the parties nor the body designated by them nor the arbitrators have chosen the place of arbitration, the seat shall be at the place of the court which would have jurisdiction over the case but for arbitration.

3. If more than one court would have jurisdiction in the sense of the preceding subsection, the seat of the arbitral tribunal is at the place of the first judicial authority seized as provided in Art. 3.

> 1. If one of the parties is non-Swiss in the sense of Art. 176 of the PIL Statute, then the twelfth chapter of that Statute (Art. 176 to 194) applies.
> This article applies to domestic arbitration in Concordat cantons (Art. 1) only. Subsections 2 and 3 are mandatory, see Art. 1 subs. 3 Concordat.

Jurisdiction of Judicial Authority at the Seat of the Arbitral Tribunal

Art. 3[1]

Subject to Art. 45 subsection 2, the superior court of common civil jurisdiction of the canton in which the seat of the arbitration is located has jurisdiction to:
(a) appoint arbitrators if they have not been designated by the parties or by the body chosen by the parties;
(b) decide on challenges of arbitrators, their removal and re-placement;
(c) extend the term of the arbitrators;
(d) assist in executing measures for taking evidence on the arbitral tribunal's request;
(e) accept deposit of the arbitral award and notify it;
(f) give judgment on actions for annulment or revision of awards;
(g) declare the award enforceable.

> 1. If one of the parties is non-Swiss in the sense of Art. 176 of the PIL Statute, then the twelfth chapter of that Statute (Art. 176 to 194) applies exclusively.
> This article applies to domestic arbitration in Concordat cantons (Art. 1) only.

Chapter II. Agreement to Arbitrate

Arbitration Agreements and Clauses

Art. 4[1]

1. An agreement to arbitrate is made by an arbitration agreement or an arbitration clause.

2. In an arbitration agreement the parties submit an existing dispute to arbitration.

3. An arbitration clause may refer only to future disputes arising from a particular legal relationship.

> 1. If one of the parties is non-Swiss in the sense of Art. 176 of the PIL Statute, then the twelfth chapter of that Statute (Art. 176 to 194) applies exclusively.
> This article applies in domestic arbitration in Concordat cantons (Art. 1) only where this article is mandatory, see Art. 1 subs. 3 Concordat.

Arbitrability

Art. 5[1]

Any right at the free disposal of the parties is arbitrable unless the case is subject to the exclusive jurisdiction of a State authority pursuant to a mandatory legal provision.

> 1. If one of the parties is non-Swiss in the sense of Art. 176 of the PIL Statute, Art. 177 of that Statute applies exclusively.
> This article applies in domestic arbitration in Concordat cantons (Art. 1) only where the article is mandatory, see Art. 1 subs. 3 Concordat.

Form

Art. 6[1]

1. The agreement to arbitrate must be in writing.

2. It may result from a written declaration to adhere to the statutes of a juridical person provided that the declaration expressly refer to the arbitration clause contained in the statutes or rules made pursuant to them.

1. If one of the parties is non-Swiss in the sense of Art. 176 of the PIL Statute, Art. 178 of that Statute applies exclusively.
This article applies in domestic arbitration in Concordat cantons (Art. 1) only where the article is mandatory, see Art. 1 subs. 3 Concordat.

Exclusion of Lawyers

Art. 7[1]

Any provision in an arbitration clause prohibiting the use of lawyers in an arbitration whether as arbitrators, secretaries or representatives of the parties is void.

1. This article applies in domestic arbitration in Concordat cantons (Art. 1) only where the article is mandatory, see Art. 1 subs. 3 Concordat.

Jurisdiction of the Arbitral Tribunal[1]

Art. 8[1]

1. If the validity of the agreement to arbitrate or its content or scope are challenged before the arbitral tribunal, it decides on its own jurisdiction by an interim or final award.

2. A plea of lack of jurisdiction of the arbitral tribunal must be raised prior to any defence on the merits.

1. If one of the parties is non-Swiss in the sense of Art. 176 of the PIL Statute, then the twelfth chapter of that Statute (Art. 176 to 194) applies exclusively.
This article applies in domestic arbitration in Concordat cantons (Art. 1) only where the article in mandatory, see Art. 1 subs. 3 Concordat.

Remedy as to Jurisdiction

Art. 9[1]

An interim award whereby the arbitral tribunal accepts or declines jurisdiction may be challenged immediately by action for annulment as provided in Art. 30 (b).

1. If one of the parties is non-Swiss in the sense of Art. 176 of the PIL Statute, then the twelfth chapter of that Statute (Art. 176 to 194) applies exclusively.
This article applies in domestic arbitration in Concordat cantons (Art. 1) only where the article is mandatory, see Art. 1 subs. 3 Concordat.

Chapter III. Designation, Appointment and Term of Arbitrators. Lis Pendens

Number of Arbitrators

Art. 10[1]

1. The arbitral tribunal shall consist of three arbitrators unless the parties have agreed on a different uneven number or on a sole arbitrator.

2. The parties may, however, agree to designate an even number of arbitrators without a chairman being designated.

> 1. If one of the parties is non-Swiss in the sense of Art. 176 of the PIL Statute, then the twelfth chapter of that Statute (Art. 176 to 194) applies. Art. 179 of the PIL Statute provides for analogous application of cantonal law in the absence of an agreement of the parties.
> This article applies directly in domestic arbitration in Concordat cantons (Art. 1) only.

Designation by the Parties

Art. 11[1]

1. The parties may designate the arbitrator or arbitrators by common consent in the agreement to arbitrate itself or in a later agreement. They may also cause them to be designated by a body of their choice.

2. If an arbitrator is designated only by reference to his office, the designation shall be deemed to refer to the holder of the office at the time of acceptance of the mandate as arbitrator.

3. Unless otherwise agreed, each party designates an equal number of arbitrators, and the arbitrators so designated unanimously elect a chairman.

4. Where the arbitrators are even in number, the parties shall agree either to give a casting vote to the chairman, or to require an unanimous or qualified majority vote from the tribunal.[2]

1. If one of the parties is non-Swiss in the sense of Art. 176 ff. of the PIL Statute, Art. 179 subs. 2 provides for analogous application of cantonal law in the absence of an agreement of the parties.

This article applies in domestic arbitration in Concordat cantons (Art. 1) only.

2. If one of the parties is non-Swiss in the sense of Art. 176 of the PIL Statute, then the twelfth chapter of that Statute (Art. 176 to 194) applies.

This paragraph applies in domestic arbitration in Concordat cantons only.

Appointment by the Judicial Authority

Art. 12

If the parties cannot agree on the designation of a sole arbitrator, if one of them fails to designate the arbitrator or arbitrators as required, or if the designated arbitrators cannot agree on a chairman, the judicial authority provided in Art. 3 shall make the appointment on petition by one of the parties, unless the agreement provides for another appointing body.

1. If one of the parties is non-Swiss in the sense of Art. 176 of the PIL Statute, then the twelfth chapter of that Statute (Art. 176 to 194) applies. Art. 179 subs. 2 provides for analogous application of cantonal law in the absence of an agreement of the parties.

This article applies directly in domestic arbitration in Concordat cantons (Art. 1) only where it is mandatory, see Art. 1 subs. 3.

Lis Pendens

Art. 13[1]

1. The arbitration is pending:
(a) from the time when one of the parties seizes the arbitrator or arbitrators designated in an arbitrator clause; or
(b) if there is no such designation in the arbitration clause, from the time when one of the parties commences the procedure for the designation of the arbitrators as provided in the arbitration clause; or
(c) if there is no such provision in the arbitration clause, from the time when one of the parties petitions the competent judicial authority; or
(d) if there is no arbitration clause, on the signing of the arbitration agreement.

2. If the arbitration rules accepted by the parties or the arbitration clause provide for a conciliation procedure, the commencement of this procedure shall be assimilated with the commencement of the arbitral proceedings.

1. If one of the parties is non-Swiss in the sense of Art. 176 of the PIL Statute, Art. 181 of the PIL Statute applies exclusively.

This article applies in domestic arbitration in Concordat cantons (Art. 1) only where the article is mandatory, see Art. 1 subs. 3 Concordat.

Acceptance by the Arbitrators

Art. 14[1]

1. The arbitrators must accept their mandate.

2. The arbitral tribunal shall be deemed to be properly constituted only when all the arbitrators have accepted their mandate with respect to the case submitted to them.

1. If one of the parties is non-Swiss in the sense of Art. 176 of the PIL Statute, Art. 179 subs. 2 of the PIL Statute provides for analogous application of cantonal law in the absence of an agreement of the parties.

This article applies directly in domestic arbitration in Concordat cantons (Art. 1) only.

Secretary

Art. 15[1]

1. With the agreement of the parties, the arbitral tribunal may designate a secretary.

2. Articles 18 to 20 shall be applicable to the challenge of a secretary.

1. If one of the parties is non-Swiss in the sense of Art. 176 of the PIL Statute, Art. 179 subs. 2 of the PIL Statute provides for analogous application of cantonal law in the absence of an agreement of the parties.

This article applies directly in domestic arbitration in Concordat cantons (Art. 1) only.

Term

Art. 16[1]

1. The parties may, either in an agreement to arbitrate or in a later agreement, impose a time limit on the authority of the arbitral tribunal.

2. In this case, the term may be extended each time for a certain period either by agreement between the parties, or by a decision of the judicial authority provided in Art. 3 on petition by one of the parties or by the arbitral tribunal.

3. If the petition is by one of the parties, the other party must be heard.

> 1. If one of the parties is non-Swiss in the sense of Art. 176 of the PIL Statute, Art. 179 subs. 2 of the PIL Statute provides for analogous application of cantonal law in the absence of an agreement of the parties.
> This article applies directly in domestic arbitration in Concordat cantons (Art. 1) only.

Unjustifiable Delay

Art. 17[1]

The parties may at any time petition the judicial authority provided in Art. 3 with respect to unjustifiable delay on the part of the arbitral tribunal.

> 1. If one of the parties is non-Swiss in the sense of Art. 176 of the PIL Statute, Art. 179 subs. 2 of the PIL Statute provides for analogous application of cantonal law in the absence of an agreement of the parties.
> This article applies directly in domestic arbitration in Concordat cantons (Art. 1) only.

Chapter IV. Challenge, Removal and Replacement of Arbitrators

Challenge of Arbitrator

Art. 18[1]

1. The parties may challenge an arbitrator on any grounds which the Statute on the Organization of the Federal Judiciary provides for the mandatory or voluntary withdrawal of the federal judges,[2] and on any grounds in the arbitration rules to which the parties have submitted.

2. Any arbitrator who has been deprived of the exercise of civil rights or who has been sentenced to deprivation of liberty for an infamous crime or misdemeanor may also be challenged.

3. A party may not challenge an arbitrator designated by him unless the ground for such objection arises after such designation, or he establishes that he was not aware of it at the time of designation.

> 1. If one of parties is non-Swiss in the sense of Art. 176 of the PIL Statute, Art. 180 of the PIL Statute applies exclusively.
> This article applies in domestic arbitration in Concordat cantons (Art. 1) only where the article is mandatory, see Art. 1 subs. 3 Concordat.
>
> 2. See appendix II, Art. 4, 22 and 23.

Challenge of the Arbitral Tribunal

Art. 19[1]

1. The arbitral tribunal as such may be challenged if one of the parties has exercised an overriding influence on the designation of its members.

2. A new arbitral tribunal is established according to the method provided for in Art. 11.

3. The parties may still designate as an arbitrator any member of the tribunal that was challenged.

1. If one of the parties is non-Swiss in the sense of Art. 176 of the PIL Statute, Art. 180 of the PIL Statute applies exclusively.
This article applies in domestic arbitration in Concordat cantons (Art. 1) only where the article is mandatory, see Art. 1 subs. 3 Concordat.

Time Limit

Art. 20¹

The challenge must be made before an appearance on the merits, or as soon as the challenging party has knowledge of the grounds for challenge.

1. If one of the parties is non-Swiss in the sense of Art. 176 of the PIL Statute, Art. 180 of the PIL Statute, Art. 187 189 and 190 of the Pil Statute applies exclusively.
This article applies in domestic arbitration in Concordat cantons (Art. 1) only where the article is mandatory, see Art. 1 subs. 3 Concordat.

Dispute

Art. 21¹

1. In case of dispute, the judicial authority provided for in Art. 3 shall decide on the challenge.

2. The parties may present evidence.

1. If one of the parties is non-Swiss in the sense of Art. 176 of the PIL Statute, Art. 180 of the PIL Statute applies exclusively.
This article applies in domestic arbitration in Concordat cantons (Art. 1) only where the article is mandatory, see Art. 1 subs. 3 Concordat.

Removal

Art. 22¹

1. Any arbitrator may be removed by a written agreement of the parties.

2. The judicial authority provided for in Art. 3 on petition of one of the parties may also remove an arbitrator for cause.

205

1. If one of the party is non-Swiss in the sense of Art. 176 of the PIL Statute, Art. 179 subs. 2 of the PIL Statute provides for analogous application of cantonal law in the absence of an agreement of the parties.

This article applies directly in domestic arbitration in Concordat cantons (Art. 1) only where the article is mandatory, see Art. 1 subs. 3 Concordat.

Replacement

Art. 23[1]

1. If an arbitrator dies, resigns, is challenged or removed he shall be replaced according to the method adopted for his designation or appointment.

2. If such replacement cannot take place, the new arbitrator shall be appointed by the judicial authority provided for in Art. 3, unless it follows from the agreement to arbitrate that it must be deemed to have lapsed.

3. Unless otherwise agreed, the judicial authority provided for in Art. 3, after consultation with the arbitral tribunal, shall determine the extent to which the proceedings in which the replaced arbitrator took part shall remain valid.

4. The replacement of one or several arbitrators shall not postpone the running of the time limit in which the arbitral tribunal may be required to make its award.

1. If one of the party is non-Swiss in the sense of Art. 176 of the PIL Statute, Art. 179 subs. 2 of the PIL Statute provides for analogous application of cantonal law in the absence of an agreement of the parties.

This article applies directly in domestic arbitration in Concordat cantons (Art. 1) only.

Chapter V. Procedure before the Arbitrators

Determination

Art. 24[1]

1. The rules of procedure before the arbitrators shall be determined by agreement between the parties, or if there is none, by decision of the arbitral tribunal.

2. If the rules of procedure have been determined neither by agreement between the parties nor by a decision of the arbitral tribunal, the Federal Code of Civil Procedure shall apply by analogy.

1. If one of the parties is non-Swiss in the sense of Art. 176 of the PIL Statute, Art. 182 of the PIL Statute applies exclusively.

This article applies in domestic arbitration in Concordat cantons (Art. 1) only.

Right to Be Heard

Art. 25[1]

The rules of procedure selected must in any case respect the principle of equality of the parties and permit both parties:
(a) to exercise their right to be heard and in particular to present their factual and legal arguments;
(b) to have sufficient time to become acquainted with the file;
(c) to participate at the hearings for taking of evidence or argument that the arbitral tribunal may conduct;
(d) to be represented or assisted by a representative of their choice.

1. If one of the parties is non-Swiss in the sense of Art. 176 of the PIL Statute, Art. 182 and 190 to 192 of the PIL Statute apply exclusively.

This article applies in domestic arbitration in Concordat cantons (Art. 1) only where the article is mandatory, see Art. 1 subs. 3 Concordat.

Provisional Orders

Art. 26[1]

1. The ordinary judicial authorities alone have jurisdiction to make provisional orders.

2. However, the parties may voluntarily submit to a provisional order proposed by the arbitral tribunal.

1. If one of the parties is non-Swiss in the sense of Art. 176 of the PIL Statute, Art. 182 of the PIL Statute applies exclusively.

This article applies in domestic arbitration in Concordat cantons (Art. 1) only where the article is mandatory, see Art. 1 subs. 3 Concordat.

CONCORDAT

Assitance of the Judicial Authorities

Art. 27[1]

1. The arbitral tribunal shall itself take evidence.

2. If necessary, the arbitral tribunal may request the assistance of the judicial authority provided for in Art. 3. That authority proceeds under cantonal law.

1. If one of the parties is non-Swiss in the sense of Art. 176 of the PIL Statute, Art. 182 and 183 of the PIL Statute apply exclusively.
This article applies in domestic aribtration in Concordat cantons (Art. 1) only where the article is mandatory, see Art. 1 subs. 3 Concordat.

Third Party Practice

Art. 28[1]

1. The intervention or calling of a third party may be admitted only by virtue of an agreement to arbitrate between the third party and the parties in dispute.

2. Moreover, third party practice is subject to the consent of the arbitral tribunal.[2]

1. This article applies in domestic arbitration in Concordat cantons (Art. 1) only where the article is mandatory, see Art. 1 subs. 3 Concordat.

2. What is meant is 'the arbitrators'.

Set-off

Art. 29[1]

1. Where one of the parties pleads a set-off on the basis of a legal relationship for which the arbitral tribunal lacks jurisdiction under the terms of the agreement to arbitrate, and the parties do not agree to extend the arbitration to that legal relationship, the proceedings shall be stayed, and a reasonable time shall be allowed to the party making the exception to establish it before the court having jurisdiction.

2. When the court having jurisdiction has made a determination, the proceedings are resumed upon motion of one of the parties.

3. If the arbitral tribunal has been given a time limit in which to make its award, such period shall not continue to run during the stay of proceedings.

> 1. This article applies in domestic arbitration in Concordat cantons (Art. 1) only where the article is mandatory, see Art. 1 subs. 3 Concordat.

Advance on Costs

Art. 30[1]

1. The arbitral tribunal may order an advance of foreseeable costs and may make the procedural process dependent thereon. It shall determine the amount to be advanced by each party.

2. If one of the parties fails to advance the sums required, the other party may either advance all the costs or forego the arbitration. In the latter course, the parties are no longer bound by the agreement to arbitrate with respect to the dispute in question.

> 1. If one of the parties is non-Swiss in the sense of Art. 176 of the PIL Statute, the arbitration rules agreed by the parties may deal with the point, Art. 182 of the PIL Statute. Otherwise Art. 182 of the PIL Statute should give the arbitral tribunal the required power.
>
> This article applies in domestic arbitration in Concordat cantons (Art. 1) only.

Chapter VI. Arbitral Award

Deliberation and Award

Art. 31[1]

1. All arbitrators must participate in all deliberations and decisions of the arbitral tribunals.

2. The award is made by a simple majority of votes, unless the agreement to arbitrate requires unanimity or a qualified majority. Art. 11 subsection 4 is reserved.

3. The arbitral tribunal decides according to the rules of the applicable law, unless the parties have, in the agreement to arbitrate, authorized it to judge ex aequo et bono.

4. The arbitral tribunal may not award a party more or other than claimed, unless a particular provision of law authorizes it to do so.

> 1. If one of the parties is non-Swiss in the sense of Art. 176 of the PIL Statute Art. 187, 189 and 190 of the PIL Statute apply exclusively.
> This article applies in domestic aribtration in Concordat cantons (Art. 1) only where the article is mandatory, see Art. 1 subs. 3 Concordat.

Partial Awards

Art. 32[1]

Unless the parties agree otherwise, the arbitral tribunal may make several awards.

> 1. If one of the parties is non-Swiss in the sense of Art. 176 of the PIL Statute, Art. 188 of the PIL Statute applies exclusively.
> This article applies in domestic arbitration in Concordat cantons (Art. 1) only.

Content of the Award

Art. 33[1]

1. The arbitral award shall specify:
(a) the names of the arbitrators;
(b) the designation of the parties;
(c) the seat of the arbitration;
(d) the relief prayed for by the parties or, in default of such, the question to be determined;
(e) the factual, legal, and, as the case may be, ex aequo et bono reasons for the decision, unless the parties expressly waive this requirement;
(f) the decision on the merits;
(g) the decision as to the amount and burden of costs.

2. The award shall be dated and signed by the arbitrators. The signature of the majority of the arbitrators shall suffice if there is a statement in the award that the minority refuses to sign.

3. If the mandate of the arbitral tribunal is to designate one or more arbitrators, subs. 1 (c) of this article does not apply.

1. If one of the parties is non-Swiss in the sense of Art. 176 of the PIL Statute, Art. 189 of the PIL Statute applies exclusively.

This article applies in domestic arbitration in Concordat cantons (Art. 1), where the whole article except subs. 1 g is mandatory.

Consent Award

Art. 34[1]

If the parties settle their dispute in arbitration, the arbitral tribunal records this in the form of an award.

1. If one of the parties is non-Swiss in the sense of Art. 176 of the PIL Statute, Art. 189 of the PIL Statute applies exclusively.

This article applies in domestic arbitration in Concordat cantons (Art. 1) only.

Deposit and Notification

Art. 35[1]

1. The arbitral tribunal shall attend to the deposit of the award with the judicial authority provided in Art. 3.

2. The award shall be deposited in the original, where subsection 4 applies, together with as many copies as there are parties.

3. If the award is not drafted in one of the official languages of the Swiss Confederation,[2] the authority with whom it is deposited may require an authenticated translation of the award.

4. Such authority shall notify the parties of the award and shall inform them of the date of deposit.

5. The parties may waive deposit. They may likewise waive notification of the award by the judicial authority; in this case, the notification shall be attended to by the arbitral tribunal.

1. If one of the parties is non-Swiss in the sense of Art. 176 of the PIL Statute, Art. 193 of the PIL Statute applies exclusively.

This article applies in domestic arbitration in Concordat cantons (Art. 1) only.

2. German, French or Italian.

Chapter VII. Action for Annulment and Revision

I. Action for Annulment
Grounds

Art. 36[1]

An action for annulment of the arbitral award may be brought before the judicial authority provided for in Art. 3 where it is alleged that:
(a) the arbitral tribunal was not properly constituted;
(b) that the arbitral tribunal mistakenly accepted or declined jurisdiction;
(c) that it awarded points not submitted to it or, subject to Art. 32, failed to make a determination on one of the items in the claim;
(d) that there was a breach of one of the mandatory procedural rules referred to in Art. 25;
(e) that the arbitral tribunal awarded to one of the parties more or other than claimed, without being authorized to do so by a provision of law;
(f) that the award is arbitrary in that it was based on findings which were manifestly contrary to the facts appearing in the file, or in that it constitutes a clear violation of law or fairness;
(g) that the arbitral tribunal made its award after the expiration of the time limit imposed upon it to accomplish its mission;
(h) that the conditions of Art. 33 were not complied with or that the order is unintelligible or contradictory;
(i) that the fees of the arbitrators fixed by the arbitral tribunal are manifestly excessive.

1. If one of the parties is non-Swiss in the sense of Art. 176 of the PIL Statute, Art. 190 to 192 of the PIL Statute apply exclusively.
   This article applies in domestic arbitration in Concordat cantons (Art. 1) only where the article is mandatory, see Art. 1 subs. 3 Concordat.

Deadline

Art. 37[1]

1. The action for annulment must be brought within 30 days of the notification of the award.

2. The action shall be admissible only if all arbitral remedies provided in the agreement of the parties have been exhausted.

1. If one of the parties is non-Swiss in the sense of Art. 176 of the PIL Statute, Art. 191, 192 of the PIL Statute and Art. 92 of the Swiss Federal Statute on the Organization of the Federal Judiciary (Appendix II) apply exclusively.

This article applies in domestic arbitration in Concordat cantons (Art. 1) only where the article is mandatory, see Art. 1 subs. 3 Concordat.

Suspensive Effect of Action

Art. 38[1]

The action shall not have suspensive effect. However, the judicial authority provided for in Art. 3 may grant such effect on one of the parties' request.

1. This applies to domestic arbitrations in Concordat cantons (Art. 1) only where it is mandatory, see Art. 1 subs. 3 Concordat.

Remand to the Arbitral Tribunal

Art. 39[1]

The judicial authority seized of the action may, having heard the parties, and if it sees fit, remand the award to the arbitral tribunal and impose a deadline to amend or supplement the award.

1. This article applies to domestic arbitrations in Concordat cantons (Art. 1) only where it is mandatory, see Art. 1 subs. 3 Concordat.

Decision

Art. 40[1]

1. If the judicial authority does not remand the award to the arbitral tribunal or if the award is not amended or supplemented within the deadline, the judicial authority shall give judgment on the action for annulment, and if it finds such action well-founded it may annul the award.

2. The annulment may relate only to certain items in the award, unless the other items are dependent on them.

3. If the action is based on Art. 36 letter (i), the award shall be annulled only in respect of the fees, and the judicial authority shall itself determine the amount of such fees.

4. If the award is annulled, the arbitrators shall decide anew, unless they are challenged on the ground that they participated in the previous proceedings or on some other ground.

1. This applies to domestic arbitrations in Concordat cantons (Art. 1) only where it is mandatory, see Art. 1, subs. 3 Concordat.

II. Revision

Art. 41[1]

The award may be reviewed:
(a) If it was influenced by acts that are punishable according to Swiss law. Such acts must be established in a criminal sentence unless the criminal proceedings could not result in a conviction for reasons other than lack of evidence.
(b) If it was issued in ignorance of important facts in existence prior to the award or of evidence of decisive importance, and it was impossible for the petitioner to present such facts or evidence during the proceedings.

1. If one of the parties is non-Swiss in the sense of Art. 176 of the PIL Statute, the PIL Statute applies exclusively which does not provide for 'revision' of awards.
This applies to domestic arbitrations in Concordat cantons (Art. 1) only where it is mandatory, see Art. 1, subs. 3 Concordat.

Deadline

Art. 42[1]

The action for revision must be brought before the judicial authority provided for in Art. 3 within 60 days of the date on which the petitioner became aware of the grounds for revision. However, it may not be brought later than five years after the notification of the award.

1. This applies to domestic arbitrations in Concordat cantons (Art. 1) only where it is mandatory, see Art. 41.

Remand to the Arbitral Tribunal

Art. 43[1]

1. If the action for revision succeeds, the judicial authority shall remand the case to the arbitral tribunal for new decision.

2. Arbitrators unable to act shall be replaced in accordance with the provisions of Art. 3.

3. If it is necessary to constitute a new arbitral tribunal, the arbitrators shall be designated or appointed in accordance with Art. 10 to 12.

4. If the case is remanded to the arbitral tribunal, Art. 16 shall be applied by analogy.

> 1. This article applies to domestic arbitrations in Concordat cantons (Art. 1) only where it is mandatory, see Art. 41.

Chapter VIII. Enforcement of Arbitral Awards

Declaration of Enforceability

Art. 44[1]

1. Upon petition of one of the parties, the judicial authority provided for in Art. 3 shall declare enforceable, to the same extent as a judgment, any arbitral award:
(a) which the parties have formally accepted; or
(b) in respect of which no action for annulment has been brought within the deadline stipulated in Art. 37 subsection 1; or
(c) in respect of which an action for annulment has been brought within the deadline, but no suspensive effect was granted; or
(d) in respect of which an action for annulment has been dismissed or is statute-barred. The declaration of enforceability may not be issued if the award is contrary to Art. 5.

2. The certificate of enforceability of the arbitral award is affixed at the bottom of the award.

3. The arbitral award may not be provisionally enforced.

> 1. If one of the parties is non-Swiss in the sense of Art. 176 of the PIL Statute, Art. 193 of the PIL Statute applies exclusivley.
> This article applies in domestic arbitration in Concordat cantons (Art. 1) only where the article is mandatory, see Art. 1 subs. 3 Concordat.

Chapter IX. Final Provisions

Procedure

Art. 45[1]

1. The cantons determine the procedure before the judicial authority provided in Art. 3. Decisions on appointment, removal and replacement of arbitrators are subject to summary procedure.

2. The cantons may vest jurisdiction in part or in whole, in accordance with Art. 3 a to e and g, in a judicial authority other than that provided for in that article. In this case, the parties may, nevertheless, submit their application to the superior court of common civil jurisdiction of the canton.

> 1. If one of the parties is non-Swiss in the sense of Art. 176 of the PIL Statute, Art. 178 of the PIL Statute, Art. 178 of the PIL Statute provides for analogous application of cantonal law in the absence of an agreement of the parties.
> This article applies directly in domestic arbitration in Concordat cantons (Art. 1) only.

Consequence of Entry into Force

Art. 46

On entry into force of this Concordat in a canton, all statutory provisions of that canton concerning arbitration shall be abrogated. Article 45 is reserved.[1]

> 1. In international arbitration, Art. 176 et seq. and 195 et seq. of the PIL Statute apply. Art. 195 et seq. of the PIL Statute are not entirely clear in their application to international arbitrations.
> In domestic arbitration in Concordat cantons (Art. 1), the article is mandatory.
> In Zurich, the Concordat entered into force on July 1, 1985 only, and arbitrations then pending, including judicial remedies, were to be continued under the repealed provisions of the Zurich Cantonal Code of Civil Procedure (ZPO).

In Zurich, the combined effect of these provisions is possibly as follows: Domestic arbitrations commenced before July 1, 1985, including judicial remedies, are governed by the repealed provisions of the Cantonal Code of Civil Procedure (ZPO). Domestic arbitrations commenced on or after July 1, 1985 including judicial remedies, are governed by the Concordat. International arbitrations commenced before July 1, 1985, are governed by the repealed ZPO provisions until at least January 1, 1989, and possibly continue at the trial level under the PIL Statute, but judicial remedies pending on January 1, 1989 are decided under the repealed ZPO provisions. International arbitrations commenced after July 1, 1985 are governed by the Concordat until at least January 1, 1989 and possibly continue at the trial level under the PIL Statute, but judicial remedies pending on January 1, 1989 are decided under the Concordat.

Bibliography

Achermann, *Hubert*, Studien zu Auslegungsproblemen des Abkommens zwischen der Schweizerischen Eidgenossenschaft und dem Fürstentum Liechtenstein über die Anerkennung und Vollstreckung von gerichtlichen Entscheiden und Schiedssprüchen in Zivilsachen vom 25. April 1968. Diss. Bern (1983).

Ansay, *Tugrul*, Problems of Migrant Workers in Europe. In: The Reform of Family Law in Europe, (Deventer 1978) 323–338 (France, Federal Republic of Germany, Switzerland, Belgium, Netherlands, Luxembourg, Austria, Sweden, United Kingdom).

Arnold, *Karl*, Worker Participation in Management, Switzerland. In: Comparative Law Yearbook Vol. 4 (1980) 143–151.

Aubert, *Gabriel*, Der Arbeitsvertrag im internationalen Privatrecht der Schweiz. Schweizerische Juristische Kartothek, Karten 1985, Nr. 843.

Aubert, *Jean-François*, Renvoi in Swiss Law, American Journal of Comparative Law 5 (1956) 478–486.

Aubert, *Jean-François*, Switzerland: International Jurisdiction, American Journal of Comparative Law 8 (1959) 228.

Barmann, *Isabelle*, La condition juridique de la femme mariée en droit international privé suisse. Thèse Lausanne (1982).

Beitzke, *Günther*, Das Deliktsrecht im schweizerischen IPR-Entwurf. Schweizerisches Jahrbuch für internationales Recht 35 – Annuaire suisse de droit international (1979, ersch. 1980) 93–114.

Bischof, *Thomas*, Ausgewählte IPR-Probleme des Grundstückkaufs. Praetor (1986) Nr. 4/5; 18–22.

Brunner, *Alexander*, Allgemeine Geschäftsbedingungen im internationalen Privatrecht (AGB im IPR): unter Berücksichtigung des internationalen Zivilprozessrechts mit rechtsvergleichenden Hinweisen (materielles Recht und Kollisionsrecht) de lege lata und de lege ferenda. Diss. Zürich (1985). Handels- und Wirtschaftsrecht 19.

219

Brunschwig François; Lévy, Laurent, The Commercial Laws of the World, Switzerland. Nelson (ed.) Commercial Law VI (Switzerland).

Bucher, Andreas, Adoption, internationales Privatrecht. Schweizerische Juristische Kartothek, Karten 1980, Nr. 157–161.

Bucher, Andreas, Auslegungsregeln in der neueren Gesetzgebung des schweizerischen internationalen Privatrechts. In: Festschrift für Arthur Meier-Hayoz (1982) 45–64.

Bucher, Andreas, Zivilrechtliche Schadenersatz- und Unterlassungsklagen – Gerichtliche Zuständigkeit und Verfahrensfragen (Schweiz) In: Rechtsfragen grenzüberschreitender Umweltbelastungen, (Berlin 1984) 175–182.

Bucher, Andreas, Transnationales Recht im IPR. In: Aktuelle Fragen zum Europarecht, (Wien 1986) 11–59.

Buchner, Herbert, Zur internationalen Zuständigkeit des Konkursverwalters, speziell im deutsch-schweizerischen Verhältnis. Blätter für Schuldbetreibung und Konkurs 50 (1986) 41–53, 81–87.

Bundesgesetz über das internationale Privatrecht. Darstellung der Stellungnahmen auf Grund des Gesetzesentwurfs der Expertenkommission und des entsprechenden Begleitberichts. Bern, Bundesamt für Justiz (1980).

Bünten, Norbert, Grundzüge des schweizerischen Ehe- und Erbrechts unter Einschluss des Internationalen Privatrechts. Mitteilungen der Rhein. Notarkammer (1984) 1–12.

Burckhardt, Thomas, Zum gegenwärtigen Stand der Revision des Rechtes der internationalen Schiedsgerichte. Schweizerische Juristenzeitung 81 (1985) 297–301.

Butty, Philippe, Les règles juridiques relatives à l'implantation des filiales et des succursales de sociétés anonymes suisses dans les pays du Marché commun. Thèse Lausanne. (Genève 1983).

Campiglio, Cristina, L'esperienza svizzera in tema di clausola d'eccezione: l'art. 14 del progetto di riforma del diritto internazionale privato. Rivista di diritto internazionale privato e processuale 21 (1985) 47–88.

de Chedid, Bernard, Le transfert du siège des sociétés anonymes: étude de droit international privé. Thèse Lausanne (1983).

Council of Europe. The Practical Guide to the Recognition and Enforcement of Foreign Judicial Decisions in Civil and Commercial Law. Switzerland, 146–164. (Strasbourg, 1975).

Dallèves, Louis, Faillites internationales et droit suisse. Le dogme de la territorialité remis en question. Blätter für Schuldbetreibung und Konkurs 46 (1982) 81–91.

Dessemontet, François, Les contrats de licence en droit international privé. In: Mélanges Guy Flattet (1985) 435–453.

Dessemontet, François; *Ansay Tugrul*, Introduction to Swiss Law. (Deventer 1981).

Le divorce en droit international privé allemand, français et suisse. Actes du colloque des 11–12 mai 1979. (Paris, 1980). Travaux de l'Institut de droit comparé. – Annales de la Faculté de droit et des sciences politiques et de l'Institut de recherches juridiques, politiques et sociales de Strasbourg 30.

Le droit de la faillite internationale. Premier Séminaire de droit international et de droit européen, Neuchâtel, 11–12 octobre 1985. (Zürich 1986). Etudes suisses de droit international 46. Beiträge: PHILIPPE JUNOD, Tendances actuelles de la jurisprudence du Tribunal fédéral en matière de faillite prononcée à l'étranger avec des biens situés en Suisse. – HANS HANISCH, Procédure d'insolvabilité interne comprenant des biens situés à l'étranger. – HENRI-ROBERT SCHÜPBACH, L'exécution collective dans quelques pays d'Europe (Allemagne, Autriche, France, Italie, Liechtenstein). – LOUIS DALLEVES, Les accords bilatéraux en matière de faillite, notamment la Convention franco-suisse de 1869. – LUTZ KRAUSKOPF, Les aspects internationaux de la faillite dans le projet de revision de la LP. – PIERRE-ROBERT GILLIERON, La faillite et le concordat dans le projet de loi fédérale sur le droit international privé. – JEAN-FRANÇOIS EGLI; Deux aspects internationaux du séquestre, de lege ferenda.

Dubler, César E., Les clauses d'exception en droit international privé. Thèse Fribourg. (Genève 1983). Etudes suisses de droit international 35.

Dutoit, Bernard, Le nouveau droit international privé suisse en matière de droit de famille comparé à la récente loi yougoslave sur le droit international privé. In: Premières journées juridiques yougoslavo-suisse Lausanne et

221

Fribourg, 16–19 novembre 1983, (Zürich 1984) 7–33. Publications de l'Institut suisse de droit comparé 2.

Dutoit, Bernard, L'ordre public: caméléon du droit international privé? Un survol de la jurisprudence suisse. In: Mélanges Guy Flattet (1985) 455–472.

Dutoit, Bernard; Majoros, Ferenc, Le lacis des conflits de conventions en droit privé et leurs solutions possibles. Revue critique de droit international privé 73 (1984) 565–596.

Ebenroth, Carsten, Unternehmensrecht und Internationales Privatrecht. In: Festschrift für Arthur Meier-Hayoz (1982) 101–124.

Egger, Andrea, Le transfert de la propriété dans les successions internationales. Etude comparative de droit interne et de droit international. Thèse Neuchâtel, (Genève 1982). Etudes suisses de droit international 26

Enforcing antitrust against foreign enterprises. Procedural Problems in the Extraterritorial Application of Antitrust Laws. General Rapporteur: Cornelis Canenbley. (National Report Switzerland: Michel Haymann.) (Deventer 1981).

Erne, Monica, Vertragsgültigkeit und drittstaatliche Eingriffsnormen. Rechtsvergleichende Studie aus dem internationalen Privatrecht. Diss. Zürich. (Zürich 1985). Schweizer Studien zum internationalen Recht 41

Eulau, Peter H., Inducing Breach of Contract: A Comparison of the Laws of the United States, France, The Federal Republic of Germany and Switzerland. Boston College International and Comparative Law Journal (1978) 41–68.

The European Business World and the Extraterritorial Application of United States Economic Regulations. Hrg. von ROGER ZÄCH. Wirtschaft und Recht, 35 (1983) 67–247, Sonderheft. Beiträge: I. The U.S. Theory and Practice of Extraterritoriality: DETLEV F. VAGTS, The Scope of Application and Enforcement of U.S. Laws. – FRANK VISCHER, The United States Jurisdictional Concepts Viewed from Abroad. II. Antitrust laws: JOHN H. SHENEFIELD, Extraterritorial Application of United States Antitrust Laws: Economic Imperialism or Correcting the Evil at the Source? – FERDINAND ELSENER, Extraterritorial Application of U.S. Antitrust Laws: the Viewpoint of a European Lawyer. III. Trade and Financial Controls: ROBERT B. OWEN, Extraterritorial Application of U.S. Trade and Financial Controls: Freezings, Vestings, Embargoes etc. – HEINRICH GATTIKER, Foreign Policy Objectives and the Extraterritorial Application of Law. IV. Securities Laws: BEVIS LONGSTRETH, Toward Neutral Principles of International Securities Regulation. –

WERNER DE CAPITANI, The Swiss Banks and the United States Securities Laws. V. Legal Assistance in Switzerland: LIONEL FREI, The Service of Process and the Taking of Evidence on Behalf of U.S. Proceedings – the Problem of Granting Assistance. – GABRIELLE KAUFMANN-KOHLER, Enforcement of United States Judgments in Switzerland. – GEORG FRIEDLI, Statements on International Legal Assistance from the Viewpoint of one of the Large Swiss Banks.

Fisch, Pius, Eigentumserwerb, Eigentumsvorbehalt und Sicherungsübereignung an Fahrnis im internationalen Sachenrecht der Schweiz, der Bundesrepublik Deutschland und Frankreichs. Diss. Freiburg (Entlebuch 1985).

Flattet, Guy; Dupuis, Michel, Les conventions de droit international privé. Lausanne, Université. Travaux de l'Institut d'études de droit international de la Faculté de droit de Lausanne. 1: Obligations alimentaires (1982).

Flattet, Guy; Dupuis, Michel; Cuccio, Roanne, Les conventions de droit international privé. Lausanne, Université. Travaux de l'Institut d'études de droit international de la Faculté de droit de Lausanne. 2: Procédure civile. T.1: Entraide judiciaire (1983). T.2: Exécution des jugements (1984). T.3: Exécution des sentences arbitrales. (1985).

Forstmoser, Peter; Meier, Walter, Switzerland. In: Ellis and Storm (ed.), Business Law in Europe (1982) 513–553.

Frei, Lionel, Discovery, Secrecy, and International Mutual Assistance in Civil Matters. In: Litigation of Business Matters in the United States and International Legal Assistance, (Bern 1984) 169–214. St. Galler Studien zum Privat-, Handels- und Wirtschaftsrecht 3.

Fribourg Colloque, Freiburger Kolloquium über den schweizerischen Entwurf zu einem Bundesgesetz über das internationale Privatrecht, Freiburg (Schweiz) 27–28. April 1979 – Colloque de Fribourg relatif au projet suisse de loi fédérale sur le droit international privé (Zürich 1979). Schweizer Studien zum internationalen Recht 14.

Furgler, Dominik, Die Anknüpfung der Vertragsform im internationalen Privatrecht: der Ausgleich zwischen Parteiautonomie und Schutz des Schwächeren, insbesondere im schweizerischen IRP-Entwurf. Diss. Freiburg. (Zürich 1985).

Gessner, Anne-Françoise; Mayer, Geneviève, L'adoption dans les principales législations européennes: droit international privé suisse. Revue internationale de droit comparé 37 (1985) 865–884.

Gilléron, Pierre-Robert, Le droit de la faillite dans le droit international privé suisse de lege ferenda. In: Mélanges Guy Flattet (1985) 237–273.

Gonzenbach, Gerald C., Die akzessorische Anknüpfung. Ein Beitrag zur Verwirklichung des Vertrauensprinzips im IPR. Diss. Zürich. (Zürich 1986). Schweizer Studien zum internationalen Recht 47.

Grossen, Jaques-Michel, Aspects of de facto Marriage Under Switzerland's Private Law, 258–264. In: Eckelaar and Katz (ed.), Marriage and Cohabitation in Contemporary Societies. (Toronto 1980).

Gutzwiller, Max, Der Entwurf zu einer Kodifikation des schweizerischen International privatrechts, Zeitschrift für Schweizerisches Recht 98 I (1979) 1–31.

Gutzwiller, Max, Die Botschaft des Bundesrates zum Bundesgesetz über das internationale Privatrecht. Zeitschrift für Schweizerisches Recht 102 I (1983) 277–291.

Gutzwiller, Peter-Max, Der Trust in der schweizerischen Rechtspraxis. Schweizerisches Jahrbuch für internationales Recht 41 (1985) 53–56.

Habscheid, Walther J., Bemerkungen zur Rechtshängigkeitsproblematik im Verhältnis der Bundesrepublik Deutschland und der Schweiz einerseits und den USA andererseits. In: Festschrift für Konrad Zweigert (1981) 109–125.

Habscheid, Walther J., Zur internationalen Schiedsgerichtsbarkeit in der Schweiz. Konkurs-, Treuhand- und Schiedsgerichtswesen, (Köln 1982) 577–589.

Habscheid, Walther J., Les mesures provisoires en procédure civile – droits allemand et suisse. In: Les mesures provisoires en procédure civile, (Milano 1985) 33–53.

Hahn, Dominique, L'arbitrage commercial international en Suisse face aux règles de la CEE. Thèse Lausanne. (Genève 1983). Etudes suisses de droit international 36.

Hangartner, Yvo, (Hrsg.), Die allgemeinen Bestimmungen des Bundesgesetzes über das internationale Privatrecht. Referate und Unterlagen der Tagung vom 22. Oktober 1987 in Luzern.

Hanisch, Hans, Aktuelle Probleme des internationalen Insolvenzrechts. Schweizerisches Jahrbuch für internationales Recht 36 (1980, ersch. 1981) 109–136.

Hanisch, Hans, Gründe und Wege für eine Neuregelung des internationalen Insolvenzrechts. Liechtensteinische Juristen-Zeitung 3 (1982) 65–73.

Hanisch, Hans, Realisierung einer Forderung des deutschen Gemeinschuldners gegen einen Schuldner in der Schweiz zugunsten der deutschen Konkursmasse (zu Schweizerisches Bundesgericht, 7.12. 1981-ZIP 1982, 596). Praxis des Internationalen Privat- und Verfahrensrechts (1983) 195–198.

Hauser, Robert, Ausgewählte Probleme der definitiven Rechtsöffnung, insbesondere bei ausländischen Urteilen. recht 4 (1986) 33–39.

Haymann, Michel, Extraterritorial Application of Antitrust Law. The Swiss Approach. Revue suisse du droit international de la concurrence (1981) 17–42.

Hegnauer, Cyril, Familie und Staatsgrenzen: Kooperation und Frustration im Verhältnis zwischen Inland und Ausland. Zeitschrift für Vormundschaftswesen 38 (1983) 15–25.

Heini, Anton, Die Anknüpfungsgrundsätze in den Deliktsnormen eines zukünftigen schweizerischen IPR-Gesetzes. In: Festschrift für F.A. Mann (München 1977) 193–205.

Heini, Anton, Der Entwurf eines Bundesgesetzes über das internationale Privat- und Zivilprozessrecht (IPR-Gesetz), Schweizerische Juristenzeitung 74 (1978) 249–258.

Heini, Anton, Ausländische Staatsinteressen und internationales Privatrecht. Zeitschrift für Schweizerisches Recht 100 I (1981) 65–83.

Heini, Anton, Die Anwendung wirtschaftlicher Zwangsmassnahmen im internationalen Privatrecht In: Die Anwendung wirtschaftlicher Zwangsmassnahmen im Völkerrecht und im internationalen Privatrecht, (Heidelberg 1982) 37–55.

Heini, Anton, Zur überprüfung des anwendbaren ausländischen Rechts durch das Bundesgericht de lege ferenda. Schweizerische Juristenzeitung 80 (1984) 163–164.

Heini, Anton, Jurisdiktion und Jurisdiktionsgrenzen im internationalen Privatrecht, Schweizerisches Jahrbuch für internationales Recht 41 (1985) 93–98.

Heini, Anton, Der Grundsatz der Nachlasseinheit und das neue internationale Erbrecht der Schweiz. In: Festschrift Cyril Hegnauer (1986) 187–195.

Heinrich, Gregor, Basler Symposium über die Rolle des öffentlichen Rechts im Internationalen Privatrecht (20./21.3. 1986). Praxis des internationalen Privat- und Verfahrensrechts (1986) 194–195.

Hoyer, Hans, Die gemeinsamen Bestimmungen des schweizerischen IPR-Gesetzesentwurfs. Schweizerisches Jahrbuch für internationales Recht 35 (1979, ersch. 1980) 35–56.

Imhoff-Scheier, Anne-Cathérine, Protection du consommateur et contrats internationaux. Diss. Genf. (Genf 1981). Etudes suisses de droit international 22.

Imhoff-Scheier, Anne-Cathérine, La loi applicable à la publicité internationale en droit international privé suisse. Schweizerisches Jahrbuch für Internationales Recht 41 (1985) 57–90.

Jaccottet, Catherine, Les obligations alimentaires envers les enfants dans les Conventions de la Haye. (Berne 1982). Publications universitaires européennes. Série 2, Droit, Vol. 296.

Jagmetti, Marco, Foreign Exchange Contracts: The Swiss View. International Business Lawyer 5 (1977) 30–36.

Jagmetti, Marco, Letters of Responsibility, Switzerland: International Business Lawyer 6 (1978) 320–332.

Kaiser, Erhard, Verlängerter Eigentumsvorbehalt und Globalzession im IPR. Rechtsvergleichende Darstellung von Zession und Zessionsstatut im deutschen, österreichischen, schweizerischen, französischen, englischen und US-amerikanischen Recht (1986). Reihe Rechtswissenschaft 33.

Kaufmann-Kohler, Gabrielle, La clause d'lelection de for dans les contrats internatinaux. Diss. Basel. (Basel, Frankfurt a.M. 1980). Schriftenreihe des Instituts für internationales Recht und internationale Beziehungen, Juristische Fakultät der Universität Basel 29.

Kaufmann-Kohler, Gabrielle, Conflits en matière d'obtention de preuves à l'étranger Schweizerisches Jahrbuch für internationales Recht 41 (1985) 110–120.

226

Keller, Max; Siehr, Kurt, Allgemeine Lehren des internationalen Privatrechts. (Zürich 1986).

Kellerhals; Perrin; Voneche, Switzerland. In: Chester (ed.), Divorce in Europe, Leyden (1977) 195–210.

Klein, Frédéric-Edouard, The Law to Be Applied by the Arbitrators to the Substance of the Dispute. In: The Art of Arbitration, Essays on International Arbitration, Liber Amicorum Pieter Sanders (12. Sept. 1912–1982) 189–206.

Klein, Frédéric-Edouard, A propos de l'exécution en Suisse des sentences arbitrales étrangères. In: Festgabe zum Schweizerischen Juristentag (Basel 1985) 157–170.

Klein Frédéric-Edouard, Zur Ernennung von Schiedsrichtern durch im voraus bezeichnete Dritte. Praxis des internationalen Privat- und Verfahrensrechts (1986) 53–56.

Kleiner, Beat, Internationales Devisen-Schuldrecht: Fremdwährungs-, Euro- und Rechnungseinheitsschuld; mit Mustertexten. (Zürich 1985).

Knoepfler, François; Schweizer, Philippe, L'arbitrage international et les voies de recours: à propos du projet de Loi fédérale sur le DIP. In: Mélanges Guy Flattet (1985) 491–507.

Kupfer, Hans, Prochaines innovations dans l'échange international des actes de l'état civil. Zeitschrift für Zivilstandswesen 48 (1980) 17–19.

Lagarde, Paul, Les contrats dans le projet suisse de codification du droit international privé, Annuaire Suisse de droit international 35 (1979) 72.

Lalive, Jean-Flavien, Swiss Law and Practice in Relation to Measures of Execution Against the Property of a Foreign State. Netherlands Yearbook of International Law 10 (1979) 153–166.

Lalive, Pierre, The Transfer of Chattels in the Conflict of Laws, (Oxford 1955).

Lalive, Pierre, Tendances et méthodes en droit international privé. Cours général. (Alphen aan den Rijn 1979). Recueil des Cours de l'Académie de Droit International 1977, Bd. 2.

Lalive, *Pierre*, Sur une notion de 'Contrat international'. In: Multum non multa, Festschrift Kurt Lipstein, (Heidelberg/Karlsruhe 1980) 135–155.

Lalive, *Pierre*, Ordre public transnational (ou réellement international) et arbitrage international. Revue de l'Arbitrage (1986) 329–373.

Lang, *Georg Adolf*, La fraude à la loi en droit international privé suisse. Thèse Lausanne (1984).

Lausanne Colloque, Lausanner Kolloquium über den deutschen und den schweizerischen Gesetzenwurf zur Neuregelung des Internationalen Privatrechts, Lausanne, 14.–15. Oktober 1983, veranstaltet vom Schweizerischen Institut für Rechtsvergleichung. Lausanne. (Zürich 1984). Veröffentlichungen des Schweizerischen Instituts für Rechtsvergleichung. I. – Referate: Allgemeiner Teil des Internationalen Privatrechts, KARL KREUZER/ ALFRED E. VON OVERBECK. – Personen- unde Eherecht, G. KÜHNE/IVO SCHWANDER. – Ehegüter- unde Erbrecht, D. HEN-RICH/ANDREAS BUCHER. – Kindschaftsrecht, KURT SIEHR/ BERNARD DUTOIT. – Internationales Verfahrensrecht, PAUL VOLKEN/J. PIRRUNG. – Zusammenfassung, FRANK VISCHER/G. KEGEL.

Lehner, *Georg Rudolf*, Die Verantwortlichkeit der Leitungsorgane von Aktiengesellschaften in rechtsvergleichender und international-privatrechtlicher Sicht, unter Berücksichtigung des schweizerischen, amerikanischen, deutschen, französischen, englischen und italienischen Rechts. Diss. Basel. (Zürich 1981). Schweizer Schriften zum Handels- und Wirtschaftsrecht 54.

Lejeune, *Yves*, Le statut international des collectivités fédérées à la lumière de l'expérience suisse. Préf. de Paul de Visscher. (Paris 1984). Bibliothèque de droit international 95.

Lévy, *Laurent*, Entraide judiciaire internationale en matière civile. In: L'entraide judiciaire internationale en matière pénale, civile, administrative et fiscale, (Genève 1986) 53–114.

Maier, *Hans Jakob*, Schiedsgerichtsverfahren im deutsch-schweizerischen Handelsverkehr. Internationale Wirtschafts-Briefe (1980) 323–326

Maier, *Hans Jakob*, Verwendung allgemeiner Geschäftsbedingungen (AGB) im Handelsverkehr Deutschland–Schweiz. Handelskammer Deutschland-Schweiz (1985).

Majoros, Ferenc, Das Kollisionsrecht der Konventionskonflikte etabliert sich. Die Regel der maximalen Wirksamkeit in der doctrine des schweizerischen Bundesgerichts (Entscheidung Denysiana v. 14. März 1984). In: Festschrift Karl H. Neumayer (1985) 431–457.

Mangold, Denise, Familiennamensänderungen im Kanton Basel-Stadt unter Berücksichtigung von Fällen aus dem Bereiche des IPR. Diss. Basel (1981).

Mann, Frederick Alexander, Zur Anerkennung summarischer Verfahren des englischen Rechts (zu schweizer Bundesgericht, 20. 5. 1981, BGE 107 Ia 198). Praxis des internationalen Privat- und Verfährensrechts (1984) 44–45.

Mann, Frederick Alexander, Zur staatlichen Hoheitsgewalt über ausländische Tochtergesellschaften und Zweigniederlassungen inländischer Unternehmen. Schweizerische Juristenzeitung 82 (1986) 21–28.

McCaffrey, Stephen, The Swiss Draft Conflicts Law. American Journal of Comparative Law 28 (1980) 235–285.

Meier, Walter H., Die einfache Gesellschaft im internationalen Privatrecht. Diss. Zürich. (Zürich 1980).

Meyer, Doris Maria, Der Regress im internationalen Privatrecht. Diss. Zürich. (Zürich 1982). Schweizer Studien zum internationalen Recht 27.

Meyer, Hermine Herta, Obtaining evidence in Switzerland for use in foreign courts, American Journal of Comparative Law 3 (1954) 412–418.

Miller, A.R., International Cooperation in Litigation between the United States and Switzerland: Unilateral Procedural Accomodation in Test Tube, Minnesota Law Review 49 (1965) 1069.

Moser, Rudolf, Methodologische Fragen und ihre Beantwortung im Entwurf zu einem schweizerischen IPR-Gesetz. In: St. Galler Festgabe zum Schweizerischen Juristentag 1981, 319–339.

Festschrift für Prof. Rudolf Moser, Beiträge zum neuen IPR des Sachen-, Schuld- und Gesellschaftsrechts: MARIO M. PEDRAZZINI Ein Wort des Geleites. – FRITZ STURM Die allgemeinen Grundsätze im schweizerischen IPR- Gesetzesentwurf. Eine kritische Analyse. – HANS HANISCH Besitzlose Mobiliarsicherungsrechte im internationalen Rechtsverkehr, insbesondere im Verhältnis zwischen der Schweiz und der Bundesrepublik Deutschland. – ERNST BREM Das Immaterialgüterrecht im zukünftigen IPR-Gesetz. – ANTON HEINI Die Rechtswahl im bertragsrecht und das neue IPR-Gesetz. – IVO SCHWANDER Internationales bertragsschuldrecht – direkte Zuständigkeit und objektive Anknüpfung. – KURT SIEHR Gemeinsame Kollisionsnormen für das Recht der vertraglichen und ausservertraglichen Schuldverhältnisse. – FRANK VISCHER Das Deliktsrecht des schweizerischen IPR-Gesetzes unter besonderer Berücksichtigung der Regelung der Produktehaftpflicht. – ROLF BÄR Internationales Kartellrecht und unlauterer Wettbewerb. – PETER NOBEL Zum Internationalen Gesellschaftsrecht im IPR-Gesetz. – ANDREAS BUCHER Das Kapitel 11 des IPR-Gesetzes über die internationale Schiedsgerichtsbarkeit. – PAUL VOLKEN Neue Entwicklungen im Bereich der internationalen Zuständigkeit. Schweizer Studien zum internationalen Recht 51.

Nebel, Rolf, Internationale Verhaltensregeln über wettbewerbsbeschränkende Geschäftspraktiken. Diss. Zürich. (Zürich 1986). Schweizer Studien zum internationalen Recht 44.

Neuhaus, Paul Heinrich, Der Schweizer IPR-Entwurf – Ein internationales Modell?, Rabels Zeitschrift für ausländisches und internationales Recht 43 (1979) 277–289.

Nussbaum, Arthur, American-Swiss Private International Law, (New York 1958).

Nussbaum, Werner, Das internationale Konkursrecht der Schweiz de lege lata et ferenda. Diss. Bern. (Zürich 1980). Schweizer Studien zum internationalen Recht 20.

Nussbaum, Werner, Anerkennung und Vollstreckung eines auf dem Gebiet des früheren Königreichs Württemberg eröffneten Konkurses in der Schweiz. Schweizerische Juristenzeitung 80 (1984) 355–358.

Ott, Günter, Der deutsche und der schweizerische Entwurf eines Gesetzes über das internationale Privat- und Prozessrecht auf dem Prüfstand. Das Standesamt (1984) 29–36.

Ottrubay, Stephan, Die Eintragung des Eigentumsvorbehalts unter Berücksichtigung des internationalen Rechts und der internationalen Harmonisierungsbestrebungen. Diss. Freiburg/Schweiz (1980) Arbeiten aus dem Juristischen Seminar der Universität Freiburg/Schweiz 50.

von Overbeck, Alfred E., American-Swiss Succession: The Meaning of Art. 6 of the 1850 Treaty, American Journal of Comparative Law 18 (1970) 595–611.

von Overbeck, Alfred E., Der schweizerische Entwurf eines Bundesgesetzes über das internationale Privatrecht, Rabels Zeitschrift für ausländisches und internationales Recht 42 (1978) 601–633.

von Overbeck, Alfred E., Zwischenbericht über die schweizerische IPR- Reform, Zeitschrift für Rechtsvergleichung (1978) 194–208.

von Overbeck, Alfred E., Le divorce en droit international privé suisse. Annales de la Faculté de droit et des sciences politiques et de l'Institut de recherches juridiques, politiques et sociales de Strasbourg 30 (1979) 89 ff.

von Overbeck, Alfred E., Le divorce en droit international privé suisse. In: Le divorce en droit international privé allemand, français et suisse, (Paris 1980) 89–114.

von Overbeck, Alfred E., La compétence internationale directe et indirecte dans le projet de loi suisse sur le droit international privé. In: Festschrift Konrad Zweigert (1981) 307–320.

von Overbeck, Alfred E., Les questions générales du droit international privé à la lumière des codifications et projets récents. Recueil des cours de l'Académie de droit international (1982) III, 176; 9–258.

von Overbeck, Alfred E., Der schweizerische Regierungsentwurf eines Bundesgesetzes über das internationale Privatrecht. Praxis des internationalen Privat- und Verfahrensrechts (1983) 49–52.

von Overbeck, Alfred E., La convention de La Haye du 1 juillet 1985 relative à la loi applicable au trust et à sa reconnaissance. Schweizerisches Jahrbuch für internationales Recht 41 (1985) 30–38, 47–52.

Pestalozzi, Gmuer & Heiz, Switzerland Law Digest. In: Martindale-Hubbell Law Directory (New York, yearly).

Pocar, Fausto, Les régimes matrimoniaux et les successions dans le projet suisse de codification du droit international privé. Schweizerisches Jahrbuch für internationales Recht 35 (1979, ersch. 1980) 57–71.

Poudret, Jean-François, La clause arbitrale par référence selon la Convention de New York et l'art. 6 du Concordat sur l'arbitrage. In: Mélanges Guy Flattet (1985) 523–538.

Pouvoir exécutif et pouvoir législatif, La responsabilité pré- et post-contractuelle, droit international public et privé. Recueil des travaux présentés aux deuxièmes journées juridiques yougoslavo-suisses, Belgrade, 19 au 21 mars 1986 (Zürich 1986). Publications de l'Institut suisse de droit comparé. 5. Beiträge: BERNARD DUTOIT, Le droit internationale privé moderne des contrats – comparaison du projet suisse de droit international privé avec la loi yougoslave du 15 juillet 1982, 219–237.

de Preux, Patrick, La Professio juris (étude de l'article 22 LRDC). Thèse Lausanne (1981).

Die Rechtsprechung des Bundesgerichts im Internationalen Privatrecht und in verwandten Rechtsgebieten. Eine systematische Auswertung. Von Max Keller u.a. (Zürich 1982).

Répertoire de droit international privé suisse Présentation systématique et synthétique du droit commun et conventionnel, de la jurisprudence et des sources doctrinales principales. Par Bernard Dutoit e.a. Bern. Vol. I: Le contrat international; L'arbitrage international (1982). Vol. 2: Les conventions bilatérales sur les conflits de jurisdiction, la reconnaissance et l'exécution des jugements étrangers (1983). Vol. 3: Les principales conventions d'établissement touchant le droit international privé (1986).

Reymond, Claude, Problèmes actuels de l'arbitrage commercial international. Revue économique et sociale 40 (1982) 5 ff.

Reymond, Claude, Souveraineté de l'état et participation à l'arbitrage. Revue de l'arbitrage (1985) 517–542.

von Rhein, Roderich, Zur Anerkennung und Vollstreckung von schweizerischen Gerichtsentscheidungen, Schiedssprüchen und Vergleichen in der Bundesrepublik Deutschland. Schweizerische Juristenzeitung 82 (1986) 141–145.

Riesenfeld, S. A., Domestic Effects of Foreign Liquidation and Rehabilitation Proceedings in the Light of Comparative Law, In: Internationales Privatrecht und Rechtsvergleichung im Ausgang des 20. Jahrhunders. Bewahrung oder Wende? Festschrift für Gerhard Kegel (Frankfurt a.M. 1977) 433–449.

Rochat, Christian, La dislocation du statut personnel. Etude de droit internationale privé. Thèse Lausanne (1986).

Roesle, Eugen A., Die internationale Vereinheitlichung des Rechts der Bankgarantien. Diss. Zürich. (Zürich 1983). Schriften zum Bankenwesen. 26.

Rohr, Andreas, Der Konzern im IPR unter besonderer Berücksichtigung des Schutzes der Minderheitsaktionäre. Diss. Freiburg i.Ue. (Zürich 1983). Schweizer Studien zum internationalen Recht 32.

Schaub, Rudolf P., Zur Problematik des internationalen Konkursrechts der Schweiz. Kritische Bemerkungen zur Bundesgerichtspraxis und zum Entwurf eines internationalen Konkursrechts. Zeitschrift für Schweizerisches Recht 101 I (1982) 21–60.

Schluep, Walter R., Switzerland. In: World Law of Competition B 6 (New York 1981).

Schluep, Walter R., The Swiss Act on Cartels and the Practice of the Swiss Cartel Commission Concerning Economic Concentration. In: Hopt (ed.), Legal and Economic Analyses on Multinational Enterprises (European Merger Control) (1982) 123–151.

Schluep, Walter R., Wirksamer Wettbewerb (1987).

Schluep, Walter R.; Baudenbacher Carl, Corporation Law and the Law of Intangible Property in Swiss Law. In: Newman (ed.), The Unity of Law II (Brussels 1978) 355–370.

Schnitzer, Adolf F., Gegenentwurf für ein schweizerisches IPR-Gesetz. Schweizerische Juristenzeitung 76 (1980) 309–316.

Schnitzer, Adolf F., Grundsätzliche Bemerkungen zum Internationalen Privatrecht von heute und morgen. Praxis des internationalen Privat- und Verfahrensrechts (1984) 233–237.

Schnitzer, Adolf F.; Châtelain, Susan, Die Kodifikationen des internationalen Privatrechts. Zeitschrift für Rechtsvergleichung 25 (1984) 276–307.

Schnitzer, Adolf F.; Châtelain, Susan, Das überforderte Kollisionsrecht. Schweizerische Juristenzeitung 81 (1985) 105–113.

Schnyder, Anton K.; Die Anwendung des zuständigen fremden Sachrechts im internationalen Privatrecht; unter besonderer Würdigung des Entwurfs zu einem schweizerischen IPR-Gesetz. Diss. Zürich. (Zürich 1981). Schweizer Studien Zum internationalen Recht 23.

Schnyder, Anton K., Staatsverträge im Internationalen Privat- und Zivilverfahrensrecht der Schweiz. (Zürich 1983).

Schnyder, Anton K., Schweizerische Unternehmen und ausländisches Forum – insbesondere im Verhältnis zu den USA. Schweizerische Aktiengesellschaft 57 (1985) 137–144.

Schnyder, Anton K., Das neue IPR-Gesetz, Einführung in das Bundesgesetz vom 18. Dezember 1987 über das Internationale Privatrecht (IPRG). (Zürich 1988).

Schoch, Magdalena, Conflict of Laws in a Federal State: The Experience of Switzerland, Harvard Law Review 55 (1942) 738–749.

Schönle, Herbert; Thévenoz, Luc, La lettre de garantie pour connaissement (letter of indemnity) dans les opérations de crédit documentaire. Zeitschrift für Schweizerisches Recht 105 I (1986) 47–78.

Schulthess, Hans Conrad, Der verfahrensrechtliche ordre public in der internationalen Schiedsgerichtsbarkeit in der Schweiz. Diss. Zürich (1981).

Schulze, Carsten, Die Kodifikation des Vertragsstatuts im internationalen Privatrecht. Diss. Basel. (Basel, Frankfurt a.M. 1980). Schriftenreihe des Instituts für internationales Recht und internationale Beziehungen, Juristische Fakultät der Universität Basel 30.

Schwander, Ivo, Internationales Privatrecht: Allgemeiner Teil: Skriptum. (St. Gallen 1985).

Schwander, Ivo, Das internationale Familienrecht der Schweiz: unter besonderer Berücksichtigung des Entwurfs des Bundesrates vom 10. 11. 1982/1. 2. 1983 zu einem Bundesgesetz über das internationale Privatrecht. Habschr. Freiburg/Schweiz, (St. Gallen 1985).

Schwander, Ivo, Das IPR der Produktehaftung. In: Produkthaftung, (Bern 1986) 197–235. Schweizerische Beiträge zum Europarecht 29.

Schwander, Ivo, Einige Berührungspunkte des internationalen Privatrechts mit anderen Rechtsdisziplinen. recht 4 (1986) 1–7.

Siehr, Kurt, Zum Entwurf eines schweizerischen Bundesgesetzes über das internationale Privatrecht, Recht der Internationalen Wirtschaft 25 (1979) 729–737.

Siehr, Kurt, Eigentumsvorbehalt im deutsch-schweizerischen Rechtsverkehr. Praxis des internationalen Privat- und Verfahrensrechts (1982) 207–210.

Siehr, Kurt, Internationales Kindesrecht. Schweizerische Juristenzeitung 78 (1982) 173–184.

Simonius, Pascal, Privatrechtliche Forderung und Staatenimmunität. In: Festgabe zum Schwiezerischen Juristentag, (Basel 1985) 335–351.

Stampfli, Lorenz, Le transfert de technologie. Les efforts actuels pour une réglementation internationale. Diss. rer. pol. Genève. (Berne 1980). Publications universitaires européennes. Série 31, Sciences politiques. 18.

von Steiger Werner, Zur Kodifikation des internationalen Privatrechts. Erste Betrachtungen zum Entwurf eines Bundesgesetzes über das internationale Privatrecht (IPR-Gesetz), Zeitschrift des Bernischen Juristenvereins (1979) 41–64.

Stojan, Teddy S., Die Anerkennung und Vollstreckung ausländische Zivilurteiler in Handelssachen unter Berücksichtigung des IPR-Gesetzes. Diss. Zürich. (Zürich 1986). Zürcher Studien zum Verfahrensrecht. 72.

Stojanvic, Srdjan. Die Parteiautonomie und der internationale Entscheidungs einklang unter besonderer Berücksichtigung des internationalen Ehegüterrechts. Diss. Freiburg i. Ue. (Zürich 1983). Schweizer Studien zum internationalen Recht 29.

Stucki, Hans Ulrich; Altenburger, Peter R., Product Liability. A Manual of Practice in Selected Nations – Switzerland (London 1981).

Sturm, Fritz, Zur Reform des internationalen Familien- und Erbrechts in der Schweiz und in der Bundesrepublik Deutschland. Zeitschrift für das gesamte Familienrecht 31 (1984) 744–752.

Sturm, Fritz, Parteiautonomie als bestimmender Faktor im internationalen Familien- und Erbrecht. In: Festschrift Ernst Wolf (1985) 637–658.

Szasz, Ivan, Recognition of the Legal Effects of Foreign Civil Procedure, In: Festschrift zum 70. Geburtstag von Max Guldener, (Zürich 1973) 309–327.

Trutmann, Verena, Arbeitsrecht und Internationales Privatrecht. Mitteilungen des Institutes für Schweizerisches Arbeitsrecht (1986) 64–80.

Tschanz, Pierre-Yves, Contrats d'Etat et mesures unilatérales de l'Etat devant l'arbitre international. Revue critique de droit international privé 74 (1985) 47–84.

L'unification du droit privé suisse au XIXe siècle. Méthodes et problèmes. Rapports du 6e séminaire organisé par la Conférence universitaire romande dans le cadre de l'enseignement du 3e cycle de droit 1985. Universités de Berne, Fribourg, Genève, Lausanne et Neuchâtel, Douanne du 17 au 21 septembre 1985. Responsable: Pio Caroni. (Fribourg 1986).

Vischer, Frank, Drafting National Legislation and Conflict of Laws: The Swiss Experience. In: Contemporary Perspectives in Conflicts of Laws, Essays in honor of David F. Caters. (Durham 1977) 131–145.

Vischer, Frank, Wo sollten die Schwerpunkte einer IPR-Reform liegen? (Heidelberg 1982). Schriftenreihe der Juristischen Studiengesellschaft Karlsruhe 151.

Vischer, Frank, Status und Wirkung aus der Sicht des schweizerischen IPR. In: Festschrift Wolfram Müller-Freienfels (1986) 661–690

Festschrift für Frank Vischer, (1983). Beiträge (Auszug): II. Internationales Recht: – ANDREAS BUCHER, Ueber die räumlichen Grenzen der Kollisionsnormen. – PETER MAX GUTZWILLER, Zur internationalen Zuständigkeit im Arbeitsvertragsrecht. – ANTON HEINI, Vertrauensprinzip und Individualanknüpfung im internationalen Vertragsrecht. – GABRIELLE KAUFMANN-KOHLER, Compétence internationale et bouleversements politiques. – MAX KELLER, Schutz des Schwächeren im Internationalen Vertragsrecht. – FRANÇOIS KNOEPFLER, L'article 7h LRDC est-il interprèté conformément à la ration legis? – FRANCIS A. MANN, Einheitsrecht und internationales Privatrecht. – WOLFRAM MÜLLER-FREIENFELS, Übernationales Ziel und nationale Kodifikation internationalen Privatrechts heute. – ALFRED E. VON OVERBECK, La théorie des 'règles de conflit facultatives' et l'autonomie de la volonté. – PAUL PIOTET, Application de la convention franco-suisse de 1869 à la succession d'un français domicilié en Suisse qui n'a jamais eu de domicile en France? – WILLIS L.M. REESE, The Influence of Substantive Policies on Choice of Law. – PASCAL SIMONIUS, Der ausländische Staatsbetrieb als schweizerisches Rechtssubjekt. – PAUL VOLKEN, Von Analogien und ihren Grenzen im internationalen Privatrecht der Schweiz.

Vischer, Frank; von Planta, Andreas, Internationales Privatrecht. (Basel/Frankfurt a.M. 1982).

Volken, Paul, Aktuelle Fragen des internationalen Kindesrechtes. Zeitschrift für Zivilstandswesen 48 (1980) 163–171; ital. 196–204; frz. 9–17.

236

Volken, Paul, The Vienna Convention: Scope, Interpretation, and Gap-Filling. In: International Sale of Goods, (New York 1986) 19–53.

Volken, Paul, Le nom en droit international privé suisse. Zeitschrift für Zivilstandswesen 54 (1986) 46–51; dt. 65–71.

Volken, Paul, Das Zivilstandswesen im neuen schweizerischen IPR-Gesetz. Zeitschrift für Zivilstandswesen 54 (1986) 336–345.

Voyame, Joseph, Das SchKG im grenzüberschreitenden Rechtsverkehr – la LP à travers les frontières nationales. Blätter für Schuldbetreibung und Konkurs 47 (1983) 161–169, 201–204.

Walder-Bohner, Hans Ulrich, Frage der Anfechtung von Schiedsgerichtsentscheiden durch Rechtsmittel. Ein Gegenvorschlag zum Entwurf des Bundesrates für ein Bundesgesetz über das Internationale Privatrecht. Schweizerische Juristenzeitung 79 (1983) 356.

Walder-Bohner, Hans Ulrich, Die international konkursrechtlichen Bestimmungen des Entwurfes des Bundesgesetzes über das internationale Privatrecht (IPR-Gesetz) und die Auswirkungen auf die konkursrechtliche Praxis in der Schweiz. Juristenzeitung 7 (1986) 51–60.

Walser, Hermann, Die Behandlung der freien Stiftungsmittel im Zusammenhang mit dem Inkrafttreten des 'VG'. Referat, gehalten im Juni 1983, Luzern. (Zürich 1983).

Weber, Rolf H., Parteiautonomie im internationalen Sachenrecht? Rabels Zeitschrift für ausländisches und internationales Privatrecht 44 (1980) 510–530.

Weber, Wolfgang F., Die kollisionsrechtliche Behandlung von Wettbewerbsverletzungen mit Auslandsbezug. Eine Darstellung unter besonderer Berücksichtigung des österreichischen IPR-Gesetzes, des Schweizer Expertenentwurfs eines IPR-Gesetzes sowie der Möglichkeit von Harmonisierungsmassnahmen im Kollisions- und Wettbewerbsrecht für die Europäische Gemeinschaft. (Frankfurt a.M. 1982).

Wehrli, Daniel, Rechtsprechung zum Schweizerischen Konkordat über die Schiedsgerichtbarkeit. Mit Hinweisen auf Entscheide zum New Yorker Übereinkommen vom 10. Juni 1958. (Zürich 1985).

Wirth, Markus H., Attachment of Swiss bank accounts: A remedy for international debt collection. The Business Lawyer 36 (1981) 1029–1040.

Index and Glossary

(*English*, *French*, *German*, *Italian*)

	Article of PIL statute
Ablehnung eines Schiedsrichters (G), ricusa di un arbitro (I), challenge of an arbitrator (E), récusation d'un arbitre (F)	180
Abschluss der Ehe (G), celebrazione del matrimonio (I), conclusion of the marriage (E), célébration du mariage (F)	53
Absence (F), scomparsa (I), disappearance (E), Verschollenheit (G)	41
Abstammung (G), discendenza (I), descent (E), naissance (F)	66
Abtretung durch Vertrag (G), cessione contrattuale (I), contractual assignment (E), cession contractuelle (F)	145
Abusive (E), abusif (F), missbräuchlich (G), abusivo (I)	5
Accomplished (E), accompli (F), durchgeführt (G), compiuto (I)	11
Acknowledgement of paternity (E), reconnaissance d'enfant (F), Anerkennung eines Kindes (G), riconoscimento di filglio (I)	71, 72
Act of judicial assistance (E), acte d'entraide judiciaire (F), Rechtshilfehandlung (G), atto d'assistenza giudiziaria (I)	11
Acte	
– illicite (F), unerlaubte Handlung (G), atto illecito (I), unlawful act (E)	142
– juridique (F), Rechtsgeschäft (G), negozio giuridico (I), legal transaction (E)	36
– d'entraide judiciaire (F), Rechtshilfehandlung (G), atto d'assistenza giudiziaria (I), act of judicial assistance (E)	11
Action	
– for annulment (E), recours (F), Anfechtung (G), impugnazione (I)	190, 191

239

	Article
– directe (F)	131, 141
– en contestation de l'état de collocation (F), Kollokationsklage (G), azione di impugnazione della graduatoria (I), lawsuit on the schedule of claims (E)	172
Actions	
– ou mesures (F), Klagen oder Massnahmen (G), azioni o provvedimenti (I), lawsuits or measures (E)	46
– réelles (F), Klagen betreffend dingliche Rechte (G), azioni concernenti diritti reali (I), lawsuits on real rights (E)	97, 98
actio Pauliana (L), undue preference (E), action révocatoire (F), Anfechtungsklage (G), azione revocatoria (I)	171
Activités professionnelles ou commerciales (F), geschäftliche Tätigkeit (G), attività economica (I), business activities (E)	20
Administration des preuves (F), Beweisaufnahme (G), assunzione delle prove (I), taking of evidence (E)	184
Adjustment (E)	143
Administration de la faillite (F), Konkursverwaltung (G), amministrazione del fallimento (I), receiver in bankruptcy (E)	166
Adoption (E) (F) (D), adozione (I)	75
Advances of alimony (E)	81
Adversarial proceedings (E), procédure contradictoire (F), kontradiktorisches Verfahren, Verhandlungsmaxime (G), contraddittorio (I)	182
Affidavit (E)	11
Agent (E), représentant (F), Vertreter (G), rappresentante (I)	126, 158
Agent without a mandate (E)	112
Agreement fails, is inoperative or cannot be implemented (E), convention d'arbitrage est caduque, inopérante ou non susceptible d'être appliquée (F), Schiedsvereinbarung ist hinfällig, unwirksam oder nicht erfüllbar (G), caducità, inefficacia o inadempibilità del patto d'arbitrato (I)	7
Aircraft, air transportation (E)	105, 107, 116
Alimony (E)	62
Amiable compositeur (F)	187
Amministrazione del fallimento (I), receiver in bankruptcy (E), administration de la faillite (F), Konkursverwaltung (G)	166

	Article
Anbieter (G), fornitore (I), marketer (E), fournisseur (F)	114
Ancillary measures (E), effets accessoires (F), Nebenfolgen (G), effetti accessori (I)	63
Anerkennung eines Kindes (G), riconoscimento di figlio (I), acknowledgement of paternity (E), reconnaissance d'enfant (F)	71, 72
Anerkennungszuständigkeit (G)	26
Anfechtung (G), impugnazione (I), action for annulment (E), recours (F)	189
Anfechtungsklage (G), azione revocatoria (I), actio Pauliana (L), undue preference (E), action révocatoire (F)	171
Angemessene Frist (G), congruo termine (I), reasonable time (E), délai convenable (F)	9
Annulment of marriage (E)	59
Antitrust (E)	137
Anzuwendendes Recht (G), diritto applicabile (I), applicable law (E), droit applicable (F)	1
Applicable (E) (F), anwendbar (G), applicabile (I)	20
Applicable law (E), droit applicable (F), anzuwendendes Recht (G), diritto applicabile (I)	1
Applies by analogy (E), s'applique par analogie (F), gilt sinngemäss (G), si applica per analogia (I)	85
Appointment, removal, replacement of arbitrators (E)	179
Approvisionnement économique du pays (F), wirtschaftliche Landesversorgung (G), approvvigionamento economico del paese (I), economic national defense (E)	163
Arbeitnehmererfindung (G)	122
Arbitrability (E), arbitrabilité (F), Schiedsfähigkeit (G), compromettibilità (I)	177
Arbitrable dispute (E), différend arbitrable (F), schiedsfähige Streitsache (G), controversia compromettibile (I)	7
Arbitrage (F), Schiedsgerichtsbarkeit (G), arbitrato (I), arbitration (E)	1, 7, 176 to 194
Arbitral procedure (E)	182
Arbitral tribunal (E)	179
Arbitration (E), arbitrage (F), Schiedsgerichtsbarkeit (G), arbitrato (I)	1, 7, 176 to 194
Arbitration agreement (E)	7
Arbitration clause (E)	124
Are recognized (E), sont reconnus (F), werden anerkannt (G), sono riconosciuti (I)	50

Article

Arrestprosequierung (G), convalida del sequestro (I), validation of attachment (E), validation de séquestre (F)   4
Ascertaining foreign law (E)   16
Assistance of the state judiciary authorities (E)   183, 184
Assunzione delle prove (I), taking of evidence (E), administration des preuves (F), Beweisaufnahme (G)   184
Association (E) (F)   150
Asylum (E)   24
Atomic energy (E)   131
Attachment (E), séquestre (F), Arrest (G), sequestro (I)   4
Atteintes aux intérêts personnels (F), Persönlichkeitsverletzung (G), lesioni arrecate alla personalità (I), violation of the right of personality (E)   33
Attestazione della forza di cosa giudicata (I)   193
Atti d'assistenza giudiziaria (I), acts of judicial assistance (E), actes d'entraide judicaire (F), Rechtshilfehandlung (G)   11
Attività economica (I), business activities (E), activités professionnelles ou commerciales (F), geschäftliche Tätigkeit (G)   20
Atto illecito (I), unlawful act (E), acte illicite (F), unerlaubte Handlung (G)   142
Au-delà des demandes dont il était saisi (F), Streitpunkte, die ihm nicht unterbreitet wurden (G), punti litigiosi che non gli erano stati sottoposti (I), ultra petita (L), beyond the questions submitted to it (E)   190
Aufsichtsbehörde (G), autorità di vigilanza (I), supervisory authority (E), autorité de surveillance (F)   32
Ausländische Entscheidungen (G), decisioni straniere (I), foreign decisions (E), décisions étrangères (F)   1, 65
Auteur de l'atteinte (F), Urheber der Verletzung (G), l'autore della lesione (I), damaging party (E)   139
Autolimitazione (I)   14
Autorité de surveillance (F), Aufsichtsbehörde (G), autorità di vigilanza (I), supervisory authority (E)   32
Autorités judiciaries ou administratives suisses (F), schweizerische Gerichte oder Behörden (G), tribunali e autorità svizzeri (I), Swiss judicial or administrative authorities (E)   1
Award on the merits (E)   189
Azioni concernenti diritti reali (I), lawsuits on real rights (E), actions réelles (F), Klagen betreffend dingliche Rechte (G)   97, 98

242

Azione   *Article*

 – di impugnazione della graduatoria (I), lawsuit on the
   schedule of claims (E), action en contestation de
   l'état de collocation (F), Kollokationsklage (G)   172
 – revocatoria (I), actio Pauliana (L), undue preference
   (E), action révocatoire (F), Anfechtungsklage (G)   171

Bankruptcy (E), faillite (F), Konkurs (G), fallimento (I)   166 to 175
Bankruptcy and composition (E), faillite et concordat (F),
   Konkurs und Nachlassvertrag (G), fallimento e con-
   cordato (I)   1
"Battle of the forms", contract formation (E)   123
Beklagter (G), convenuto (I), defendant, respondent in
   arbitration (E), défendeur (F)   7
Begriffe (G), definizioni (I), definitions (E), notions (F)   150
Beschränkung der Vertretungsbefugnis eines Organs (G),
   limitazione del potere di rappresentanza di un organo
   (I), limitations of the power of representation of an
   officer (E), restrictions du pouvoir de représentation
   d'un organe (F)   158
Bestimmtes Rechtsverhältnis (G), determinato rapporto
   giuridico (I), specific legal relationship (E), rapport de
   droit déterminé (F)   5
Beteiligungspapiere und Anleihen (G), titoli di par-
   tecipazione e di prestiti (I), shares and bonds (E),
   titres de participation et d'emprunts (F)   151
Betriebliche Interessen (G), interessi aziendali (I), opera-
   tional interests (E), intérêts d'entreprise (F)   136
Betroffen (G), interessato (I), concerned, involved (E),
   lésé (F)   136
Beweisaufnahme (G), assunzione delle prove (I), taking of
   evidence (E), administration des preuves (F)   184
Beyond the questions submitted to it (E), au delà des
   demandes dont il était saisi (F), Streitpunkte, die ihm
   nicht unterbreitet wurden (G), punti litigiosi che non
   gli erano stati sottoposti (I), ultra petita (L)   190
Biens
 – en transit (F), Sachen im Transit (G), cose in transito
   (I), res in transitu (L), goods in transit (E)   101
 – transportés en Suisse (F), Sachen, die in die Schweiz
   gelangen (G), cose che giungono in Svizzera (I),
   goods entering Switzerland (E)   102

Article

Bill of lading (E), connaissement (F), Konnossement (G),
connossamento (I)   106
Bills and Notes (E)   112, 116
"Binnenbeziehung" (G)   61
Birth (E)   66
Branch office (E), succursale (F), (I), Zweigniederlassung
(G)   21, 160
Bürgschaft (G), cautionnement (F), cauzionamento (I)   124
Business
    – activities (E), activités professionnelles ou commer-
    ciales (F), geschäftliche Tätigkeit (G), attività
    economica (I)   20
    – establishment (E), établissement (F), Niederlassung
    (G), stabile organizzazione (I)   20, 21
But (F), Zweck (G), scopo (I), policy (E)   18
By analogy (E), par analogie (F), sinngemäss (G), per
analogia (I)   167

Call to the creditors (E), appel aux créditeurs (F), Schul-
denruf (G)   170
Campo d'applicazione (I), field of Application (E), champ
d'application (F), Geltungsbereich (G)   1
Capacità giuridica (I), capacity to have rights (E), jouis-
sance des droits civils (F), Rechtsfähigkeit (G)   34
Capacity
    – to act (E), exercice des droits civils (F), Handlungs-
    fähigkeit (G), capacità d'agire (I)   35
    – to arbitrate (E)   177
    – to commit an unlawful act (E)   142
    – to dispose for cause of death (E)   94
    – to exercise rights (E)   35
    – to have rights (E), jouissance des droits civils (F),
    Rechtsfähigkeit (G), capacità giuridica (I)   34
Caractère de droit public (F), öffentlichrechtlicher Charak-
ter (G), carattere di diritto pubblico (I), characterized
as public law (E)   13
Cartels (F), Kartelle (G), cartelli (I), antitrust (E)   137
Célébrer le mariage, célébration du mariage (F), Ehe-
schliessung, Abschluss der Ehe (G), celebrare il ma-
trimonio, celebrazione del matrimonio (I), conduct a
marriage ceremony, conclusion of the marriage (E)   43, 53, 55
Certificate of enforceability (E)   193
Certificates (E), documents (F), Urkunden (G), documenti
(I)   96

244

	Article
Cession contractuelle (F), Abtretung durch Vertrag (G), cessione contrattuale (I), contractual assignment (E)	145
Challenge of an arbitrator (E), récusation d'un arbitre (F), Ablehnung eines Schiedsrichters (G), ricusa di un arbitro (I)	180
Champ d'application (F), Geltungsbereich (G), campo di applicazione (I), field of application (E)	1
Change of name (E)	38, 39
Characteristic performance (E), prestation caractéristique (F), charakteristische Leistung (G), prestazione caratteristica (I)	171
Charakteristische Leistung (G), prestazione caratteristica (I), characteristic performance (E), prestation caractéristique (F)	171
Child (E), enfant (F), Kind (G), figlio (I)	20, 66 to 85
Choice of jurisdiction clause (E)	5
Circular letters, prospectuses (E)	156
Citation en conciliation (F), Sühneverfahren (G), procedura di conciliazione (I), conciliation proceeding (E)	9
Citizenship (E), nationalité (F), Staatsangehörigkeit (G), cittadinanza (I)	22
Claim (E), créance (F), Forderung (G), credito (I)	105, 143, 145, 156
Claims of financial interest (E), matière patrimoniale (F), vermögensrechtliche Ansprüche (G), pretese patrimoniali (I)	5, 6
Clearly evident (E), de façon certaine (F), eindeutig (G), univocamente (I)	53, 116
Closely connected (E), lien étroit (F), enger Zusammenhang (G), strettamente connesso (I)	19
Collision at sea (E)	129
Collocation, état de (F), Kollokationsplan (G), graduatoria (I), schedule of claims (E)	172
Commercial transactions, protection of (E)	36
Common law marriage (E)	43
Communication (F), Eröffnung (G), notificato che sia (I), notification (E)	190
Companies (E), sociétés (F), Gesellschaften (G), società (I)	21, 150 to 165
Compensation (F), Verrechnung (G), compensazione (I), set-off (E)	148
Compétence	
– directe (F)	2
– indirecte (F)	25, 26

	Article
Composition and bankruptcy (E)	166 to 175
Conception of child (E)	34
Concerned, involved (E) lésé (F), betroffen (G), interessata (I)	136
Conciliation proceeding (E), citation en conciliation (F), Sühneverfahren (G), procedura di conciliazione (I)	9
Conclusion	
– of arbitration clause (E)	178
– of marriage (E)	43, 53
– of contract (E)	123, 124
Concurrence déloyale (F), unlauterer Wettbewerb (G), concorrenza sleale (I), unfair competition (E)	136
Conditions de fond (F), materiell-rechtliche Vorraussetzungen (G), presupposti materiali (I), substantive prerequisites (E)	44
Conduct a marriage ceremony (E), célébrer le mariage (F), Eheschliessung (G), celebrare il matrimonio (I)	43
"Conflit mobile" (F)	35, 39, 69, 100
Conflict of laws rules (E), règles de droit international privé (F), Kollisionsrecht (G), norme di diritto internazionale privato (I)	91
Conflict of laws in time (E)	198
Congruo termine (I), reasonable time (E), délai convenable (F), angemessene Frist (G)	9
Connaissement (F), connossamento (I), Konnossement (G), bill of lading (E)	106
Connexité (F), sachlicher Zusammenhang (G), materialmente connesse (I), factually connected (E)	8
Conservatory measures (E), mesures conservatoires (F), sichernde Massnahmen (G), provvedimenti conservativi (I)	88, 168
Constitutional complaint (E), recours de droit public (F), staatsrechtliche Beschwerde (G), ricorso di diritto pubblico (I)	191
Constitution of arbitral tribunal	179
Contract formation "battle of the forms" (E)	123
– association (E)	21
Contract (E), contrat (F), Vertrag (G), contratto (I)	112 to 126, 143 to 148
– construction (E)	117
– services (E)	117
– storage (E)	117
– immovable property (E)	119
– intellectual property (E)	122

Article

- for assignment of a claim, contractual assignment
  (E), cession contractuelle (F), Abtretung durch Vertrag (G), cessione contrattuale (I)   145
- to grant the use of a thing or a right (E), contrats
  portant sur l'usage d'une chose ou d'un droit (F),
  Gebrauchsüberlassungsverträge über eine Sache oder
  ein Recht (G), contratti di cessione d'uso di una cosa
  o di un diritto (I)   117
- with consumers (E), contrats conclus avec des consommateurs (F), Verträge mit Konsumenten (G),
  contratti con consumatori (I)   114, 120
- to pass title (E), contrats d'aliénation (F), Veräusserungsverträge (G), contratti di alienazione (I)   117

Contraddittorio (I), adversarial proceedings (E), procédure contradictoire (F), kontradiktorisches Verfahren
(G)   182

Controversie ereditarie (I), inheritance litigation (E), litiges
successoraux (F), erbrechtliche Streitigkeiten (G)   86

Contradictoire (F)   182

Contrats
- d'aliénation (F), Veräusserungsverträge (G), contratti di alienazione (I), contracts to pass title
  (E)   117
- de garantie ou de cautionnement (F), Garantie- und
  Bürgschaftsverträge (G), contratti di garanzia o
  fideiussione (I), guarantee and surety contracts (E)   117
- de mariage (F), Ehevertrag (G), convenzione matrimoniale (I), marital property contract (E)   53
- conclus avec des consommateurs (F), Verträge mit
  Konsumenten (G), contratti con consumatori (I),
  contracts with consumers (E)   114, 120
- portant sur l'usage d'une chose ou d'un droit (F),
  Gebrauchsüberlassungsverträge über eine Sache oder
  ein Recht (G), contratti di cessione d'uso di una cosa
  o di un diritto (I), contracts to grant the use of a
  thing or a right (E)   117

Contratti
- di alienazione (I), contracts to pass title (E), contrats
  d'aliénation (F), Veräusserungsverträge (G)   117
- di cessione d'uso di una cosa of di un diritto (I),
  contracts to grant the use of a thing or a right (E),
  contrats portant sur l'usage d'une chose ou d'un droit
  (F), Gebrauchsüberlassungsverträge über eine Sache
  oder ein Recht (G)   117

Article

– di garanzia o fideiussione (I), guarantee and surety
contracts (E), contrats de garantie ou de cautionnement (F), Garantie- und Bürgschaftsverträge (G)   117
Controversia
   – comprommettibile (I), arbitrable dispute (E), différend
arbitrable (F), schiedsfähige Streitsache (G)   7
   – in materia di pretese patrimoniali (I), dispute of
financial interest (E), différend en matière pa-
trimoniale (F), Rechtsstreit um vermögensrechtliche
Ansprüche (G)   5
Convalida del sequestro (I), validation of attachment
(E), validation de séquestre (F), Arrestprosequierung
(G)   4
Convention d'arbitrage (F), Schiedsvereinbarung (G),
patto d'arbitrato (I), arbitration agreement (E)   178
Convenuto (I), defendant, respondent (E), défendeur (F),
Beklagter (G)   7
Convenzione matrimoniale (I), marital property contract
(E), contrat de mariage (F), Ehevertrag (G)   53
Cooperative corporation (E), société coopérative (F),
Genossenschaft (G), società cooperativa (I)   150
Corporate migration (E)   163
Correspective wills (E)   95
Corporations (E)   21, 150 to 165
Cose
   – che giungono in Svizzera (I), goods entering Switzer-
land (E), biens transportés en Suisse (F), Sachen, die
in die Schweiz gelangen (G)   102
   – in transito (I), res in transitu (L), goods in transit
(E), biens en transit (F), Sachen im Transit (G)   101
Counterclaim (E), demande reconventionnelle (F), Wider-
klage (G), domanda riconvenzionale (I)   8
Country (E), Etat (F), Staat (G), Stato (I)   22
Country with more than one internal state law (E)   16
Créances (F), Forderungen (G), crediti (I), claims (E)   105
Crediti (I), claims (E), créances (F), Forderungen (G)   105
Credit insurers (E)   144
Currency (E), monnaie (F), Währung (G), moneta (I)   147

Damaging nuisance (E), immissions dommageables (F),
schädigende Einwirkungen (G), immissioni nocive (I)   138
Damaging party (E), auteur de l'atteinte (F), Urheber der
Verletzung (G), l'autore della lesione (I)   139

	Article
"Data", local (E)	142
Deadline, time limit (E)	12
Death (E)	34
Debitor cessus (L)	146
Decisioni parziali (I), partial award (E), sentence partielle (F), Teilentscheid (G)	188
Décisions étrangères (F), ausländische Entscheidungen (G), decisioni straniere (I), foreign decisions (E)	1
Declaration of disappearance or death (E)	41, 42
Decline jurisdiction (E), décliner sa compétence (F), Zuständigkeit ablehnen (G), declinare la propria competenza (I)	5
De façon certaine (F), eindeutig (G), univocamente (I), clearly evident (E)	116
Défendeur procède au fond sans faire de réserve (F), vorbehaltlose Einlassung (G), incondizionata costituzione in giudizio del convenuto (I), unconditional appearance (E)	6
Definitions (E), notions (F), Begriffe (G), definizioni (I)	20 to 24, 150
Degno di protezione e manifestamente preponderante (I), legitimate and clearly overriding (E), légitime et manifestement prépondérant (F), schützenswert und offensichtlich überwiegend (G)	19
Délai convenable (F), angemessene Frist (G), congruo termine (I), reasonable time (E)	9
Délais (F), Fristen (G), termini (I), time limits (E)	12
Delicts, unlawful acts (E)	129
Demande reconventionnelle (F), Widerklage (G), domanda riconvenzionale (I), counterclaim (E)	8
Deposit and certificate of enforceability (E), dépôt et certificat de force exécutoire (F), Hinterlegung und Vollstreckbarkeitsbescheinigung (G), deposito e attestazione della forza di cosa (I)	193
Dépositaire (F), Verwahrer (G), depositario (I), keeper (E)	117
"Dépéçage" (F)	123, 142, 166
Dépôt et certificat de force exécutoire (F), Hinterlegung und Vollstreckbarkeitsbescheinigung (G), deposito e attestazione dell' esecutività (I), deposit and certificate of enforceability (E)	193
Dernier domicile (F), letzter Wohnsitz (G), ultimo domicilio (I), last domicile (E)	96
Descent (E), naissance (F), Abstammung (G), discendenza (I)	66

	Article
Dessins ou modèles industriels (F)	110
Différend	
– en matière patrimoniale (F), Rechtsstreit über vermögensrechtliche Ansprüche (G), controversia in materia di pretese patrimoniali (I), dispute of financial interest (E)	5
– arbitrable (F), schiedsfähige Streitsache (G), controversia compromettibile (I), arbitrable dispute (E)	7
Dimora (I), residence (E), résidence (F), Aufenthalt (G)	59
Direct claim (E)	141
Direct international jurisdiction (E)	26
Diritti e doveri coniugali (I), marital rights and duties (E), effets du mariage (F), eheliche Rechte und Pflichten (G)	46
Diritti immateriali (I), intellectual property (E), propriété intellectuelle (F), Immaterialgüterrecht (G)	109
Diritto (I), rules of law (E), règles de droit (F), Recht (G)	187
– applicabile al divorzio (I), law governing divorce (E), le droit applicable au divorce (F), auf die Scheidung anzuwendendes Recht (G)	63
– del foro (I), lex fori (L), law at the place of the court (E), droit du for (F), Recht am Gerichtsort (G)	110
– delle obligazioni (I), law obligations (E), droit des obligations (F), Obligationenrecht, Schuldrecht (G)	112
– dello Stato di destinazione (I), lex loci destinationis (L), law of the country of destination (E), droit de l'Etat de destination (F), Recht des Bestimmungsstaates (G)	101
– dello Stato di partenza (I), lex loci expeditionis (L), law of the country of dispatch (E), droit de l'Etat de l'expédition (F), Recht des Abgangsstaates (G)	102
– del luogo di situazione (I), lex rei sitae, lex situs (L), law of the site, law at the location of the goods (E), droit du lieu de situation (F), Recht am Ort der gelegenen Sache (G)	99, 100
– di risposta (I), right to present an opposing view (E), droit de résponse (F), Gegendarstellungsrecht (G)	139
– nazionale commune (I), lex patriae communis (L), law of the country of their common citizenship (E), si les parents et l'enfant ont la nationalité d'un même État, droit de cet Etat (F), gemeinsames Heimatrecht (G)	68

	Article
Disappearance (E), absence (F), Verschollenerklärung (G), scomparsa (I)	41
Discendenza (I), descent (E), naissance (F), Abstammung (G)	66
Discovery, interrogatories, affidavits, letters rogatory (E)	11
Display of prices (E)	135
Dispositions commmunes (F), gemeinsame Bestimmungen (G), disposizioni communi (I), general provisions (E)	1 to 32
Dispositions for cause of death (E), dispositions pour cause de mort (F), Verfügungen von Todes wegen (G), disposizioni a causa di morte (I)	93
Dispute	
− of financial interest (E), différend en matière patrimoniale (F), Rechtsstreit über vermögensrechtliche Ansprüche (G), controversia in materia di pretese patrimoniali (I)	5
− in company law (E)	151
Distribution	
− of the estate (E), liquider la succession (F), erbrechtliche Auseinandersetzung (G), liquidare la successione (I)	51
− of marital property (E), dissolution du régime matrimonial (F), güterrechtliche Auseinandersetzung (G), liquidazione del regime dei beni (I)	51
Divorce and separation (E)	59
Document of title (E), titre représentant la marchandise (F), Warenpapier (G), titolo rappresentante merci (I)	106
Documents (F), Urkunden (G), documenti (I), certificates (E)	96
D'office (F), von Amtes wegen (G), d'ufficio (I), ex officio (L)	16
Domanda riconvenzionale (I), counterclaim (E), demande reconventionnelle (F), Widerklage (G)	8
Domicile, habitual residence, business establishment of an individual (E)	20
Domiciled at the same time (E), domiciliés en même temps (F), gleichzeitig Wohnsitz haben (G), simultaneamente domicilati (I), lex domicilii communis (L)	54
Droit	
− applicable (F), anzuwendendes Recht (G), diritto applicabile (I), applicable law (E)	1

251

		Article
– d'auteur (F)		110
– de l'Etat de destination (F), Recht des Bestimmungs-staates (G), diritto dello Stato di destinazione (I), lex loci destinationis (L), law of the country of destination (E)		101
– de l'Etat de l'expédition (F), Recht des Abgangs-staates (G), diritto dello Stato di partenza (I), lex loci expeditionis (L), law of the country of dispatch (E)		102
– de résponse (F), right to present an opposing view (E), Gegendarstellungsrecht (G), diritto di risposta (I)		139
– des obligations (F), Obligationenrecht (Schuldrecht) (G), diritto delle obbligazioni (I), obligations (E)		112
– des sociétés (F), Gesellschaftsrecht (G), diritto societario (I), company law (E)		151
– du for (F), Recht am Gerichtsort (G), diritto del foro (I), lex fori (L), law at the place of the court (E)		110
– diritto (I)		99
– du lieu de situation (F), Recht am Ort, Recht des Staates, in dem sich das Grundstück befindet (G), diritto dello Stato di situazione (I), lex rei sitae, lex situs (L), law at the location of the goods, law of the country of the site of the property (E)		99, 100
Droits		
– civils (F)		34
– de l'homme (F), human rights (E), Menschenrechte (G), diritti dell'uomo (I) (F)		33
D'ufficio (I), ex officio (L), d'office (F), von Amtes wegen (G)		16
D'une façon certaine (F), eindeutig (G), univocamente (I), clearly evident (E)		53
Durchführung des Rückgriffs (G), esercizio del regresso (I), implementation of recovery (E), exercice du recours (F)		144
Economic national defense (E), approvisionnement économique du pays (F), wirtschaftliche Landesversorgung (G), approvvigionamento economico del paese (I)		163
Economic espionage (E)		135

Effets   *Article*

- accessoires (F), Nebenfolgen (G), effetti accessori (I), ancillary measures (E)   63
- du mariage (F), eheliche Rechte und Pflichten (G), diritti e doveri coniugali (I), marital rights and duties (E)   46

Effects
- of marriage (E)   46
- of parent-child relationship (E)   79

Eheliche Rechte und Pflichten (G), diritti e doveri coniugali (I), marital rights and duties (E), effets du mariage (F)   46

Eheschliessung (G), celebrare il matrimonio (I), conduct a marriage ceremony (E), célébrer le mariage (F)   43

Ehevertrag (G), convenzione matrimoniale (I), marital property contract (E), contrat de mariage (F)   53

Eigentumsvorbehalt (G), réserve de propriété (F), riserva di proprietà (I), retention of title, chattel mortgage (E)   102, 103

Eindeutig (G), univocamente (I), clearly evident (E), d'une façon certaine (F)   53, 116

Emergency trust (E)   163

Employment contract (E)   115, 121, 122, 126, 145

En équité (F), nach Billigkeit (G), secondo equità (I), ex aequo et bono (L)   187

Enforceability (E)   28

Enger Zusammenhang (G), strettamente connesso (I), lien étroit (F), closely connected (E)   19

Entrave á la concurrence (F), Wettbewerbsbehinderung (G), ostacoli alla concorrenza (I), restraint of competition (E)   137

Equal treatment (E)   182

Erbrechtliche
- Auseinandersetzung (G), liquidare la successione (I), distribution of the estate (E), liquider la succession (F)   51
- Streitigkeiten (G), controversie ereditarie (I), inheritance litigation (E), litiges successoraux (F)   86

Eröffnung (G), notificato che sia (I), notification (E), communication (F)   190

Erfüllungsmodalitäten (G)   125

Eröffnungsstatut (G)   92

Article

Esercizio del regresso (I), implementation of recovery (E), exercise du recours (F), Durchführung des Rückgriffs (G) — 144

Esiguamente – più strettamente connessa (I), slight – much closer connection (E), lien très lâche – relation beaucoup plus étroite (F), geringer – viel engerer Zusammenhang (G) — 15

Estate (E), succession, biens successoraux (F), Nachlass (G), successione, beni successorali (I) — 92, 96

Etablissement (F), Niederlassung (G), stabile organizzazione (I), business establishment (E) — 20

Etat (F), Staat (G), Stato (I), country (E) — 22

  – dans lequel ces immeubles sont situés (F), Ort der gelegenen Sache (G), Stato di situazione dei medesimi (I), forum rei sitae (L), place where the property is situated (E) — 58

Etendue de la responsabilité (F), Umfang der Haftung (G), estensione della responsalilità (I), scope of liability (E) — 142

Ex aequo et bono (L), en équité (F), nach Billigkeit (G), secondo equità (I) — 187

"Exclusion agreement" (E) — 192

Exception clause (E) — 15

Exercice

  – des droits civils (F), Handlungsfähigkeit (G), capacità di agire (I), capacity to act (E) — 35

  – du recours (F), Durchführung des Rückgriffs (G), esercizio del regresso (I), implementation of recovery (E) — 144

Execution of the will (E) — 92

Exequatur (L) — 25, 28

Ex officio (L), d'office (F), von Amtes wegen (G), d'ufficio (I) — 16

Exports (E) — 103

Ex post facto law (E) — 196

Extinction of a claim (E) — 148

Factually connected (E), connexité (F), sachlicher Zusammenhang (G), materialmente connesso (I) — 8

Fahrnis (G) — 98

Faillite et concordat (F), Konkurs und Nachlassvertrag (G), fallimento e concordato (I), bankruptcy and composition (E) — 1

	Article
Falsus procurator (L)	126
Favor	
– divortii (L)	61
– laesi (L)	135, 138, 139
– matrimonii (L)	43, 44
– negotii (L)	36, 56
– recognitionis (L)	27, 70, 73, 78
– testamenti (L)	94
– validitatis (L)	56, 70
Field of application (E), champ d'application (F), Geltungsbereich (G), campo di applicazione	1
Filiation (E) (F)	66
Firmenschutz (G), protezione del nome o della ditta (I), protection of name and business designation (E), protection du nom et de la raison sociale (F)	157
For	
– d'origine (F), Heimatzuständigkeit (G), foro di origine (I), forum originis (L), place of citizenship (E)	47
– du lieu de situation (F), Zuständigkeit am Ort der gelegenen Sache (G), foro del luogo di situazione (I), forum rei sitae (L), jurisdiction at place of assets (E)	88
Foreign	
– acknowledgement (E), reconnaissance intervenue à l'étranger (F), im Ausland erfolgte Anerkennung (G), riconoscimento all'estero (I)	73
– adoptions and similar measures (E)	78
– decisions (E), décisions étrangères (F), ausländische Entscheidungen (G), decisioni straniere (I)	1
– decisions concerning a declaration or disclaimer of parent-child relationship (E)	70
– decisions, measures, certificates and rights concerning the estate (E)	96
– decisions on claims arising from the public issue of shares or bonds by means of a prospectus, circular letters, or similar publications (E)	165
– divorce or separation decrees (E), décisions étrangères de divorce ou de séparation de corps (F), ausländische Entscheidungen über die Scheidung oder Trennung (G), decisioni straniere in materia di divorzio o separazione (I)	65
– law (E)	13, 16
– receiver in bankruptcy (E)	166, 171, 173

Form
  - of contract (E)   124
  - of assignment (E)   145
  - of marital property contract (E)   56
  - of wills (E)   93
Fornitore (I), marketer (E), fournisseur (F), Anbieter (G)   114
Foro
  - del luogo di situazione (I), forum rei sitae (L),
    jurisdiction at place of assets (E), for du lieu de
    situation (F), Zuständigkeit am Ort der gelegenen
    Sache (G)   88
  - di origine (I), forum originis (L), place of citizenship
    (E), for d'origine (F), Heimatzuständigkeit (G)   47
Forum
  - arresti (L), Swiss place of attachment (E), for suisse
    du séquestre (F), schweizerischer Arrestort (G),
    luogo svizzero del sequestro (I)   4
  - loci executionis (L), court at the place of perform-
    ance of the contract (E), tribunal du lieu d'exécution
    (F), Gericht am Erfüllungsort (G), tribunale del
    luogo di adempimento (I)   113
  - necessitatis (L), subsidiary jurisdiction (E), for de
    nécessité (F), Notzuständigkeit (G), foro di necissità
    (I)   3
  - non conveniens (L)   3
  - originis (L), place of citizenship (E), for d'origine
    (F), Heimatzuständigkeit (G), foro di origine (I)   47
  - rei sitae (L), jurisdiction at place of assets, place
    where the property is situated (E), for du lieu de
    situation (F), Zuständigkeit am Ort der gelegenen
    Sache (G), foro del luogo di situazione (I)   58, 88
Foundation (E)   150
Fournisseur (F), Anbieter (G), fornitore (I), marketer (E)   114
Fraus legis (L)   45, 159
Fristen (G), termini (I), time limits (E), délais (F)   12

Garantie- und Bürgschaftsverträge (G), contratti di garan-
    zia o fideiussione (I), guarantee and surety contracts
    (E), contrats de garantie ou de cautionnement (F)   117
Gebrauchsüberlassungsverträge über eine Sache oder ein
    Recht (G), contratti di cessione d'uso di una cosa o di
    un diritto (I), contracts to grant the use of a thing or a
    right (E), contrats portant sur l'usage d'une chose ou
    d'un droit (F)   117

	Article
Gegendarstellungsrecht (G), diritto di risposta (I), right to present an opposing view (E), droit de réponse (F)	139
Geltungsbereich (G), campo di applicazione (I), field of application (E), champ d'application (F)	1
Gemeinsame Bestimmungen (G), disposizioni comuni (I), general provisions (E), dispositions communes (F)	1
Gemeinsames Heimatrecht (G), diritto nazionale comune (I), lex patriae communis (L), law of the country of their common citizenship (E), si les parents et l'enfant ont la nationalité d'un même État, droit de cet Etat (F)	68
General or collective partnership (E)	150
General provisions (E), dispositions communes (F), Gemeinsame Bestimmungen (G), disposizioni comuni (I)	1
Geneva Convention on bills and notes (E)	1, note after 149
Genügender Zusammenhang (G), sufficiente connessione (I), sufficient connection (E), lien suffisant (F)	3
Gericht am Erfüllungsort (G), tribunale del luogo di adempimento (I), court at the place of performance of the contract (E), tribunal du lieu d'exécution (F)	113
Gerichte am Ort (G), tribunali del luogo (I), forum rei sitae (L), courts at the site (E), tribunaux de lieu (F)	97
Geringer – viel engerer Zusammenhang (G), esiguamente – più strettamente connessa (I), slight – much closer connection (E), lien très lâche – relation beaucoup plus étroite (F)	15
Gesamtverweisung (G)	14
Geschäftliche Tätigkeit (G), attività economica (I), business activities (E), activités professionnelles ou commerciales (F)	20
Geschäftssitz (G), sede commerciale (I), seat (E), siège commercial (F)	109
Gesellschaften (G), società (I), companies (E), sociétés (F)	21, 150, 151
Gewöhnlicher Aufenthalt (G), dimora abituale (I), habitual residence (E), résidence habituelle (F)	20
Gilt sinngemäss (G), si applica par analogia (I), applies by analogy (E), s'applique par analogie (F)	85
Gleichzeitig Wohnsitz haben (G), simultaneamente domiciliati (I), lex domicilii communis (L), domiciled at the same time (E), domiciliés en même temps (F)	48, 54
Gold clause (E)	147

                                                                    Article

Goods
  – entering Switzerland (E), biens transportés en Suisse
    (F), Sachen, die in die Schweiz gelangen (G), cose
    che giungongo in Svizzera (I)   102
  – in transit (E), biens en transit (F), Sachen im Transit
    (G), cose in transito (I), res in transitu (L)   101
Graduatoria (I), schedule of claims (E), état de collocation
    (F), Kollokationsplan (G)   172
Gravi motivi inerenti all'interessato (I) party has no im-
    portant countervailing reasons (E), importants motifs
    tenant à l'intéressé (F), wichtige Gründe auf Seiten des
    Betroffenen (G)   11
Gründerhaftung (G)   151
Guarantee and surety contracts (E), contrats de garantie ou
    de cautionnement (F), Garantie- und Bürgschaftsver-
    träge (G), contratti di garanzia o fideiussione (I)   117
Guardianship (E)   85
Guest statutes (E)   133
Güterrechtliche Auseinandersetzung (G), liquidazione del
    regime dei beni (I), distribution of marital property
    (E), dissolution du régime matrimonial (F)   51

Habitual residence (E), résidence habituelle (F), gewöhn-
    licher Aufenthalt (G), dimora abituale (I)   20
Heimatort (G), luogo di origine (I), place of citizenship
    (E), lieu d'origine (F)   22
Heimatzuständigkeit, Heimatgerichtsstand (G), foro
    d'origine (I), jurisdiction at the place of citizenship
    (E), for d'origine (F)   23, 47, 67,
                                                                    76, 80, 87

Im Ausland erfolgte Anerkennung (G), riconoscimento
    avvenuto all'estero (I), foreign acknowledgement (E),
    reconnaissance intervenue à l'étranger (F)   73
Im internationalen Verhältnis (G), nell'ambito inter-
    nazionale (I), in international matters (E), en matière
    internationale (F)   1
Immaterialgüterrecht (G), diritti immateriali (I), intellectu-
    al property (E), propriété intellectuelle (F)   109
Immissions dommageables (F), schädigende Einwirkungen
    (G), immissioni nocive (I), damaging nuisance (E)   138
Immovable property (E)   97, 119

	Article
Implementation of recovery (E), exercice du recours (F), Durchführung des Rückgriffs (G), esercizio del regresso (I)	144
Important countervailing reasons (of the party concerned) (E), importants motifs tenant à l'intéressé (F), wichtige Gründe auf Seiten des Betroffenen (G), gravi motivi inerenti all'interessato (I)	11
Imports, import goods (E)	102
Impossible or highly impracticable (E), impossible ou qu'on ne peut raisonnablement exiger (F), nicht möglich oder unzumutbar (G), non è possibile o non può essere ragionevolmente preteso (I)	3
Impugnazione (I), action for annulment (E), recours (F), Anfechtung (G)	190
Incondizionata constituzione in giudizio del convento (I), unconditional appearance (E), défendeur procède au fond sans faire de réserve (F), vorbehaltlose Einlassung (G)	6
Independence of an arbitrator (E), indépendance (F), Unabhängigkeit (G), indipendenza (I)	180
"Indirect" international jurisdiction (E)	26
Individual (E), personne physique (F), natürliche Person (G), persona fisica (I)	20, 33
In dubio pro validitate (L)	56
Inheritance law (E)	86
In international matters (E), en matière internationale (F), im internationalen Verhältnis (G), nell'ambito internazionale (I)	1
Inheritance litigation (E), litiges successoraux (F), erbrechtliche Streitigkeiten (G), controversie ereditarie (I)	86
Injunctions (E)	31
In limine litis (L)	178
Institution that fulfills a public function (E)	144
Instruction de la cause (F)	184
Insurance contracts (E)	117, 141
Intellectual property, industrial property (E), propriété intellectuelle (F), Immaterialgüterrecht (G), diritti immateriali (I)	109
Intercantonal conflicts (E)	22
Interessi aziendali (I), operational interests (E), intérêts d'entreprise (F), betriebliche Interessen (G)	136
Intérêts d'entreprise (F), betriebliche Interessen (G), interessi aziendali (I), operational interests (E)	136

	Article
Interlocal law (E)	16
International	
– arbitration (E)	176
– conflict of laws (E)	163
– organizations (E)	154
– treaties (E), traités internationaux (F), völkerrechtliche Verträge (G), trattati internazionali (I)	1
Interpersonal law (E)	16
Interrogatories (E)	11
Interzessionsverbot (G)	48
Inventory	
– of estate (E)	89
– of bankrupt debtor's assets (E)	170
Jouissance des droits civils (F), Rechtsfähigkeit (G), capacità giuridica (I), capacity to have rights (E)	34
Jour du mariage (F), Zeitpunkt der Eheschliessung (G), momento della celebrazione del matrimonio (I), time of the marriage (E)	55
Judicial assistance	
– to arbitral tribunal (E)	185
– to foreign authorities (E)	11
Juge naturel (F)	2
Jurisdiction	
– at place of assets (E), for du lieu de situation (F), Zuständigkeit am Ort der gelegenen Sache (G), foro del luogo di situazione (I), forum rei sitae (L)	88
– at place of citizenship (E)	47, 60, 67, 76, 80, 87
– of foreign authorities (E)	26
Jurisdictionally improper fora (E)	4
Kartell (G), cartel (F), cartello (I), restraint of competition (E)	137
Keeper (E), dépositaire (F), Verwahrer (G), depositario (I)	117
Kernenergiehaftpflicht (G)	130
Klagen	
– betreffend dingliche Rechte (G), azioni concernenti diritti reali (I), lawsuits on real rights (E)	97, 98
Kollisionsrecht (G), norme di diritto internazionale privato (I), conflict of laws rules (E), règles de droit international privé (F)	91

	Article
Kollokationsplan (G), graduatoria (I), schedule of claims (E), état de collocation	172
Kommorientenvermutung (G)	34
Kompetenz-Kompetenz of arbitral tribunal (E)	186
Konkurs und Nachlassvertrag (G), fallimento e concordato (I), bankruptcy and composition (E), faillite et concordat (F)	1, 166 to 175
Konkursverwaltung (G), amministrazione del fallimento (I), l'administration de la faillite (F), receiver in bankruptcy (E)	166
Konsumentenverträge (G)	114
Kontradiktorische Verfahren (G), contraddittorio (I), adversarial proceedings (E), procédure contradictoire (F)	182

Labor contract (E)	115
Last domicile (E), dernier domicile (F), letzter Wohnsitz (G), ultimo domicilio (I)	96
Law	
– at the location of the goods (E), droit du lieu de situation du meuble (F), Recht am Ort der gelegenen Sache (G), diritto del luogo di situazione (I), lex rei sitae (L)	100
– at the place of the court (E), droit du for (F), Recht am Gerichtsort (G), diritto del foro (I), lex fori (L)	110
– governing divorce (E), le droit applicable au divorce (F), auf die Scheidung anzuwendendes Recht (G), diritto applicabile al divorzio (I)	63
– of nations (E)	1
– of the country of destination (E), droit de l'Etat de destination (F), Recht des Bestimmungsstaates (G), diritto dello Stato di destinazione (I), lex loci destinationis (L)	101
– of the country of dispatch (E), droit de l'Etat de l'expédition (F), Recht des Abgangsstaates (G), diritto dello Stato di partenza (I), lex loci expeditionis (L)	104
– of the country of common citizenship (E), si les parents et l'enfant ont la nationalité d'un même État, droit de cet Etat (F), gemeinsames Heimatsrecht (G), diritto nazionale commune (I), lex patriae communis (L)	68
– of the site (E), droit du lieu (F), Recht am Ort (G), diritto del luogo (I), lex situs, lex rei sitae (L)	99, 119

Lawsuits
- on real rights (E), actions réelles (F), Klagen betreffend dingliche Rechte (G), azioni concernenti diritti reali (I)   97, 98
- on the schedule of claims (E), action en contestation de l'état de collocation (F), Kollokationsklage (G), azione di impugnazione della graduatoria (I)   172
- or measures (E), actions ou mesures (F), Klagen oder Massnahmen (G), azioni o provvedimenti (I)   46
- on real rights in immovable property (E)   97
Lease (E)   117
Legal transaction (E), acte juridique (F), Rechtsgeschäft (G), negozio giuridico (I)   36
Legge
- applicabile (I), applicable law (E), droit applicable (F), anzuwendendes Recht (G)   1
Legitimate and clearly overriding (E), légitime et manifestement prépondérant (F), schützenswert und offensichtlich überwiegend (G), degno di protezione e manifestamente preponderante (I)   19
Legitimatio per subsequens matrimonium (L)   74
Lending, loan agreements (E)   117
Lesioni arrecate alla personalità (I), violation of the right of personality (E), atteintes aux intérêts personnels (F), Persönlichkeitsverletzung (G)   33
Letters rogatory (E)   11
Letzter Wohnsitz (G), ultimo domicilio (I), last domicile (E), dernier domicile (F)   96
Letztwillige Verfügung oder Erbvertrag (G), testamento o contratto successorio (I), will or successorial pact (E), testament ou pacte successoral (F)   87
Lex
- contractus (L)   116, 148
- domicilii (L)   38, 41, 44, 61
- domicilli communis (L), domiciled at the same time (E), domiciliés en même temps (F), gleichzeitig Wohnsitz haben (G), simultaneamente domicilati (I)   48, 54
- "Friedrich"   119, 154
- fori (L), law at the place of the court (E), droit du for (F), Recht am Gerichtsort (G), diritto del foro (I)   110

	Article
– loci destinationis (L), law of the country of destination (E), droit de l'Etat de destination (F), Recht des Bestimmungsstaates (G), diritto dello Stato di destinazione (I)	101
– loci delicti commissi (L), diritto dello Stato in cui l'atto è stato commesso (I), law of the country where the unlawful act was committed (E), droit de l'Etat dans lequel l'acte illicite a été commis (F), Recht des Staates, in dem die unerlaubte Handlung begangen worden ist (G)	133
– loci expeditionis (L), law of the country of dispatch (E), droit de l'Etat de l'expédition (F), Recht des Abgangsstaates (G), diritto dello Stato di partenza (I)	102
– (loci) rei sitae, lex situs (L), law at the location of the goods, law of the site (E), droit du lieu de situation du meuble (F), Recht am Ort der gelegenen Sache (G), diritto del luogo di situazione (I)	99, 100
– mercatoria (L)	187
– patriae communis (L), law of the country of their common citizenship (E), si les parents et l'enfant ont la nationalité d'un même État, droit de cet Etat (F), gemeinsames Heimatrecht (G), diritto nazionale commune (I)	68
– rei sitae, lex situs (L), law of the country of the site of the property (E), droit du lieu de leur situation (F), Recht des Staates, in dem sich das Grundstück befindet (G), legge dello Stato di situazione (I)	119
– societatis (L), law applicable to the company (E), droit applicable à la société (F), das auf die Gesellschaft anwendbare Recht (G), diritto applicabile alla società (I)	155
– stabuli (L)	134
Liabilities of the estate (E)	92
Liability for foreign companies (E), responsabilité pour une société étrangère (F), Haftung für ausländische Gesellschaften (G), responsabilità per società straniere (I)	159
Liabilty insurer (E)	131, 141
License agreement (E)	122
Liechtenstein Anstalt (G)	150, 159
Lieferungsmodalitäten (G)	125

Article

Lien étroit – suffisant (F), enger – genügender Zusammenhang (G), stretta – sufficiente connessione (I), close – sufficient connection (E)   3, 19

Lien très lâche – relation beaucoup plus étroite (F), geringer – viel engerer Zusammenhang (G), esiguamente – più strettamente connessa (I), slight – much closer connection (E)   15

Lieu dans lequel le travailleur accomplit son travail (F), Ort, wo der Arbeitnehmer seine Arbeit verrichtet (G), luogo in cui il lavoratore compie il suo lavoro (I), place where the employee performs his work (E)   115

Life (E)   34

Limitation of the powers of representation of an officer (E), restrictions du pouvoir de représentation d'un organe (F), Beschränkung der Vertretungsbefugnis eines Organs (G), limitazione del potere di rappresentanza di un organo (I)   158

Limited Liability Corporation (E)   150

Limited Partnership (E)   150

Limited Partnership with shares (E)   150

Limited real rights (E)   98

"Limping marriages" (E)   44

Liquidazione del regime die beni (I), dissolution of marital property (E), distribution du régime matrimonial (F), güterrechtliche Auseinandersetzung (G)   51

Liquidare la successione (I), distribution of the estate (E), liquider la succession (F), erbrechtliche Auseinandersetzung (G)   51

Liquider la succession (F), erbrechtliche Auseinandersetzung (G), liquidare la successione (I), distribution of the estate (E)   51

Lis pendens (L), litispendance (F), Rechtshängigkeit (G), litispendenza (I)   181

Litiges successoraux (F), erbrechtliche Streitigkeiten (G), controversie ereditarie (I), inheritance litigation (E)   86

Loan agreement (E)   117

"Local data" (E)   136, 142

Loi

   – d'application immédiate (F)   18, 34

   – d'ordre public (F)   18

   – uniforme (F)   1, 49

Luogo in cui il lavoratore compie il suo lavoro (I), place where the employee performs his work (E), lieu dans lequel le travailleur accomplit son travail (F), Ort, wo der Arbeitnehmer seine Arbeit verrichtet (G)   115

	Article
Maintenance obligations (E)	49, 83
Making of contract (E)	123
Mandate (E), mandat (F), Auftrag (G), mandato (I)	117
Mandatory	
– application of Swiss law (E)	18
– provisions of a foreign law (E)	19
Mareva injunction (E)	4
Marital	
– property contract (E) contrat de mariage (F), Ehevertrag (G), convenzione matrimoniale (I)	51, 53, 56
– rights and duties (E), effets du mariage (F), eheliche Rechte und Pflichten (G), diritti e doveri coniugali (I)	46
Marketer (E), founisseur (F), Anbieter (G), fornitore (I)	114
Marques (F), trademarks (E), Marken (G), marche (I)	110
Marriage (E) (F)	43
Materiell-rechtliche Voraussetzungen (G), presupposti materiali (I), substantive prerequisites (E), conditions de fond (F)	44
Materialmente connesse (I), factually connected (E), connexité (F), sachlicher Zusammenhang (G)	8
Mater semper certa est (L)	68
Matrimonium claudicans (L)	44
Means of transportation (E), moyens de transport (F), Transportmittel (G), mezzi di trasporto (I)	107
Médias à caractère périodique (F), periodisch erscheinende Medien (G), mezzi di communicazione sociale periodici (I), recurrent media (E)	139
Mesures	
– conservatoires (F), sichernde Massnahmen (G), provvedimenti conservativi (I), conservatory measures (E)	89, 168
– provisoires (F), vorsorgliche Massnahmen (G), provvedimenti cautelari (I), provisional measures (E)	10, 62
Mezzi	
– di communicazione sociale periodici (I), recurrent media (E), médias à caractère périodique (F), periodisch erscheinende Medien (G)	139
– di trasporto (I), means of transportation (E), moyens de transport (F), Transportmittel (G)	107
Migratory marriage (E)	45
Mini-bankruptcy (E), mini-faillite (F), Mini-Konkurs (G), mini-fallimento (I)	170, 171
Missbräuchlich (G), abusivamente (I), abusive (E), abusif (F)	5

	Article
Mittelpunkt der Lebensbeziehungen (G)	20
Modalities of performance and inspections (E)	125
Monnaie (F), Währung (G), moneta (I), currency (E)	147
More than one person liable (E)	140
Mort civile (F)	34
Movable goods (E), meubles (F), bewegliche Sachen (G), cose mobili (I)	98, 100
Multiple citizenship (E)	23
Mutability of marital property law (E)	53
Mutual (E), réciproque (F), gegenseitig (G), reciproche (I)	95
Nach Billigkeit (G), secondo equità (I), ex aequo et bono (L), en équité (F)	187
Nachlass, Nachlassgüter (G), successione, beni successorali (I), estate (E), succession, biens successoraux (F)	92
Nachlassverfahren (G), procedimento successorio (I), probate proceedings (E), règlement de la succession (F)	86
Naissance (F), Abstammung (G), discendenza (I), descent (E)	66
Näherberechtigung (G)	3, 15
Name (E) (G)	37
Nasciturus pro iam nato habetur (L)	34
Nationalité (F), cittadinanza (I), citizenship (E), Staatsangehörigkeit (G)	22
Natürliche Person (G), persona fisica (I), individual (E), personne physique (F)	20, 33
Naturalization (E)	22
Nebenfolgen (G), effetti accessori (I), ancillary measures (E), effets accessoires (F)	63
Negozio giuridico (I), legal transaction (E), acte juridique (F), Rechtsgeschäft (G)	36
Niederlassung (G), stabile organizzazione (I), business establishment (E), établissement (F)	20, 139
Niederlassungskonkurs (G)	166
Noncontentious jurisdiction (E)	31
Norme di diritto internazionale privato (I), conflict of laws rules (E), règles de droit international privé (F), Kollisionsrecht (G)	91
Notification (E), communication (F), Eröffnung, Zustellung (G), notificazione (I)	190
Notions (F), Begriffe (G), definizioni (I), definitions (E)	20 to 24, 150
Nottebohn case (E)	22

	Article
Notzuständigkeit (G), foro di necessità (I), subsidiary jurisdiction (E), for de nécessité (F), forum necessitatis (L)	3
Novation (E) (F)	148
Nuclear energy (E)	130
Nuclear liability (E)	130
Nuclear plant or shipment (E)	130
Nuisance (E)	99, 138
Nullity of marriage (E)	59
Oath (E)	11
Obligations alimentaires (F)	49, 83
Obligations, law of (E), droit des obligations (F), Obligationenrecht, Schuldrecht (G), diritto delle obbligazioni (I)	112
Oeffentlichrechtlicher Charakter (G), carattere di diritto pubblico (I), characterized as public law (E), caractère de droit public (F)	13
Office, branch office (E)	21
Operational interests (E), intérêts d'entreprise (F), betriebliche Interessen (G), interessi aziendali (I)	136
Ordinamento procedurale arbitrale, regolamento d'arbitrato (I), rules of arbitration (E), règlement d'arbitrage (F), Verfahrensordnung, Schiedsordnung (G)	180
Ordinary partnership (E)	150
Ordre public (F), ordre public (Vorbehaltsklausel) (G), ordine pubblico (I), public policy exception (E)	17, 18, 27, 190
Ort	
– der gelegenen Sache (G), Stato di situazione dei medesimi (I), forum rei sitae (L), place where the property is situated (E), Etat dans lequel ces immeubles sont situés (F)	58
– wo der Arbeitnehmer seine Arbeit verrichtet (G), luogo in cui il lavoratore compie il suo lavoro (I), place where the employee performs his work (E), lieu dans lequel le travailleur accomplit son travail (F)	115
Ostacoli alla concorrenza (I), restraint of competition (E), entrave à la concurrence (F), Wettbewerbsbehinderung (G)	137
Out-of-court settlement (E)	30
Pacte de réserve de propriété (F)	103

	Article
Papiers-valeurs (F), titoli di credito (cartevalori) (I), securities (E), Wertpapiere (G)	105
Par analogie (F), sinngemäss (G), per analogia (I), by analogy (E)	167
Parent-child relationship (E), filiation (F), Kindesverhältnis (G), filiazione (I)	66 to 85
Parte non risponde a una proposta (I), party does not answer an offer (E), partie ne répond pas à l'offre (F), Partei schweigt auf einen Antrag (G)	123
Parteien (G), parti (I), parties (E) (F)	19, 189
Partial award (E), sentence partielle (F), Teilentscheid (G), decisone parziale (I)	188
Partie ne répond pas à l'offre (F), Partei schweigt auf einen Antrag (G), parte non risponde a una proposta (I), party does not answer an offer (E)	123
Parties (E) (F), Parteien (G), parti (I)	189
Party does not answer an offer (E), partie ne réspnd pas à l'offre (F), Partei schweigt auf einen Antrag (G), parte non risponde a una proposta (I)	123
Patent (E) (G), brevet (F), brevetto (I)	110, 122
Pending matter (E)	9, 181
Permanent establishment in tax law (E)	20
Per analogia (I), by analogy (E), par analogie (F), sinngemäss (G)	167
Periodicals, libel and defamation (E)	139
Periodisch erscheinende Medien (G), mezzi di communicazione sociale periodici (I), recurrent media (E), médias à caractère périodique (F)	139
Perpetuatio fori (L)	64
Person, individual (E), Person, natürliche Person (G), personne, personne physique (F), persona, persona fisica (I)	22, 33
Persönlichkeit (G), personalità (I), personality, personhood, right of personality (E), personnalité (F)	34, 139
Personality, personhood, (E), personnalité (F), Persönlichkeit (G), personalità (I)	34
Personenrechtliche Verhältnisse (G), rapporti di diritto delle persone (I), matters of personal status (E), en matière de droit des personnes (F)	33
Persons	
– liable in company law (E)	151
– without citizenship (E), apatride (F), Staatenloser (G), apolidi (I)	24

Place   *Article*

- of citizenship (E), lieu d'origine (F), Heimatort (G), luogo di origine (I)   22, 47
- where the employee performs his work (E), lieu dans lequel le travailleur accomplit son travail (F), Ort, wo der Arbeitnehmer seine Arbeit verrichtet (G), luogo in cui il lavoratore compie il suo lavoro (I)   115
- where the property is situated (E), Etat dans lequel ces immeubles sont situés (F), Ort der gelegenen Sache (G), stato di situazione dei medesimi (I), forum rei sitae (L)   58

Probate proceedings (E), règlement de la succession (F), Nachlassverfahren (G), procedimento successorio (I)   86

Procedimento successorio (I), probate proceedings (E), règlement de la succession (F), Nachlassverfahren (G)   86

Professio iuris (L)   87

Propriété intellectuelle, propriété industrielle (F), Immaterrialgüterrecht (G), diritti immateriali (I), intellectual property, industrial property (E)   109

Plea of lack of jurisdiction (E)   6, 186

Pledge of movables, of rights (E)   98, 105

Plurality of debtors (E)   143

Policy (E), but (F), Zweck (G), scopo (I)   18

Portée de la règle de conflict (F), Umfang der Verweisung (G), estensione del rinvio (I), scope of conflicts rule (E)   13

Preamble (E), préamble (F), Präambel (G), preambula (I)   1

Preliminary
- arbitral award (E)   186
- injunctions (E)   31
- question, incidental question (E)   29, 34, 37

Prescription (F), Verjährung (G), prescrizione (I), statute of limitations (E)   148

Prescription, statute of limitations (E)   13, 148

Presentation of an opposing view (E), droit de réponse (F), Gegendarstellungsrecht (G), diritto di risposta (I)   139

Press and media (E)   139

Presupposti materiali (I), substantive prerequisites (E), conditions de fond (F), materiell-rechtliche Voraussetzungen (G)   44

Prestation caractéristique (F), charakteristische Leistung (G), prestazione caratteristica (I), characteristic performance (E)   117

	Article
Principal and agent (E)	126
Private law – public law (E)	13
Probate, inheritance law (E)	92, 96
Procedure before arbitral tribunal (E)	182
Procédure contradictoire (F), kontradiktorisches Verfahren (G), contraddittorio (I), adversarial proceedings (E)	182
Produktehaftung (G), vizi di un prodotto (I), products liability (E), responsabilité du fait d'un produit (F)	135
Products liability (E), responsabilité du fait d'un produit (F), Produktehaftpflicht (G), prestese derivanti da vizi di un prodotto (I)	135
Professio iuris (L)	90, 91, 95
Proper law of the contract (E)	117
Property (E)	98
Prorogatio fori (L)	5
Prospectus, liability for (E), Prospekthaftung	151, 156
Protection	
– of legal transactions (E), sécurité des transactions (F), Verkehrsschutz (G), protezione del commercio giuridico (I)	36
– of name and business designation (E), protection du nom et de la raison sociale (F), Firmenschutz (G), protezione del nome o della ditta (I)	157
Provisional measures (E), mesures provisoires (F), vorsorgliche Massnahmen (G), provvedimenti cautelari (I)	10, 62, 183
Provvedimenti	
– cautelari (I), provisional measures (E), mesures provisoires (F), vorsorgliche Massnahmen (G)	10, 62, 183
– conservativi (I), conservatory measures (E), mesures conservatoires (F), sichernde Massnahmen (G)	89, 168, 183
Publication of judgment (E)	142
Public	
– deed (E)	119
– international law, law of nations (E)	1
– issue of shares or bonds (E)	156
– law (E)	13
– law entities (E)	154
Publisher, libel and defamation (E)	139
Punitive damages (E)	135
Quasi in rem jurisdiction (E)	4
Qui elegit iudicem elegit ius (L)	116

	Article
Radio and other media (E)	139
Radioactivity (E)	138
Rail transportation (E)	116
Rapport de droit (F), Rechtsverhältnis (G), rapporto guiridico (I), legal relationship (E)	5
Rappresentante (I), agent (E), représentant (F), Vertreter (G)	158
Reale Verbandspersönlichkeit (G)	154
Real rights (E)	97, 98
Reasonable time (E), délai convenable (F), angemessene Frist (G), congruo termine (I)	9
Receiver in bankruptcy (E), administration de la faillite (G), Konkursverwaltung (G), amministrazione del fallimento (I)	166
Recht (G), diritto (I), rules of law (E), règles de droit (F)	187
– am Gerichtsort (G), diritto del foro (I), lex fori (L), law at the place of the court (E), droit du for (F)	110
– am Ort der gelegenen Sache (G), diritto del luogo di situazione (I), lex rei sitae (L), law at the location of the goods, law of the site (E), droit du lieu de situation du meuble (F)	99, 100
– des Abgangsstaates (G), diritto dello Stato di partenza (I), lex loci expeditionis (L), law of the country of dispatch (E), droit de l'Etat de l'expédition (F)	104
– des Staates, in dem sich das Grundstück befindet (G), diritto dello Stato di situazione (I), lex rei sitae, lex situs (L), law of the country of the site of the property (E), droit du lieu de leur situation (F)	119
Rechtshängigkeit (G), litispendenza (I), lis pendens (L), litispendence (F)	9, 181
Rechtsfähigkeit (G), capacità giuridica (I), capacity to have rights (E), jouissance des droits civils (F)	34
Rechtsgeschäft (G), negozio giuridico (I), legal transaction (E), acte juridique (F)	36
Rechtshilfehandlungen (G), atti d'assistenza giudiziaria (I), acts of judicial assistance (E), actes d'entraide judiciaire (F)	11
Rechtskraftsbescheinigung, Vollstreckbarkeitsbescheinigung (G)	193
Reconnaissance	
– en Suisse (F), Anerkennung in der Schweiz (G), riconoscimento in Svizzera (I), acknowledgement made in Switzerland (E)	72

Article

– intervenue à l'étranger (F), im Ausland erfolgte Anerkennung (G), riconoscimento avvenuto all'estero (I), foreign acknowledgement (E)   73

Recours (F), Anfechtung (G), impugnazione (I), action for annulment (E)   190

– de droit public (F), staatsrechtliche Beschwerde (G), ricorso di diritto publico (I), constitutional complaint (E)   191

Recognition and enforcement of foreign decisions (E)   25 to 32

Recovery among debtors (E), Recours entre codébiteurs (F), Rückgriff zwischen Schuldnern (G), Regresso tra debitori (I)   144

Recurrent media (E), médias à caractère périodique (F), periodisch erscheinende Medien (G), mezzi di comunicazione sociale periodici (I)   139

Récusation d'un arbitre (F), Ablehnung eines Schiedsrichtes (G), ricusa di un arbitro (I), challenge of an arbitrator (E)   180

Refugee (E), réfugié (F), Flüchtling (G), rifugiato (I)   24

Register

– of civil status (E), registre de l'Etat civil (F), Zivilstandsregister (G), registro dello stato civile (I)   14, 32, 40

– of commerce (E), registre du commerce (F), Handelsregister (G), registro di commercio (I)   157

Règlement de la succession (F), Nachlassverfahren (G), procedimento successorio (I), probate proceedings (E)   86

Règlement d'arbitrage (F), Verfahrensordnung (G), ordinamento procedurale arbitrale, regolamento d'arbitrato (I), rules of arbitration, arbitration rules (E)   180

Règles

– de sécurité et de comportement (F), Sicherheits- und Verhaltensvorschriften (G), norme di sicurezza e di condotta (I), regulation of safety and conduct (E)   142

– de droit (F), Recht (G), diritto (I), rules of law (E)   187

– de droit international privé (F), Kollisionsrecht (G), norme di diritto internazionale privato (I), conflict of laws rules (E)   91

Regresso tra debitori (I), recovery among debtors (E), recours entre codébiteurs (F), Rückgriff zwischen Schuldnern (G)   144

Regulations of safety and conduct (E), règles de sécurité et de comportement (F), Sicherheits- und Verhaltensvorschriften (G), norme di sicurezza e di condotta (I)   142

Refugees (E)   24

Reinstatement of original state (E), restitutio in integrum
(L)   142
Religious marriage ceremony (E)   43
Renonciation au recours (F), Verzicht auf Rechtsmittel
(G), rinuncia all'impugnazione (I), waiver of annul-
ment (E)   192
Rent, lease (E)   117
Renvoi (F), Verweisung (G), rinvio (I)   13, 14, 37, 90
Représentant (F), Vertreter (G), rappresentante (I), agent
(E)   126
Representation (E), représentation (F)   158
Réserve de l'ordre public (F), Vorbehaltsklausel (G),
clausola di riserva (I), public policy exception (E)   17
Residence, habitual (E), résidence habituelle (F), gewöhn-
licher Aufenthalt (G), dimora abituale (I)   20, 59, 85
Res
 – in transitu (L), goods in transit (E), biens en transit
(F), Sachen im Transit (G), cose in transito (I)   101
 – iudicata (L)   193
Réserve de propriété (F), Eigentumsvorbehalt (G), riserva
di proprietà (I), retention of title (E)   102
Respondent in arbitration (E), défendeur à l'arbitrage arbitrage (F), Beklagte im Schiedsverfahren (G), convenuto nel procedimento arbitrale (I)   7
Responsabilité
 – pour une société étrangère (F), Haftung für ausländische Gesellschaften (G), responsabilità per
società straniere (I), liability for foreign companies
(E)   159
 – du fait d'un produit (F), Produktehaftung (G), re-
sponsabilita per vizi di un prodotto (I), products
liability (E)   135
Responsibility arising from the public issue of shares and
bonds (E)   151
Restraint of competition, antitrust (E), entrave à la concurrence (F), Wettbewerbsbehinderung (G), ostacoli
alla concorrenza (I)   137
Restrictions du pouvoir de représentation d'un organe (F),
Beschränkung der Vertretungsbefugnis eines Organs
(G), limitazione del potere di rappresentanza di un
organo (I), limitation of the power of representation of
an officer (E)   158
Retention of title (E), réserve de propriété (F), Eigentumsvorbehalt (G), riserva di proprietà (I)   102

273

Article

Riconoscimento
- all'estero (I), foreign acknowledgement (E), reconnaissance intervenue à l'étranger (F), im Ausland erfolgte Anerkennung (G) 73
- in Svizzera (I), acknowledgement made in Switzerland (E), reconnaissance en Suisse (F), Anerkennung in der Schweiz (G) 72
Ricorso di diritto pubblico (I), constitutional complaint (E), recours de droit public (F), staatsrechtliche Beschwerde (G) 191
Ricusa di un arbitro (I), challenge of an arbitrator (E), récusation d'un arbitre (F), Ablehnung eines Schiedsrichters (G) 180
Right
- of personality (E), personnalité (F), Persönlichkeit (G), personalità (I) 139
- to be heard (E) 182
- to direct claim (E), action directe (F) 131
- to present an opposing view (E), droit de réponse (F), Gegendarstellungsrecht (G), diritto di risposta (I) 139
Rinuncia all'impugnazione (I), waiver of annulment (E), renonciation au recours (F), Verzicht auf Rechtsmittel (G) 192
Rinvio (I), renvoi (F), Verweisung (G) 13, 14, 37, 90, 187
Riserva de proprietà (I), retention of title (E), réserve de propriété (F), Eigentumsvorbehalt (G) 102
Road transportation, highway transportation (E) 116
Royalties (E), droits de licence (F), Lizenzgebühren (G), spese di licenza (I) 122
Rückgriff zwischen Schuldnern (G), regresso tra debitori (I), recovery among debtors (E), recours entre codébiteurs (F) 144
Rules
- of arbitration (E), règlement d'arbitrage (F), Verfahrensordnung, Schiedsordnung (G), ordinamento procedurale arbitrale, regolamento d'arbitrato (I) 180
- of law (E), règles de droit (F), Recht (G), diritto (I) 187

Sachen
- die in die Schweiz gelangen (G), cose che giungono in Svizzera (I), goods entering Switzerland (E), biens transportés en Suisse (F) 102

274

	Article
– im Transit (G), cose in transito (I), res in transitu (L) goods in transit (E), biens en transit (F)	101
Sachlicher Zusammenhang (G), materialmente connesse (I), factually connected (E), connexité (F)	8
Sachnormverweisung (G)	14
Sale (E), vente (F), Verkauf (G), compravendita (I)	118
Schädigende Einwirkungen (G), immissioni nocive (I), damaging nuisance (E), immissions dommageables (F)	138
Schedule of claims (E), état de collocation (F), Kollokationsplan (G), graduatoria (I)	166, 170, 172
Schiedsfähige Streitsache (G), controversia compromettibile (I), arbitrable dispute (E), différend arbitrable (F)	7
Schiedsgerichtsbarkeit (G), arbitrato (I), arbitration (E), arbitrage (F)	1, 7, 176 to 194
Schiedsvereinbarung (G), patto di arbitrato (I), arbitration agreement (E), convention d'arbitrage (F)	178
Schiedsvereinbarung ist hinfällig, unwirksam oder nicht erfüllbar (G), caducità, inefficacia o inadempibilità del patto d'arbitrato (I), agreement fails, is inoperative or cannot be implemented (E), convention est caduque, inopérante ou non susceptible d'être appliquée (F)	7
Schuldrecht, Obligationenrecht (G), diritto delle obbligazioni (I), law of obligations (E), droit des obligations (F)	112 to 149
Schuldwährung (G)	147
Schützenswert und offensichtlich überwiegend (G), degno di protezione e manifestamente preponderante (I), legitimate and clearly overriding (E), légitime et manifestement prépondérant (F)	19
Schutzstaat (G)	122
Schweigen (G), silenzio (I), silence (E), silence (F)	123
Scomparsa, dichiarazione di (I)	41
Scope of conflicts rule (E), portée de la règle de conflit (F), Umfang der Verweisung (G), estensione del rinvio (I)	13
Scope	
– of liability (E), étendue de la responsabilité (F), Umfang der Haftung (G), estensione della responsabilità (I)	142
– of the law on succession and distribution of the estate (E)	92
Scopo (I), policy (E), but (F), Zweck (G)	18
Sealing as a conservatory measure (E)	89

	Article
Seat (E), siège commercial (F), Geschäftssitz (G), sede commerciale (I)	21, 109
Seat (E), siège, Sitz (G), sede (I)	21, 176
– of company (E)	21
– of arbitral tribunal (E)	7
Sea transportation, maritime transportation (E)	116
Secondo equità (I), ex aequo et bono (L), en équité (F), nach Billigkeit (G)	187
Sécurité des transactions (F), Verkehrsschutz (G), protezione del commercio giuridico (I), protection of legal transactions (E)	36
Securities (E), papiers-valeurs (F), Wertpapeire (G), titoli di credito (cartevalori) (I)	105
Security interest (E)	103, 105, 106
Sede (I), seat (E), siège (F), Sitz (G)	21, 176
Sede commerciale (I), seat (E), siège commercial (F), Geschäftssitz (G)	109
Seized (E), saisi (F), angerufen (G), adito (I)	88
Sentence partielle (F), Teilentscheid (G), decisioni parziali (I), partial award (E)	188
Séquestre (F), Arrest (G), sequestro (I), attachment, Mareva injunction (E)	4
Services, contract for (E)	117
Set-off (E), compensation (F), Verrechnungsvertrag, (Aufrechnung) (G), compensazione (I)	8, 141, 148
Settlement in court – out of court (E)	30
Share corporation (E)	162
Shares and bonds (E), titres de participation et d'emprunts (F), Beteiligungspapiere und Anleihen (G), titoli di partecipazione e di prestiti (I)	151
Ships, vessels (E)	105, 107
Sicherheits- und Verhaltensvorschriften (G), norme di sicurezza e di condotta (I), regulations of safety and conduct (E), règles de sécurité et de comportement (F)	142
Sichernde Massnahmen (G), provvedimenti conservativi (I), conservatory measures (E), mesures conservatoires (F)	89, 168
Sicherungsrecht (G)	103
Siège (F), Sitz (G), sede (I), seat (E)	21, 176
Siège commercial (F), Geschäftssitz (G), sede commerciale (I), seat (E)	109
Silence in response to an offer (E), silence après réception d'une offre (F), Schweigen auf einen Antrag (G), silenzio su una proposta (I)	123

	Article
Sitz (G), sede (I), seat (E), siège (F)	21, 176
Slight – much closer connection (E), lien très lâche – relation beaucoup plus étroite (F), geringer – viel engerer Zusammenhang (G), esigua – più stretta connessione (I)	15
Société (F), Gesellschaft (G), società (I), company (E)	21, 150, 151
Sole distributorship agreements (E)	117
Solidarity of debtors, joint debtors (E)	140
"Soziale Einbettung" (G)	133
Space, outer (E), espace cosmique (F), Weltraum (G), spazio (I)	129
Special sales regulations (E)	135
Specific legal relationship (E), rapport de droit déterminé (F), bestimmtes Rechtsverhältnis (G), determinato rapporto giuridico (I)	5
Staat (G), Stato (I), country, state (E), Etat (F)	22, 177
Staatsangehörigkeit (G), cittadinanza (I), citzenship (E), nationalité (F)	22
Staatsrechtliche Beschwerde (G), ricorso di diritto pubblico (I), constitutional complaint (E), recours de droit public (F)	191
Stabile organizzazione (I), business establishment (E), établissement (F), Niederlassung (G)	20
Stato civile (I), civil status (E), état civil (F), Zivilstand (G)	32
Statute of limitations, prescription (E), prescription (F), Verjährung (G), prescrizione (I)	12, 128, 148
Stretta connessione (I), close connection (E), lien étroit (F), enger Zusammenhang (G)	19
Subsidiary jurisdiction (E), for de nécessité (F), Notzuständigkeit (G), foro di necessità (I)	3
Substance v. procedure (E)	148
Substantive prerequisites (E), conditions de fond (F), materiell-rechtliche Voraussetzungen (G), presupposti materiali (I)	44
Succession (F), Nachlass (G), successione (I), estate (E)	92
Succursale (F) (I), branch office (E), Zweigniederlassung (G)	21, 160
Sufficient connection (E), lien suffisant (F), genügender Zussammenhang (G), sufficiente connessione (I)	3
Sühneverfahren (G), procedura di conciliazione (I), conciliation proceeding (E), citation en conciliation (F)	9
Summons (E)	11
Supervisory authority (E), autorité de surveillance (F), Aufsichtsbehörde (G), autorità di vigilanza (I)	32

	Article
Supplement to or modification of divorce decrees (E)	64
Support and alimony (E)	49, 83
Survivorship (E)	34
Swiss branch offices of foreign companies (E)	160
Swiss public policy exception (E), réserve de l'ordre public suisse (F), schweizerischer Ordre public (Vorbehaltsklausel) (G), (clausola di riserva) ordine pubblico svizzero (I)	17

Taking of evidence, proof procedure (E), administration des preuves (F), Beweisaufnahme (G), assunzione delle prove (I)	184
Technology transfer (E)	122
Teilentscheid (G), decisioni parziali (I), partial award (E), sentence partielle (F)	188
Television and other media (E)	139
Telex, telefax and other means of communication (E)	5, 178
Temporary restraining order (E)	10
Termini (I), time limits (E), délais (F), Fristen (G)	12
Territoriality of bankruptcy (E)	166
Testament ou un pacte successoral (F), letztwillige Verfügung oder Erbvertrag (G), testamento o contratto successorio (I), will or successorial pact (E)	87
Time limits (E), délais (F), Fristen (G), termini (I)	12
Title	
– passing of (E)	99 to 107
– retention of (E)	103
– document of (E)	106
Titoli	
– di credito (cartevalori) (I), securities (E), papiers-valeurs (F), Wertpapiere (G)	105
– di partecipazione e di prestiti (I), shares and bonds (E), titres de participation et d'emprunts (F), Beteiligungspapiere und Anleihen (G)	151
– rappresentanti merci (I), documents of title (E), titres représentant la marchandise (F), Warenpapiere (G)	106
Titres	
– représentant la marchandise (F), Warenpapiere (G), titoli rappresentanti merci (I), document of title (E)	106
– de participation et d'emprunts (F), Beteiligungspapiere und Anleihen (G), titoli di partecipazione e di prestiti (I), shares and bonds (E)	151

278

	Article
Torts, unlawful acts (E)	112, 129 to 148
Trademark (E), marque (F), Marke (G), marchio (I)	110, 122
Traffic accidents (E), accidents de la circulation routière (F), Strassenverkehrsunfälle (G), incidenti della circolazione stradale (I)	134
Traités internationaux (F), internationale Staatsverträge (G), tratti internazionali (I), international treaties (E)	1
Transfer	
– of a claim by operation of law (E)	146
– of company from Switzerland to foreign country (E)	163
– of company from abroad to Switzerland (E)	161
Transportmittel (G), mezzi di trasporto (I), means of transportation (E), moyens de transport (F)	107
Tribunal du lieu d'exécution (F), Gericht am Erfüllungsort (G), tribunale del luogo di adempimento (I), court at the place of performance of the contract (E)	113
Tribunale del luogo di adempimento (I), court at the place of performance of the contract (E), tribunal du lieu d'exécution (F), Gericht am Erfüllungsort (G)	113
Tribunal del luogo (I), forum rei sitae (L), courts at the site (E), tribunaux de lieu (F), Gerichte am Ort (G)	97
Tribunaux de lieu (F), Gerichte am Ort (G), tribunali del luogo (I), forum rei sitae (L), courts at the site (E)	97
Trattati internazionali (I), international treaties (E), traités internationaux (F), internationale Staatsverträge (G)	1
Treble damages (E)	137
Trust (E)	150
Ultra petita (L), beyond the questions submitted to it (E), au-delà des demandes dont il était saisi (F), Streitpunkte, die ihm nicht unterbreitet wurden (G), punti litigiosi che non gli erano stati sottoposti (I)	190
Ultra vires (L)	158
Umfang	
– der Haftung (G), condizioni e estensione della responsabilità (I), scope of liability (E), étendue de la responsabilité (F)	142
– der Verweisung (G), estensione del rinvio (I), scope of conflicts rule (E), portée de la règle de conflit (F)	13
Unconditional appearance (E), défendeur procède au fond sans faire de réserve (F), vorbehaltlose Einlassung (G), incondizionata costituzione in giudizio del convenuto (I)	6

	Article
Unerlaubte Handlung (G), atto illecito (I), unlawful act, tort (E), acte illicite (F)	142
Unfair competition (E), concurrence déloyale (F), unlauterer Wettbewerb (G), concorrenza sleale (I)	136
Uniform substantive law (E)	1
Univocamente (I), clearly evident (E), de façon certaine (F), eindeutig (G)	53, 116
Unjust enrichment (E), enrichissement illégitime (F), ungerechtfertigte Bereicherung (G), indebito arrichimento (I)	127
Unlauterer Wettbewerb (G), concorrenza sleale (I), unfair competition (E), concurrence déloyale (F)	136
Unlawful act, tort (E), acte illicite (F), unerlaubte Handlung (G), atto illecito (I)	142
Urheber der Verletzung (G), l'autore della lesione (I), damaging party (E), auteur de l'atteinte (F)	139
Urkunden (G), documenti (I), certificates (E), documents (F)	96
Validation of attachment (E)	4
Veräusserungsverträge (G), contratti di alienazione (I), contracts to pass title (E), contrats d'aliénation (F)	117
Verfahrensordnung, Schiedsordnung (G), ordinamento procédurale arbitrale, regolamento arbitrale (I), rules of arbitration (E), règlement d'arbitrage (F)	180
Verfügungen von Todes wegen (G), disposizioni a causa di morte (I), dispositions for cause of death (E), dispositions pour cause de mort (F)	93
Verhandlungsmaxime (G)	16
Verjährung (G), prescrizione (I), statute of limitations (E), prescription (F)	141
Verkehrsschutz (G), protezione del commercio giuridico (I), protection of legal transactions (E), sécurité des transactions (F)	36
Verletzung der Persönlichkeitsrechte (G), lesioni arrecate alla personalità (I), violation of the right of personality (E), atteintes aux intérêts personnels (F)	33
Vermögensrechtliche Ansprüche (G), pretese patrimoniali (I), claims of financial interest (E), en matière patrimoniale (F)	16
Verschollenerklärung (G), dichiarazione di scomparsa (I), declaration of disappearance (E), déclaration d'absence (F)	41

	Article
Vertrag (G), contratto (I), contract (E), contrat (F)	116
– mit Konsumenten (G), con consumatori (I), with consumers (E), avec des consommateurs (F)	114, 120
Vertreter (G), rappresentante (I), agent (E), représentant (F)	158
Verwahrer (G), depositario (I), keeper (E), dépositaire (F)	117
Verweisung (G), rinvio (I), renvoi (F)	13, 14, 37, 90, 187
Verzicht auf Rechtsmittel (G), rinuncia all'impugnazione (I), waiver of annulment (E), renonciation au recours (F)	192
Vienna convention on the law of international sales (E)	1, 118
Violation of the right of personality (E), atteintes aux intérêts personnels (F), Verletzung der Persönlichkeitsrechte (G), lesioni arrecate alla personalità (I)	33
Visiting rights (E)	62
Vollstreckbarkeitsbescheinigung (G), deposito e attestazione dell'esecutività (I), deposit and certificate of enforceability (E), dépôt et certificat de force exécutoire (F)	193
Von Amtes wegen (G), d'ufficio (I), ex officio (L), d'office (F)	16
Vorbehaltlose Einlassung (G), incondizionata costituzione in giudizio del convenuto (I), unconditional appearance (E), défendeur procède au fond sans faire de réserve (F)	6
Vorsorgliche Massnahmen (G), provvedimenti cautelari (I), provisional measures (E), mesures provisoires (F)	10, 62
Währung (G), moneta (I), currency (E), monnaie (F)	147
Waiver of annulment (E), renonciation au recours (F), Verzicht auf Rechtsmittel (G), rinuncia all'impugnazione (I)	192
Waiver of a claim (E)	148
Waiver of action for annulment of arbitral award, exclusion agreement (E)	192
Warehouse receipt (E), certificat de dépôt (F), Lagerschein (G), certificato di diposito (I)	106
Warenpapier (G), titolo rapresentante merci (I), document of title (E), titre représentant la marchandise (F)	106
Wertpapiere (G), titolo di credito (cartevalori) (I), securities (E), papiers-valeurs (F)	105

Article

Wettbewerbsbehinderung (G), ostacoli alla concorrenza
(I), restraint of competition (E), entrave à la concurr-
ence (F)   137
Widerklage (G), domanda riconvenzionale (I), counter-
claim (E), demande reconventionelle (F)   8
Will or successorial pact (E), testament ou pacte successor-
al (F), letztwillige Verfügung oder Erbvertrag (G),
testamento o contratto successorio (I)   87
Willensvollstreckung (G)   92
Wirtschaftliche Landesversorgung (G), approvvigionamen-
to economico del paese (I), economic national defense
(E), approvisionnement économique du pays (F)   163
Work accident insurance (E)   144

Zivilstandsregister (G), registro dello stato civile (I), register of civil status (E), registre de l'état civil (F)   14, 32
Zuständigkeit am Ort der gelegenen Sache (G), foro del
luogo (I), forum rei sitae (L), jurisdiction at place of
assets (E), for du lieu de situation (F)   88
Zustellung (G), notificazione (I), notification (E), com-
munication (F)   190
Zweck (G), scopo (I), policy (E), but (F)   18
Zweigniederlassung (G), branch office (E), succursale
(F) (I)   21, 160